More Is Caught Than Taught:
A guide to quality child care

More Is Caught Than Taught:
A guide to quality child care

A. Jack Guillebeaux
Author

Phyllida Burlinghame
Project Writer

Dr. Alan Gribben
Elsie J. Williams
Editors

Federation of Child Care Centers of Alabama

Federation of Child Care Centers of Alabama
Post Office Box 214
Montgomery, Alabama 36101

Published by the Federation of Child Care Centers of Alabama, Inc.
P.O. Box 214, Montgomery, Alabama 36101

ISBN 0-9658522-0-2
Copyright © 1998 by Federation of Child Care Centers of Alabama
No part of this book may be reproduced in any form without permission from the publisher, except for the quotation of brief passages in reviews.

Printer: Herff Jones Yearbooks, Montgomery, Alabama

Photographs copyright © by Federation of Child Care Centers of Alabama

All Rights Reserved
Library of Congress Catalog Card Number: 97-60988
Printed in the United States of America
First Edition

Table of Contents

About FOCAL . . . . Page IX
Acknowledgments . . . . Page X
Photographs . . . . Page XII
Preface . . . . Page XIII
Introduction . . . . Page XV
Getting Started Module . . . . Page 1
    Expected Outcomes . . . . Page 2
    Preparing . . . . Page 2
    Who will participate? . . . . Page 2
    How long will it take? . . . . Page 3
    Where will it take place? . . . . Page 3
    When will it take place? . . . . Page 3
    How will you document this module? . . . . Page 3
    What will you need to bring to these meetings . . . . Page 4
    Challenges of this Module . . . . Page 4
    Putting this Module into Action . . . . Page 5
    Step One: Organizing the Site Team . . . . Page 5
    Basic approach in establishing the Site Team . . . . Page 6
    Initial Site Team Meeting . . . . Page 6
    Step Two: Recruit Staff, Parents, and Community Leaders . . . . Page 8
    Step Three: Bring All MCTT Participants Together . . . . Page 12
    1. What MCTT is and how we will use it at our center. . . . . Page 12
    2. Roles of Participants . . . . Page 13
    3. How We Will BE Together . . . . Page 14
    Resources . . . . Page 15
    Support Materials . . . . Page 15
    Program Talking Sheet . . . . Page 17
    Program Blueprint . . . . Page 19
Vision Module . . . . Page 41
    What Is this Module? . . . . Page 41
    Expected Outcomes . . . . Page 42
    Preparing . . . . Page 43
    Who will participate? . . . . Page 43
    How long will it take? . . . . Page 43
    Where will it take place? . . . . Page 43
    When will it take place? . . . . Page 43

How will you document this module?	Page	43
What will you need to bring to the session?	Page	44
Challenges of this Module	Page	44
Putting this Module into Action	Page	45
The Vision Session	Page	45
Additional options.	Page	47
Resources	Page	49
Support Materials	Page	49
Environment Module	Page	59
What Is this Module?	Page	59
Expected Outcomes	Page	61
Preparing	Page	61
Who will participate?	Page	61
How long will it take?	Page	61
Where will it take place?	Page	62
How will you document this module?	Page	62
What will you need to bring to the session?	Page	62
Putting this Module into Action	Page	64
Environment Site Visits	Page	67
Environment Meeting #2	Page	68
Additional Options:	Page	70
Resources	Page	72
Internalized Oppression Module	Page	83
What Is this Module?	Page	83
Expected Outcomes	Page	85
Preparing	Page	85
Who will participate?	Page	85
How long will it take?	Page	86
Where will it take place?	Page	86
When will it take place?	Page	86
How will you document this module?	Page	86
What will you need to bring to these meetings	Page	86
Challenges of this Module	Page	87
Putting this Module into Action	Page	88
Step One: Organizing the Site Team	Page	88
Points for discussion	Page	100
Discuss next steps.	Page	103
Resources	Page	104

Session Contract for participants	Page 114
Session Contract for facilitators	Page 116
How To BE Together Module	Page 119
What Is this Module?	Page 119
Expected Outcomes	Page 121
Preparing	Page 122
How long will it take?	Page 122
Where will it take place?	Page 122
When will it take place?	Page 122
How will you document this module?	Page 122
What will you need to bring to the session?	Page 122
Challenges of this Module	Page 123
Putting this Module into Action	Page 124
How To Be Together Session	Page 124
Resources	Page 136
The Cooperative Mode	Page 141
Early Childhood Theory Module	Page 147
What Is this Module?	Page 147
Expected Outcomes	Page 149
Preparing	Page 150
Who will participate?	Page 150
How long will it take?	Page 150
Where will it take place?	Page 150
When will it take place?	Page 150
How will you document this module?	Page 151
What will you need to bring to these meetings	Page 151
Challenges of this Module	Page 151
Putting this Module into Action	Page 152
Step One: Organizing the Site Team	Page 152
Early Childhood Theory Meeting #2	Page 154
Additional Options:	Page 157
Resources	Page 158
Support Materials	Page 159
Curriculum Module	Page 171
What Is this Module?	Page 171
Expected Outcomes	Page 174
Preparing	Page 174
Who will participate?	Page 174

How long will it take?	Page 174
Where will it take place?	Page 175
When will it take place?	Page 175
How will you document this module?	Page 175
What will you need to bring to the session?	Page 175
Challenges of this Module	Page 176
Putting this Module into Action	Page 176
Resources	Page 183
Support Materials	Page 185
Work Planning Module	Page 195
What Is this Module?	Page 195
Expected Outcomes	Page 195
Preparing	Page 195
Who will participate?	Page 195
How long will it take?	Page 196
Where will it take place?	Page 196
When will it take place?	Page 196
How will you document this module?	Page 197
What will you need to bring to these meetings	Page 197
Challenges of this Module	Page 198
Putting this Module into Action	Page 198
Step One: Organizing the Site Team	Page 198
Resources	Page 199
Support Materials	Page 199
Comprehensive Planning Diagram	Page 203
Appendix A -- Facilitator's Guide	Page 211
Appendix B -- Internalized Oppression	Page 219
Appendix B -- Internalized Oppression: How do we free ourselves of it?	Page 222
Appendix B -- Internalized Oppression: Identification Crisis	Page 225
Appendix C -- The Cooperative Mode	Page 229
Appendix D -- More Is Caught Than Taught Resource Guide	Page 237

ABOUT FOCAL

Sophia Bracy Harris,
Executive Director, FOCAL

We are proud to share *More Is Caught Than Taught* (*MCTT*) with you – our friends, supporters, allies, and others who care about the well-being of children. This guide represents our wisdom drawn from over twenty five years of supporting, working with, and challenging community-based child care programs. We welcome this opportunity to share some of our lessons learned and add to all of our work in creating a more just and caring world for our children to inherit.

Since the early 1970's, The Federation of Child Care Centers of Alabama (FOCAL) has fought for the survival and betterment of community-based child care. In 1972 a group of African-American center directors met in Selma, Alabama to found an organization that would speak for their interests. Since that time FOCAL has continued to work with grass-roots child care providers on everything from the most detailed one-on-one training to mobilizing communities to have a voice on the national level. FOCAL members include child care providers all over Alabama, from a center located down a winding road on the border of Mississippi, to home providers nestled in the mountains of Northern Alabama, to centers dotting Alabama's coast. FOCAL has touched the lives of thousands of providers and the tens of thousands of families whose children they care for.

Years of struggle gave birth to *More Is Caught Than Taught* as a tool for improving child care. We have learned that all of the resources and technical knowledge in the world are no substitute for understanding ourselves and creating a vision for our future. Over the years we have struggled with the negative messages we carry around: "I am dumb," "I don't write well, so I can't plan lessons," and our lack of vision for our children's growth: "What's the use of talking about my vision for the future when I can't change what happens today?" We have struggled with generational poverty and feelings of hopelessness in poor communities. We knew we needed a way for people to confront their barriers and be empowered to change their own lives. *More Is Caught Than Taught* is our tool in that struggle.

More Is Caught Than Taught is a guide for all of us: African-American, Native American, Caucasian, rich, poor, child care providers, community people, and many others. It is a means of collectively examining our histories, transforming those lessons into personal understanding, and using that understanding to grow in new directions. Without this examination, we perpetuate cycles of poverty, racism, discrimination, and abuse because we never become conscious enough to learn to challenge those systems. Our families, our communities, and even our nations will never survive without a better understanding of our histories and a vision for our future. We are proud for you to join us on this journey of transformation.

ACKNOWLEDGMENTS

Sophia Bracy Harris,
Executive Director, FOCAL

This publication had its inception work begun in 1980, evolved into the Peer Education Project in 1984, and began to look like a book in 1993. During these years many people generously contributed love, caring, and commitment, as well as knowledge, experience, and energies to the creation of these pages. A few of these people will be mentioned here, but most will not. To you, the unmentioned, we acknowledge your invaluable contributions to this publication and the years of your work upon which it is built. Though unnamed, you are remembered. Because we desire to recognize all who have contributed to *More Is Caught Than Taught*, and yet cannot, we find solace in the fact that you found your own reasons to support FOCAL in the past, and we trust that you will continue to do so.

The principal acknowledgment for this book goes to A. Jack Guillebeaux, who for years has been "the keeper of the vision" for *MCTT*. As staff members and other resource people came to FOCAL to help with our work, it was Jack who helped them appreciate *More Is Caught Than Taught* and find ways to help move it along a strategic and inevitable path to completion. Never wavering in his belief in the work of FOCAL and the potential of *MCTT*, Jack provided leadership, creativity, and ingenuity for this project as profound changes took place in the political landscape of Alabama, our financial circumstances, and the needs of our membership and staff. Jack, your gifts will long be remembered and valued.

It may have been luck, though I would like to think it was something more that brought special and gifted people to this project just when they were needed. Such a person was Wekesa O. Madzimoyo. Wekesa brought a strength and drive to FOCAL that both necessitated and facilitated the movement of FOCAL to clearly identify and define its position on blackness. His knowledge of African and American history, passion about the struggles of black peoples, and experience in child care made a deep impact on the work of FOCAL and was expressed in the initial design of this publication. Thanks, Wekesa, for the firm foundation.

The strategy for writing *More Is Caught Than Taught* was to lead several child care programs through the entire *More Is Caught Than Taught* process, document their experiences, and write the book based on these experiences. Three child care directors volunteered their programs to "test" *MCTT*. Over a period of nearly one year, Clara Card, Director of Joyland Child Development Center; Mary Jones, Director of Kiddyland Child Development Centers; and Karen Miller, Director of Toulminville Child Care Center, along with their supportive staffs, helped to plan and evaluate the sessions as well as participate in them. They enabled *MCTT* to be a reflection of reality.

rather than an exercise in theories. These directors and their staffs and supporters represent the essence of FOCAL – a willingness to come forth and do whatever is necessary to advance the mission of the Federation. We offer our lasting thanks to all of you.

As if on cue, Phyllida Burlingame, "appeared" in Montgomery and was recruited as project writer. Phyllida understood, appreciated and immediately connected with a role that far exceeded simply writing. She assisted in the design, organization, and the all-important evaluation of the training sessions for the pilot program. In addition to patiently supporting a writing strategy that was constantly changing and evolving out of our experiences, Phyllida brought a spirit which was, on the one hand, organized and focused, and on the other hand flexible, discerning, and accommodating. From Phyllida's work came the long-awaited body of *MCTT*. Her gift to this project cannot be measured.

For the final editing of *More Is Caught Than Taught*, we turned to Professor Alan Gribben, who heads the Department of English and Philosophy at Auburn University at Montgomery. While merely seeking someone who would take a red pen to our drafts, we found, to our great delight, another genuine "caeregiver" in the person of Dr. Gribben. Not only did Dr. Gribben give generously and sacrificially of his time to edit and sometimes extensively revise our work, but he and his teaching associate Dr. Robert C. Evans, who assisted him in editing the initial draft, carefully maintained the spirit and flavor of the many voices heard in MCTT. To you we extend our deepest appreciation.

In the final feverish weeks before publication we asked Elsie J. Williams, Managing Editor of *Teaching Tolerance*, a project of the Southern Poverty Law Center in Montgomery, to help with proofing the final drafts and editing last minute additions –which turned out to be significant. Elsie, as so many others have, far exceeded our request and expectations, as she joined Dr. Gribben in the editing process and helped us meet our publication schedule.

We acknowledge a group without whose generous financial support *More Is Caught Than Taught* would not have been possible. Primary financial support came from the Bernard van Leer Foundation, located at The Hague in the Netherlands, the Heron Foundation, the New World Foundation, Alan and Andrea Rabinowitz, Maya Miller, the Alabama Power Foundation, the Alabama Civil Justice Foundation, the Montgomery Area Community Foundation, and the Children's Trust Fund of Alabama.

Finally, we acknowledge the unending support of the members and friends of FOCAL whom we call the FOCAL family. Through workshops, meetings, and retreats, we tested each and every idea, approach, method and strategy that became *More Is Caught Than Taught*. Only through the love and patient support of this family was this publication possible, and therefore, it is to you that *More Is Caught Than Taught: A guide to quality child care* is dedicated.

PHOTOGRAPHS

Our 26-year quest to increase the quality and quantity of child care for poor Alabamians has taught us one abiding lesson; though critical, the effective "classroom" is only one milestone on our journey. The challenges are also political, economic, social and spiritual, and it takes many people doing many different things to achieve our goal. The photographs in this book represent this reality, for they show the diversity of people and activities necessary to achieve the goals of FOCAL.

Among the faces you will see parents, child care providers, community leaders, technicians, elected and appointed officials, volunteers, philanthropist, educators, social activists, and certain people who are more famous than rich. Some of the faces are of the founding mothers and fathers of FOCAL, some are faithful supporters who have passed on, some are our children, and some of the faces are our friends. You will see folks in training sessions, negotiating with officials, marching for child care, playing games, teaching children, consulting, loving, and supporting each other. If you look from just the right angle, you will see a family working, learning, loving, and celebrating.

These are the faces of FOCAL, old and young, black and white, rich and poor, united in a vision to care for our children.

PREFACE

Ann Elizabeth Gay Bishop

In most cultures around the world, the mother in the family (or the one who performs this role) is the first and primary teacher of children. The family, for the majority of children, is the first "school" and therefore the most influential educational institution they will ever "attend." As a result of the social and economic forces shaping and reshaping families in the United States, as well as the roles of individuals in families, we have joyfully witnessed fathers or other males, in the past few decades, assuming more of the responsibility of nurturing children and sharing that "first teacher" role. Yet at the same time, we have seen families pass on to child care and other educational institutions greater responsibility for the care, protection, and education of their children.

As these institutions have assumed responsibility, defined themselves, and claimed a place for themselves in our society, there has emerged the concept of "parent involvement." At its very best, parent involvement suggests that those <u>in charge</u>, or responsible for the "education" of our young, desire or are willing for parents to have some say-so in the education of our children. Regardless of how benevolent or well-intended the advocates or supporters of the notion of parent involvement are, this position, even in its most benign form, raises a question as to who is responsible for the education of children and, in its worst form, simply takes from the family significant responsibility for educating children.

In this book we affirm that parents or their surrogates are the most powerful educators of children and that their influence lasts a lifetime. We affirm that the "teacher," the individual connected to an educational entity outside of the family, is an essential key to helping children in our society achieve their full potential. We further affirm that in early childhood, when learning is taking place at a rate that will never be matched again in life, the whole environment becomes a significant "teacher" of children; this is particularly true of the adults in any child's environment. While it may not literally take a "village" to raise a child, clearly this "village" is still a great influence.

The spirit behind *More Is Caught Than Taught* addresses the universal "teachers" of children: all the adults who directly and indirectly influence children; the teacher in the child care classroom or day care home; and parents, the primary educators of children. The fundamental approach in this book is to mobilize and unify the "teachers" of children into a spiritual, social, and educational partnership, guided by a common vision in which each "teacher," showing respect and appreciation for all the others, plays an integral role in enabling children to achieve their full potential. Teaching young children is one of the most crucial jobs in the world. The task literally affects the future of the globe. It molds and forms a lifetime of experience, bringing either joy, delight, and intellectual satisfaction or drudgery, failure, and misery. It is key to the peace and progress of each individual and the future of all humanity.

Are educators of young children honored and rewarded for the extraordinary contribution they make? Are there multi-million-dollar contracts, signed posters, collectable teacher cards, and Nobel prizes for the early childhood teacher-stars among us? No, education has a low-status profession in our society, and the younger the students, the lower the status of the teachers. Teachers of young children continue to work long hours, with large numbers of children, for very poor pay. Sometimes it seems as though only those who do this valuable work grasp its supreme importance.

This book was written for the parents, the early childhood "classroom" teachers, and the elders, leaders, and workers who are also teachers of the children of our community. In reality, you, the teachers of young children, can change the world! You are in a position more powerful than kings or presidents. You mold the hearts and minds of every life in your family and classroom. You create the future each morning when you greet a child or every day when you walk into the classroom. *More Is Caught Than Taught* is a tool to help you think systematically about the kind of world you wish to live in and the kind of future you want to prepare children to experience. We have seen the recent results of genocide, starvation, prejudice, exploitation, and ignorance. What must we do to have a different world, a world in which everyone can contribute according her/his capacities, in which each is valued, in which all are the keepers of our brothers and sisters? These profound questions are often debated in international forums. That these questions can be addressed in practical, spiritual ways to you, the first teachers of young children, affirms that you are a most potent force in building a new earth. We must allow ourselves to live out this truth.

INTRODUCTION

"It takes a whole village to raise a child."

African Proverb

More Is Caught Than Taught is a holistic approach for increasing the quality of care and developmental experiences provided to children, especially poor and minority children. *MCTT* addresses the need to engage the latent energies of parents, teachers, administrators and community members and seeks to focus this energy on the challenge of acquiring more knowledge, mastering new skills, and assuming greater responsibility for the care, protection and development of young children.

The *More Is Caught Than Taught* approach calls for a) devising a vision for children; b) thoughtfully constructing a supportive environment; c) developing peer relationships and true collaboration among parents, community leaders, and caregivers; d) altering the attitudes of caregivers so that their personal lives reflect the lessons they attempt to teach young children; e) thoughtfully and systematically affirming the culture of children; f) building "peerness" in the administration of programs and personal interactions of workers; g) selecting or crafting a curriculum which reflects the vision of providers and parents; and h) involving parents and teachers in public policy and advocacy on behalf of children and the community in general.

The fundamental principle of *More Is Caught Than Taught* is that children form their identities, in large part, based upon their observations of the world around them. They listen to what is said by adults and, more importantly, they observe and mimic the behavior of adults. In an assessment of *MCTT*, Dr. Nancy Boxill of Atlanta, Georgia, writes: "The *MCTT* Curriculum expresses the belief that children are affected more powerfully by the spoken and unspoken messages adults bring to them than by any facts adults provide and teach about the world, suggesting that attitudes rather than facts become a child's tools for making sense of the world."

A little story: One summer day I was driving with my young daughter beside me in the front seat of the car. We had the windows rolled down. She must have been about three years old. Out of the corner of my eye I caught her, first reaching up to grasp the rain gutter at the top of the window, then noticing that her upper arm was not reaching the lower window frame. She then rested her arm on the lower window frame and noted that she was not able to reach the rain gutter. As she was quietly going about her "work," I realized that she was attempting to do exactly as I was doing: riding with my hand grasping the top of the window and my arm resting on the window frame. As the full impact of what I saw hit me, my heart sank. I asked myself, if she works this hard to be like me in this most mundane way, if she is so intently observant of me, even when I am not aware, what is she taking in regarding really important things: how I behave towards her mother, the language that I use when I am frustrated, what I say about certain people after I hang up the telephone, or how I talk about work at the supper table? At that moment I realized to a deeper extent than ever before that I was continuously influencing my dearly loved daughter, even when I did not intend or desire to teach.

In our child care programs we try to provide the best physical resources such as playgrounds, activity areas, toys, and games. We do our best to offer structured learning and developmental activities. Every effort is made to hire and put safe and sensitive staff before children. We commit resources for training in all areas of child care and early childhood development. All of these things we do explicitly. We have permission, nay, we feel mandated to do these things. However, we don't have a road map for calling into question the psychological and emotional state of caregivers and the negative attitudes and scripts that are out of our awareness. This is uncharted territory. We have little permission, legal ground, or experience, and we possess few tools to address the single most important element of the provision of child care: the spiritual resources of the caregiver, that part of ourselves that children catch whether we are aware of it or not.

All the positive and negative realities that we learn and carry from our family of origin make up our cultural, racial and gender scripts, and we bring these scripts to our work with children. We also bring our orientation (thinking, feeling and behavior) about some people being naturally superior and others being naturally inferior. *MCTT* calls for an examination of this notion of inherent superiority and inherent inferiority, which supports sexism, classism, and especially racism. *MCTT* calls for role models who are actively engaged in the process of identifying and discarding their own "caught" "isms" and prejudices and for adults who engage in efforts to systematically identify, confront, and eliminate the manifestation of "isms" in the environment of the child.

As you begin to consider the *More Is Caught Than Taught* program, you will ask yourself the question: Just how important are notions of inherent Superiority and inherent Inferiority (S/I) to this work? Should you even read, or spend time struggling with, this at all? Of course, this is up to you, the reader. At the Federation of Child Care Centers, we have determined that this work is essential and unavoidable in the quest to give children access to their full potential. We have concluded that this work merits the highest priority. We feel that thoughtfully, effectively, and wholeheartedly addressing this area is a matter of principle. Doing so rests at the very center of our moral and ethical positions regarding the care, protection, education, and development of children.

Caregivers often remind others that by the age of six a child learns lessons about how to function in the world which s/he will use throughout life. While we know that we can modify basic positions that we learn in early childhood, we also know that altering our scripts or attitudes becomes more difficult as we grow older. The good news is that we have an opportunity to give treasures to children in early childhood. The bad news is that without realizing it, we pass on to children our unconscious acceptance of and participation in the S/I system - our own "internalized" oppressing or oppressed attitudes. A large part of the process of passing on scripts to children in our care is through words and through conversations that we initiate with children. In addition to our verbal contact with children, we, as adults create an environment that profoundly teaches children to be like us. We surround children with our relationships with other adults and children, our taste in colors, clothes, food, music, our sense of appropriate levels of noise, degrees of orderliness, levels of conflict, resorts to silence, use of tools and weapons, and so on. As we live our lives around children and make the myriad choices that we make, we tell children, through our actions and attitudes: This is the way to get along in life"; "Do as I do"; "Make the choices that I make." Children have no alternative but to emulate the lives of adults. Their very survival depends on how well they learn these life lessons.

More Is *Caught* Than Taught — *Introduction* — Page XVII

Unfortunately, children are almost totally unprepared to observe our behavior objectively, make informed analysis, and choose ways of thinking, feeling and behaving that are appropriate and healthy. Thus, we pass on our scripts every day in every way, and children internalize our scripts in every way every day. Given that the gift of our scripts has such a profound and long-lasting impact on the lives of children, and given the fact that these scripts are passed down from one generation to the next, it is our profound obligation to become aware of our attitudes and the effects of our attitudes, and to alter ourselves such that the gift of our attitudes to children is beneficial to them.

More Is Caught Than Taught is a dimension of early childhood development that must be brought into the consciousness as well as into the administration of our programs and, even more importantly, into our homes. Our vision for children - that they be emotionally strong, honest, creative, questioning, moral, courageous, wise, and free of debilitating prejudices, habits, and addictions - demands that we consciously, explicitly, systematically and effectively transform prejudices, language, motivations and behaviors. The effects of internalized negative behavior must be rooted out of the environment that we create for the growth and development of our children. We must seek to understand internalized oppression, to identify and work to alter our own negative scripts, and to work unceasingly to find tools for change, develop support mechanisms for change, and build change into our personal relationships. The administration of programs - hiring, staff development, communications with parents, and care of facilities - must be thoughtfully and skillfully scrutinized. In the end, our children must be surrounded by adults who are willing to grow, themselves, into examples worthy of emulation. Let us remember, when it comes to children, "*More Is Caught Than Taught*."

Proceeding through the Program

The *MCTT* program is as much a process as a product. Thus, we encourage you to focus on and value <u>how</u> you are implementing the program as you look for specific outcomes. We recognize that many people will not have the experience or skills to facilitate the process of implementing the *MCTT* program. To this end we offer you a <u>Facilitators Guide</u> (Appendix A). By using this guide and similar tools, you should be able to meet the need for good facilitation. If you cannot, we recommend that a concerted effort be made to mobilize the resources necessary to obtain persons who are trained and skilled in facilitating the work of groups. Any sacrifices that you make to achieve good facilitation will be rewarded in the quality of your end product. You will find notes for the facilitation of several key modules in Appendix B. Referring to these notes as you read the modules will increase your understanding of how to administer the module as well as expected outcomes of the module. We encourage you to address the need for facilitation at the very beginning of the program. Again, we encourage you to focus on and value <u>how</u> you are implementing the program as you look for specific outcomes.

Application of *MCTT* to Non-Child-Care Programs and to Leadership and Community Development Initiatives

More Is Caught Than Taught was developed for and with individuals who are parents, caregivers, and community leaders expressly concerned with the care and development of young children. However, the rationale, strategies, approaches and tools of *MCTT* evolved over many years as FOCAL worked with a broad variety of groups and organizations throughout the nation. At the most fundamental level, it is accurate to say that the principles and philosophy of *MCTT* came first and that the *Guide* was the result of applying those principles and philosophy to child development.

The application of these principles, philosophies, and approaches of *MCTT* to strategies and programs aimed at leadership, community, and economic development initiatives continues to move forward. Beginning with our own programs, FOCAL has successfully applied the principles to programs centered on black women, economic development, and the organization of coalitions which address public policy. In addition to cooperating with several partners in the United States, FOCAL is working with Play-Train in Birmingham, England, and The Family Action Center at the University of Newcastle in New South Wales, Australia to apply the approaches of *MCTT* to their work.

Our own experiences and those of other organizations demonstrate the power of *MCTT*'s principles and the broad range of human development programs that can successfully apply *MCTT*'s approaches. FOCAL is interested in finding new partners to add to a network of groups that are seeking to increase the impact of their work by grounding it in the philosophy and practice of *More Is Caught Than Taught*.

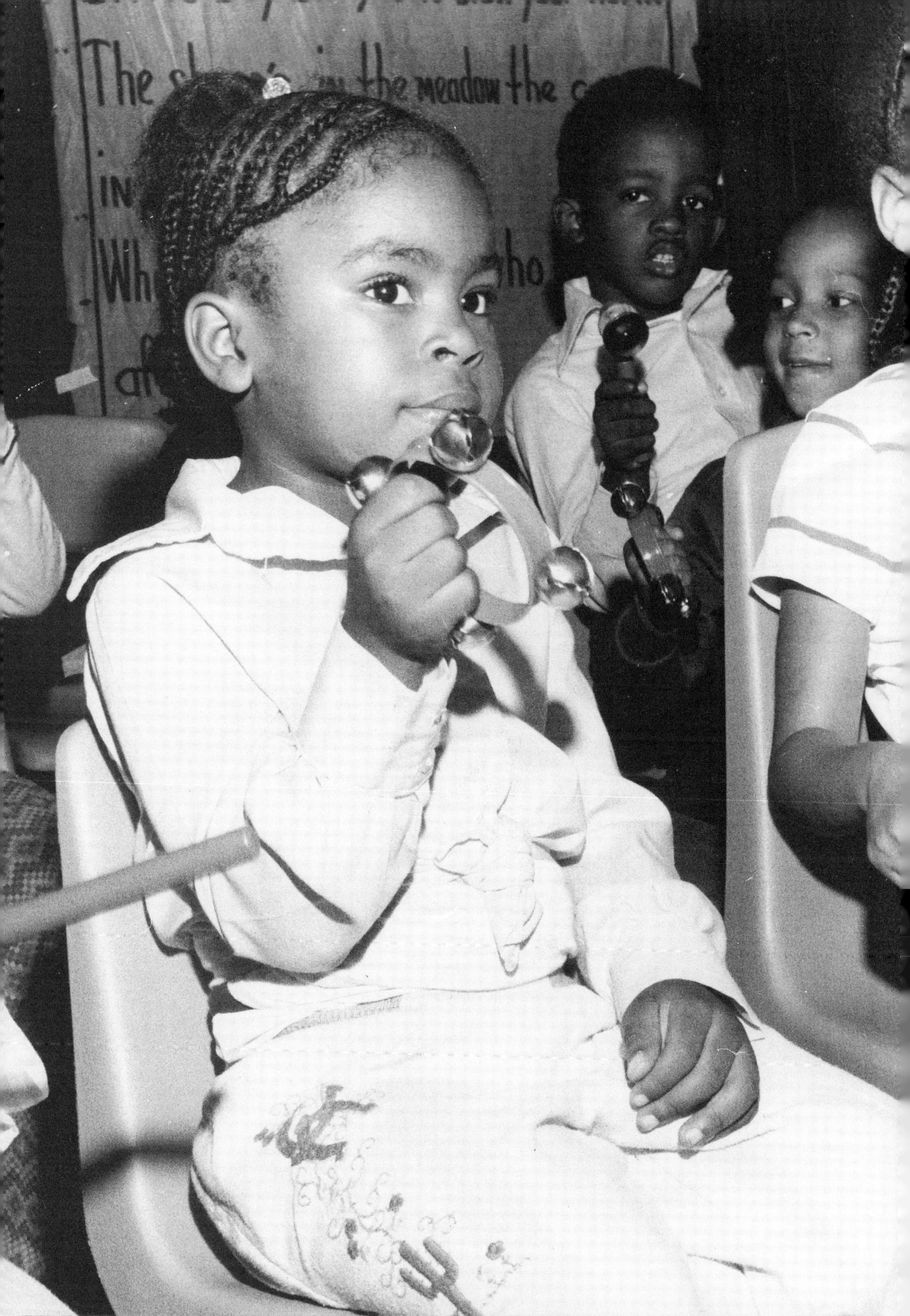

GETTING STARTED MODULE

". . . I have seen that in any great undertaking it is not enough for a man to depend simply upon himself."

– Lone Man [Isna la-wica] Teton Sioux

What Is This Module?

The "Getting Started" module is the first step, and a crucial one, along the *More Is Caught Than Taught* road. Now is the time when you take *MCTT* off the page and make it your own by applying it to your home, center, home-based program, and your community.

Note: Through this book the terms "center," "home," and "program" are used more or less interchangeably and refer to places where children are cared for and a program is organized for their development.

The *MCTT* program is built on the conviction that it takes a whole village to raise a child. Parents, child care providers, and community leaders all play a vital role in the lives, and the education, of children. All are models, all are teachers, regardless of whether we are consciously seeking those roles. Each of us, however, has something different to offer children, and if we want to build the strongest children we possibly can, we must draw on the strengths of each member of the community. This will make our children's education more comprehensive, and it will also reinforce the community through a bond of partnership.

In *MCTT*, you will forge this bond as you work together to make the child care center a place that reflects your collective vision. *MCTT* will take you through modules in which you will establish this vision; explore factors affecting the center, such as environment and internalized oppression; examine early childhood theorists and compare their visions to yours; and, finally, refashion the curriculum and the center based on what you know and have learned about the children in your community and about yourselves.

In the "Getting Started" module, you will build a strong foundation for the MCTT program by recruiting staff, parents, and community leaders as partners, emphasizing what they will bring to the process as well as what they will get from it. You will also build this foundation by introducing MCTT concepts to participants in a way that will allow them to see the program as relevant, important, and fun.

Much of the "Getting Started" module is about "nuts and bolts": creating a **Site Team**, recruiting participants, introducing the program and committing to follow it through to the end. These nuts and bolts hold the framework for MCTT together. The stronger they are, the stronger your resulting More Is Caught Than Taught program will be.

Expected Outcomes

Participants will:

- Develop a preliminary work plan
- Identify and assemble a site team
- Bring staff, parents, and community leaders into the process as partners
- Gain a thorough understanding of MCTT as individuals and as a group
- Voice and develop expectations for MCTT as a group
- Make up a plan for the first 3-4 modules of the program
- Develop a schedule for the first 3-4 modules of the program

Preparing

Who will participate?

Center staff, parents, and community leaders will all participate in the module. However, because of organizational considerations, we have found it advisable to create a site team. This should be a small group of people (6-8) who are already involved in the center and who will help in planning and implementing the MCTT program. Once you have established the site team, you will then work together to recruit other staff, parents, and community leaders. By the end of this module, you should have a full group of participants ready to move ahead through MCTT.

How long will it take?

The "Getting Started" module can take from a couple of weeks to several months, depending on the center. Because it is both introducing *MCTT* to a wider audience and laying the groundwork for the rest of the program, the "Getting Started" module can be a time-consuming phase. The importance of this module, though, is to make sure that there is a good, representative group of participants and that everyone understands and is committed to the *MCTT* program before going any further. Don't rush into the next module–wait until everyone is on the same page.

Where will it take place?

This module is made up of various meetings that can be held anywhere that is comfortable, convenient, and free of noise and other distractions. A site where chairs can be freely moved about and where newsprint can be taped to the walls is an important consideration.

When will it take place?

This module will take place in three stages. In the first stage, you will identify and recruit the site team, and you will schedule a meeting time convenient for the entire site team. In the second stage, you will meet with the site team and decide, among other things, the schedule for recruiting other *MCTT* participants. In the final stage, you will meet with all *MCTT* participants, and during this meeting you will set the schedule for the next two or three modules of the program.

How will you document this module?

It is essential to document the *MCTT* program because each module will build on the experiences and results of the one before it. Having a record of every meeting will help you in sending follow-up materials to participants, in planning for future meetings, and in evaluating the program once you have completed it. This documentation will also be very valuable in the future, as you continue to implement the changes you have identified and prioritized during the *MCTT* program.

There are various ways to document these modules, including taking good notes, audio taping, video taping, and making photographs. How you decide to document *MCTT* at your program will, of course, depend on the equipment you have access to, as well as which methods you prefer. Before ruling out any method due to lack of equipment, ask yourselves if there is anyone who might lend or otherwise provide you with the materials you seek.

> My whole life changed when I became the director of this program: the way I viewed my interaction with my children, the value I put on just having them as a part of my life. There was a time that I looked at having children and the responsibilities that I had as an awful liability, but then I became a part of these children and this community's life by caring for children, and I began to enhance my own growth with reading materials and interacting with other professionals, and I now view my children as the greatest asset that anyone could ever have.
>
> –Clara Card, Director, Joyland Child Development Center

What will you need to bring to these meetings?

Some suggestions:

- Loose paper
- Pencils or pens
- Blank newsprint paper (we find this helpful for writing up ideas where everyone can see them)
- Markers
- Masking tape
- Documentation materials and equipment
- Attendance sheet
- Agendas (enough for all participants)
- Support materials appropriate for the different meetings
- Food and drinks for a meal or snack

What else?

Is there anything else you need to think about or map out in your mind before going ahead?

Challenges of this Module

Changing the status quo is hard, even when we want to do it, and partnership means more than just saying the word. Going ahead with *MCTT* will mean a commitment to true "peerness" in your center. This may involve a new system of sharing power, assuming responsibilities, and communicating among the staff and with parents.

Part of what you will be asking from people is their voicing ideas about what can make the center better for children, for staff, and for the community. Does this mean criticizing the center as it is now? Not necessarily, but it does mean that people must have the freedom to discuss what doesn't work for them within the safety of knowing that these opinions have been asked for and will be taken seriously.

As you invite people into this process, it is necessary that overall program authority and responsibility be understood. In other words, when all voices have been solicited and heard and all positions and needs considered, who will and who will not have the power and responsibility to make real changes in the program? What will happen with the recommendations and suggestions generated by the site team and others? Putting these issues on the table and resolving them in the beginning of the program is strongly recommended.

MCTT cannot work unless there is trust and honesty among the participants. This will be developed and strengthened throughout the program, but it has to start now with the readiness and willingness to change old dynamics, resolve old disagreements, communicate in new ways, and recognize the strength in what others say and do. Asking people to join *MCTT* means being ready to change. Are you truly ready and committed?

Putting this Module into Action

Step One: Organize the Site Team

The site team will be the backbone of *MCTT* at your center. This should be a group not much larger than eight people who will join you in planning and implementing the rest of the program. At least one parent, one community leader, and one staff member should be on the site team. This group will take on the responsibility for *MCTT* at the center, and so it needs to be willing to commit time, energy, resources, and knowledge to this process. Group and individual responsibilities of the site team include:

- Determining how you will implement the *MCTT* program at your center: how each module will be presented; what materials will be used; and what the schedule will be

- Recruiting additional staff members, parents, and community leaders for the *MCTT* program

- Facilitating future modules of *MCTT*

- Documenting *MCTT* modules

- Contacting participants before meetings to remind them of the date and time and to send out any preparatory materials

- Contacting participants after meetings to send follow-up materials

- Doing anything else that is important to help the program run smoothly and ensure as much participation and equal involvement as possible

The site team will be extremely valuable in implementing *MCTT* at your center. It is crucial, however, that site team members not be considered "leaders" of the program or insiders who are giving their knowledge to other participants. *All members of MCTT should be equal partners, and all will make important contributions to the process.*

Basic Approach in Establishing the site team:

Seek out a diverse group so that you won't leave anyone or anything out as you build the program. In identifying potential members, think about how the group will work together and the strengths each person will bring.

Contact each potential site team member individually. Using the attached support materials–*MCTT* Program Talking Sheet, Site Team Description, Program Blueprint–as well as this manual, explain what *MCTT* is and why you think it's important to implement the program at your center. Tell the potential site member why s/he would be valuable to you for the process. Explain that being on the *MCTT* site team will be somewhat time-consuming, but that it will also be fun!

Set up a meeting time convenient for all those who have agreed to be members of the site team, and confirm the time with each member prior to the meeting.

Initial Site Team Meeting:

(This could be one or several meetings, depending on your schedule and the depth of your discussions)

- Distribute copies of this manual and other introductory *MCTT* materials, as well as any other materials you have identified as important.

- Share with the site team your understanding of what *MCTT* is and why you want to implement it at your center.

- Initiate a discussion concerning *MCTT*, your center, and your community. Possible questions to include:

- What does the expression "more is caught than taught" actually mean?
- What is an example of how children "catch" adult behavior and attitudes in our own center, homes, and community?
- What can the *More Is Caught Than Taught* program offer our center and our community?
- What assumptions does this program make?
- Are these assumptions valid for our center and community?
- What do we want to get out of the *MCTT* program?
- What do we realistically expect to get out of this program?
- What are our reservations and/or concerns about this program?

■ Share with the site team your understanding of the role its members will play in the *MCTT* program.

■ Continue the discussion with the focus on the site team. Possible questions include:

- How is the site team different from the rest of the *MCTT* group of participants?
- What will be expected of site team members in terms of time and energy?
- How will the site team members be partners with each other and with other *MCTT* participants?
- What is exciting about being on the site team?
- What are our reservations about being on the site team?

Before moving on, make sure that everyone feels comfortable with the concepts of *MCTT* and the site team. It's essential to the success of the program that site team members really take in the *MCTT* program and make it their own. Of course, you will all continue to learn about the program as you go through it, but answering as many questions as possible now will be helpful in the long run.

■ Develop an initial work plan with the site team by identifying who will be in charge of what aspect of *MCTT* and by setting up a preliminary time frame for the first three to four modules of the program. Some questions you might want to consider in creating your work plan include:

- Who will recruit parents and community leaders?

- Who will assemble materials and prepare for meetings?
- Who will facilitate meetings?
- How will we document meetings?
- Who will document meetings?
- Who will do follow-up to meetings?
- How long do you estimate it take to recruit a good-sized group of participants for the program?
- How many sessions or meetings do we want to devote to each module?
- How frequently will we hold these sessions?
- Do we need to buy or borrow any additional equipment or supplies that we'll need for the sessions?
- Except for more participants, is there anything else we need before moving ahead to the Vision module?

▪ Discuss the recruitment strategies included in Section 2, below, and decide as a group which strategy you'll use. Please don't feel restricted to what we have listed here. If you have a tried-and-true recruitment strategy that we haven't listed, go ahead and use it!

Step Two: Recruit Staff, Parents, and Community Leaders

Center Staff will be instrumental in seeing the *MCTT* program through at your center and in enacting whatever changes result from the program. *MCTT* will provide the staff with an opportunity to be creative, to apply their knowledge of children in new ways, and to interact differently with each other, parents, and with the children in their care.

However, staff in child care centers, as in any workplace, become comfortable with their routines and established practices, and *MCTT* represents change. It is important to recruit staff just as you do parents and community leaders. Don't assume that staff will be enthusiastic about the program just because you are, and don't simply order them to do it. This would be a violation of the *MCTT* partnership as well as an ineffectual way of securing participation and enthusiasm. People who have been through this program have found it enjoyable and exciting, and we believe that the staff at your center will also. For them to be fully invested in the program, they need to know in the beginning what it is, why you want to do it, what they will gain from it, and what each of them can give to it.

> I grew up around this community and I know a lot of people. I think that a familiar face going in and saying, "We're trying to get this program started; we think it could benefit you as well as the children in our center," then some people may feel like, "Hey, I want to be a part of that," and come out.
>
> –Coronda Davis, Teacher, Miller's Toulminville Day Care Center

The ideal in recruiting staff is to get the entire group into the program. If, however, you can't do this for any reason, be sure to include teachers from various areas of the program as well as administrators, food preparers, drivers, and so on.

Parents are the first and most fundamental educators of children, and *MCTT* is dedicated to supporting, enhancing, and augmenting that education by bringing parents into partnerships with their community. But, like all of us, parents are busy; they're juggling children and jobs, trying to make ends meet and still get some sleep at night. Many of them may not be as involved in the day care center as they would like to be, or as the center staff would like them to be.

Traditionally, parents have not been invited into the educational system–in fact they have been actively excluded from it–and so they may not have their receptors open at first. Our experience has taught us that getting parents truly involved is one of the toughest aspects of the "Getting Started" module. This doesn't mean that parents don't want to get involved; it means they may need additional support and convincing as to why their participation is valuable and essential.

In recruiting parents, try to get as diverse a group as you can, including current parents, grandparents, guardians, and parents who may no longer have children at the center. Endeavor to get a balance of men and women, if possible.

Community Leaders also play a vital role in the *MCTT* program by providing positive role models for the children; by contributing their particular visions, energies, and knowledge toward building a new future for the center, for children, and for families; by being a resource whom the center and parents can call on; and by being a bridge to the larger community.

Like parents, however, community leaders do not traditionally play more than a supporting role in child care centers. They may be invited in for presentations or mentoring programs, but they are rarely involved in decisions that affect how the center is run and what curriculum is used. For that reason, they may feel "unqualified" to participate in this way. Therefore it's important to stress to community leaders that *MCTT* is all about modeling the child care center on the vision, needs, and experiences of each particular community, and that their insight and partnership are essential for this process.

As with the other groups, it's important to get as diverse a group of community leaders as possible. Try to include educators, health care workers, artists, activists, business people, other child care providers, and anyone else who's active in the community and whose participation will improve the MCTT program. These people will continue to enrich your center in the future, because the bonds that you form with community leaders will last beyond the duration of the MCTT program.

Recruitment Strategies:

1. We recommend that you build from the ground up. Talk with each person one-on-one. Using the attached MCTT Program Talking Sheet and Program Blueprint, explain what MCTT is and why you're excited about it. Engage parents in talking about their children–what they want for them now and in the long term. Engage staff in talking about the center–how it provides for children and the ways in which it could provide more. Engage community leaders in discussing the needs of the community and their goals for it.

Help each person make connections between her/his vision and goals for children and a strong partnership among parents, child care providers, and the community. Demonstrate how MCTT can nurture and strengthen that partnership and be a powerful learning experience both at home and at the center. Strive to become one concerned individual talking with other concerned individuals about children in whom everyone has a very deep investment.

2. Meet in small groups. Get two or three staff members, parents, or community leaders together and talk with them following the model above. Encourage them to share ideas with each other and with others (we believe it's best to recruit parents, staff, and community leaders separately at this point). Increase the network in this way until all potential participants have been included.

3. Start off with larger group meetings of twelve or more staff members, parents, or community leaders.

Whatever strategy you choose, the following suggestions should be helpful.

More Is *Caught* Than Taught — Getting Started

- Get together with them in person, not over the telephone.

- Meet initially with parents and community leaders in their homes or offices, not at the child care center.

- Use the sample Talking Sheet and Program Blueprint, included here, and/or other written materials you can leave with them.

- Be familiar and comfortable with the *MCTT* program and concepts. Think about how you're going to present the process in an exciting, appealing way.

- Think about the people you recruit, and shape what you say to fit the individual listener's interests and strengths as much as possible.

- Be enthusiastic! Emphasize that *MCTT* is fun.

Additional Options:

1. After talking with them individually, conduct a group meeting with the <u>full staff</u> and the <u>site team</u>. Discuss one or several of the following questions and write ideas on newsprint in the front of the room.

- What do child care providers and parents have in common?

- What roles do child care providers play in the lives of children?

- What does "peerness" mean in a work setting?

- What was the world like when we were children? How has it changed for children today?

- What are the challenges we face as teachers that our teachers didn't face?

- How will *MCTT* help the children in our care? How will it help us as child care providers?

2. After talking with them individually, conduct a group meeting with <u>parents</u> and the <u>site team</u>. Discuss one or several of the following questions and write ideas on newsprint paper in the front of the room.

- What do parents and child care providers have in common?

- How are parents the primary teachers of their children?

- What does "partnership" really mean? How is it important?

- What was the world like when we were children? How has it changed for children today?

> The most fun has been when we get together with other people and everyone's talking and giving their ideas. We talk to people from the Board of Education and retired teachers, preachers, and councilmen. You know just meeting different people that you wouldn't ordinarily think of associating with and getting their view on things, and you find out that they have the same views as you have.
>
> –Jene Golson, Teacher, Kiddyland Child Development Center

- What are the challenges we face as parents that our parents didn't face?

- How will *MCTT* help our children? How will it help us as parents?

3. After talking with them individually, conduct a group meeting with <u>community leaders</u> and the <u>site team.</u> Discuss one or several of the following questions and write ideas on newsprint in the front of the room.

- What does the expression "It takes a whole village to raise a child" mean? What is the role of the community in the education of children?

- What was the world like when we were children? How has it changed for children today?

- What are the challenges we face as community leaders that are unique to today's world?

- What is the role of community leaders today?

- How do we reforge community connections that have broken down?

If you don't get the response you're hoping for in the beginning of the recruitment process, don't give up! Stay with it until people both understand the basics of *MCTT* and make a commitment for specific participation in the program.

Step Three: Bring All *MCTT* Participants Together

This will be your final meeting in the "Getting Started" module and an important one for galvanizing the group of *MCTT* participants at your center. We strongly encourage that you do some icebreaking exercises in the beginning to facilitate this process.

If you have already conducted separate group meetings with staff, parents, and community leaders, you might want to go straight into a discussion of *MCTT*. If you have not had these separate group meetings, it might be a good idea to discuss one or two of the sample questions listed in the "Additional Options" section, above, before going on to the *MCTT* program discussion.

1. What *MCTT* Is and How We Will Use It at Our Center

Go through an overview of the *MCTT* program, using the Program Blueprint, and briefly discuss each module so participants will know what to expect. Give participants blank *MCTT* "Work

More Is *Caught* Than Taught

Getting Started — Page 13

Planner" sheets so they can write down ideas, concerns, and priorities as you progress through the program.

Some possible questions to discuss:

- What does the expression "more is caught than taught" actually mean?

- What is an example of how children "catch" adult behavior and attitudes in our own center, homes, and community?

- What can the *More Is Caught Than Taught* program offer our center and our community?

- What assumptions does this program make?

- Are these assumptions valid for our center and community?

- What do we want to get out of the *MCTT* program?

- What are our reservations and/or worries about this program?

2. Roles of Participants

Explain the role of the site team and emphasize that every participant is an equal partner in *MCTT*. The site team members are merely the primary facilitators and organizers of the program–they are *not* the "leaders" of the program. It is important at this point to affirm and appreciate each participant's contribution.

3. How We Will "BE Together"

During the *MCTT* program, each person will encounter areas where s/he feels challenged, uncomfortable, and even angry. For the *MCTT* process to be successful, it is important to be open to these feelings in yourself and in others. Participants will come into the program with a wide array of experiences, beliefs, and priorities, and it is essential that each person's positions be given respect.

A later module will deal extensively with "How to BE Together," but in this initial stage, you need to set the gears in motion by encouraging participants to share their hearts and minds openly and candidly; to listen to each other and give full consideration to each other's thoughts, feelings and wishes; to try on new ideas and expand; and to take responsibility for helping create an atmosphere of love, caring, sensitivity, and cooperation.

4. Setting a Schedule

Set up a schedule for the next four or five meetings. This will allow people to plan ahead and to feel committed to the process from the beginning. In scheduling the meetings, make sure that the time is convenient for everyone. After having worked so hard to recruit people, you don't want to lose them now to scheduling conflicts! Of course, not everyone will be able to attend every meeting (although it would be great if they could). The important thing is to have as many participants as possible at each meeting. One way of helping people remember meetings is by setting each meeting on the same day of the week and at the same time of day.

Depending on how you have set up your timeline with the site team, these next four or five meetings might cover several modules, or cover only one or two. Either way, the important thing is to have the meeting schedule established and to secure commitments of time, energy, and partnership from all participants.

5. Next Steps

The next module is the "Vision" module, when you will identify and develop a collective vision for the children in your care. Ask participants to think about the Biblical statement, "A people without vision will perish."

Community involvement is essential to the success of the day care program. As community leaders, we can bring expertise in certain areas. We can bring resources: human, physical, and hopefully, some financial as well. In the areas of curriculum and program development, we can share our information, and we grow from the exposure and experience of working with day care employees and the kids. We can serve to empower the staff to continue in the hard work that they are doing with the kids. I think there's a lot we can do as community leaders.

–Constance Hendricks,
Community Leader, Joyland Child Development Center

More Is *Caught* Than Taught — *Getting Started* — Page 15

Resources

Books:

- Families and Early Childhood Programs, Douglas R. Powell
- A Parent's Guide to Early Childhood Education, Diane Trister Dodge and Joanna Phinney
- Teacher-Parent Relationships, J. G. Stone
- The Whole Child, Joanne Hendrick

Support Materials

- *MCTT* Program Talking Sheet
- *MCTT* Program Blueprint
- *MCTT* Site Team Description
- Agendas for all *MCTT* participants for various meetings in this module
- Expanded Agendas for the *MCTT* site team
- Blank *MCTT* Work Planner sheets to be distributed to all participants

Ice breaker exercises

Below are a few ice breaker exercises for you convenience. There are plenty of others to be found that are fun, and educational. Seek them out and make up your own.

I Used To But Now I . . .

Group members sit in a circle and one member begins by saying: "I used to . . . " and completes the phase however s/he wants. For example: "I used to be afraid of monsters." The next group member responds by saying "by now I . . . " completing the sentence however s/he wants. For example: "but now I have them over for lunch." The game continues around the circle until everyone has had a chance to speak a few times.

The Wind Blows

Group members sit in a circle with one person standing in the middle and no extra chairs. The person in the middle says: "the wind blows . . " and completes the sentence with something that s/he does, likes, or is. For example: "the wind blows for everyone who is wearing jeans." At this point all group members who are wearing jeans must stand up and move to a new chair. The person who does not get a seat and is left standing in the middle then begins the game over again saying "the wind blows . . ."

Forgotten Wallet

Group members are asked to pull an item out of their wallet or purse that has been there for a long time. Each person then tells a story about that item.

Who Are We Anyway?

For this exercise everyone needs a piece of paper and something to write with. Each group member is asked to think of an animal that s/he likes and write down three adjectives to describe it. Members are then asked to think of a color s/he likes and write down three adjectives to describe it. Finally, group members each think of a natural disaster (for example a tornado or flood) and write down three more adjectives. Group members are then told that the first set of adjectives describe themselves, the second set describe how others see them, and the third set describes how they see sex. Each member reads the adjectives and listens to the descriptions that everyone comes up with.

More Is Caught Than Taught
Program Talking Sheet

"It Takes a Whole Village To Raise a Child"

– African proverb

More Is Caught Than Taught is a program built around the wisdom of a well-known African proverb. The program provides a holistic approach for addressing the problems children face today and for preparing them to be leaders in the world of tomorrow. It does this by building partnerships among parents, child care providers, and community leaders and by using our combined knowledge, experience, and resources to strengthen the child care program and reinforce the attributes our children will need in order to thrive in the future.

The basic principle of *More Is Caught Than Taught* (*MCTT*) is that children learn through experience and observation. We all know the saying "Do what I say, not what I do," but we also know this doesn't work in reality. Children listen to adults, they watch adults, and they form their identities in large part based on what is happening around them. The home, child care center, and community are all important "schools" where children learn. *MCTT* helps participants identify and assume our role as teachers in these "schools." It assists us in developing a vision for what we want our children to learn, for what kind of children we want to grow. And it mobilizes us to create the best possible climate, offer the best possible curriculum, and present the ideal role models for the early childhood years of our children.

The main emphases of *MCTT* are:

VISION. The Bible says, "A people without vision will perish." In *MCTT* sessions, we develop a collective vision for the children of our community and specify the qualities, characteristics, skills, and knowledge we feel they must have to become leaders in the world. Through our vision, we affirm that we are the experts when it comes to the children of our own communities, and we link our dreams for our children to the qualities which will enable them to fulfill these dreams. Our vision for children is the spiritual core of the *MCTT* program. It is also a tangible listing of our goals for children that, during the rest of the program, we will be working to meet.

ENVIRONMENT. Just as plants thrive in a garden with rich soil, good sunlight, and lots of attention and watering, so do our children thrive in a warm, nurturing environment. In this part of the program we look at the physical and spiritual surroundings in which we live, work, and play, and we think about how these surroundings affect us and our children. Then we identify what environment can best grow the strong, healthy children of our vision and what we need to do to create that environment.

INTERNALIZED OPPRESSION AND HOW TO BE TOGETHER. We have all "caught," and been taught, roles that affect who we are, how we live our lives, and how we teach our children. Often, African-Americans are particularly disempowered by negative racial messages that we absorb from the world around us and internalize. *MCTT* helps participants identify, understand, and eliminate the thoughts, feelings, and dysfunctional behaviors shaped by internalized oppression and negative race, gender, age, class, and other scripts. At the same time we bring unique strengths often shaped by adversity. As we identify and address internalized oppression, we must also identify and affirm our strengths.

The program likewise invites us to envision how, given our diversity, we want to work and be together. Based on this vision, we then develop support systems that will affirm peer relationships among staff in the center, between the center and parents, and between the center and the community.

CURRICULUM. In these sessions, we select or craft a curriculum that reflects our vision of the children we want to grow, of the environment we want them to grow in, and of the peer relationships we want to model for them. Participants become familiar with early childhood principles and examine what is traditionally meant by "curriculum" and "lesson planning." We adapt these terms to encompass a wider body of knowledge, based on our life experiences, heritage, and vision. Our final result is a curriculum that is free from negative "caught" messages. Instead, it affirms our children and the type of learning which will help them grow to be strong, healthy, and happy leaders of tomorrow's world.

The *More Is Caught Than Taught* program can be accomplished in as few as twelve comprehensive sessions, or in many more, depending on time and commitment. The *MCTT* program is viewed as a process rather than a set of events. Thus, emphasis is placed on accomplishing the objectives of each module and growth along the way. We will spend as much time with each module as it takes to achieve the objectives. The process will be stimulating, educational, challenging, inspirational, and fun.

The *More Is Caught Than Taught* program was developed by FOCAL, a grassroots training and advocacy organization that has been serving child care centers in low-income and minority communities for over 25 years. FOCAL sees child care as a natural partner and essential resource to parents and families, and it sees child care programs as institutions with enormous potential for leadership and community development.

MORE IS CAUGHT THAN TAUGHT

Program Blueprint

I. **Getting Started**

   Objectives: To introduce staff, parents, and community leaders to *MCTT* and to gain a full understanding of the program; to encourage people to commit to participate in the program; to map out a plan for the program at the center.

   A. Establish a site team

   B. Develop a preliminary work plan with the site team

   C. Recruit staff, parents, and community leaders

   D. Conduct the first meeting with the entire group

      1. Introduce *MCTT* so that all have a thorough understanding of the program/process

      2. Develop and voice expectations for the *MCTT* program

      3. Develop a schedule for the first several modules of the program

II. **Vision**

   Objectives: To develop a collective vision for the care and development of the children in our charge.

   A. Conduct a "vision" session with all participants

      1. "What will the world be like in 15-20 years?" Identify the world our children will inherit.

      2. Identify individual visions of how we would like the world to be: "If I had all the resources and power, what world would I build?"

      3. "What keeps us from having this world? What are the barriers?"

      4. "Identify the qualities, characteristics, knowledge, and skills that children are going to have to possess to build the world we want."

III. **Environment**

   Objectives: To examine the environment of the children in our care and to define the characteristics of an environment needed to help grow the children of our vision.

   A. Conduct a meeting to discuss the environment of home, center, community

      1. What makes up the environment? What are its material and non-material elements?

      2. What elements of the environment are affirming to children?

   B. Visit places where child care and early childhood education are taking place

C. Conduct a meeting to discuss the site visits and define an environment that is most supportive of your vision for children

IV. **Internalized Oppression**

Objectives: To become aware of racial and other roles we have been taught and have "caught"; to become aware of dysfunctional feelings and behaviors shaped by these roles.

A. Conduct a session on Internalized Oppression

1. Identify and discuss the notion of inherent superiority and inherent inferiority which affects thinking, feeling, and behavior
2. View and discuss A Class Divided
3. Discuss internalized oppression as a condition resulting from the notion of inherent superiority and inherent inferiority
4. Discuss the alternative to the notion of inherent superiority and inherent inferiority

V. **"How To BE Together"**

Objectives: To identify and establish a basic contract or set of "rules" for being and working together based on the principles of Internalized Oppression theory.

A. Conduct a session on "How To BE Together"

1. Explore how the notion of inherent superiority and inherent inferiority manifests itself in child care programs
2. Explore the advantages and challenges of diversity
3. Discuss strategies for "being together" and encompassing diversity, such as the "Cooperative Mode"
4. Make a contract for being together in the *MCTT* program and in the center that will break down the system of superiority and inferiority

VI. **Early Childhood Theory**

Objectives: To identify and examine our own early childhood theories and to become familiar with prevailing theories; to develop a philosophy that integrates elements we like from various theories.

A. Conduct a meeting to discuss early childhood theory as it relates to us and our center

1. Explore our own "caught and taught" theories of early childhood development
2. Explore the philosophy guiding the operation of the center

B. Conduct a meeting to become familiar with the work of established early childhood theorists and to integrate their ideas with our own

1. Read and discuss the prevailing theories of early childhood development and examine their relevance to our children and our community

2. Develop a working philosophy that represents the early childhood theories of *MCTT* participants

VII. **Curriculum, Lesson Planning, and Assessment**

Objectives: To examine our current curriculum in light of early childhood theories and our particular vision for children; to reaffirm or refashion our curriculum, lesson plans, and assessment strategies so that they reflect our vision for children and include those elements that will help our children grow to become leaders in tomorrow's world.

A. Review our current curriculum, including lesson plans and assessment strategies

B. Conduct a meeting to discuss our curriculum

1. Which early childhood theory, if any, is most reflected in our curriculum?

2. How well is our vision for children reflected in our curriculum?

C. Review other curricula and compare them to ours and to our Vision Statement

D. Redesign, reaffirm, or recreate our curriculum so that it will be based on our vision, knowledge, and the insight we've gained during the *MCTT* program

VIII. **Work Plan**

Objectives: To gain increased familiarity with the tools and techniques for appropriate planning; to develop a comprehensive work plan for the rest of the *MCTT* process based on priorities identified during the first seven modules.

A. Review our own methods and strategies for short- and long-term planning

B. Review other planning methods and strategies

C. Develop a comprehensive work plan to accomplish priorities established during the *MCTT* program using the methods and strategies we believe are the most effective for our center

More Is Caught Than Taught Program

Site Teams

Definition: A site team is a group of approximately 8 people who have assumed responsibility for guiding the *MCTT* program in our community.

Membership: At least one parent, one community leader, and one staff member should be on the site team. There should be as great a diversity as possible in terms of areas of interest, expertise, and experience among the members of the site team.

Responsibilities:

- Committing energy, enthusiasm, and time to the *MCTT* program
- Determining how to implement the *MCTT* program at the center
- Recruiting additional staff members, parents, and community leaders to the *MCTT* program
- Facilitating future *MCTT* modules
- Documenting *MCTT* modules
- Preparing for *MCTT* meetings
- Doing follow-up to *MCTT* meetings
- Determining the initial schedule and work plan for implementing *MCTT* at the center

Agenda

More Is Caught Than Taught Program
Site Team Meeting

1. **Welcome**
2. **Introductions**
3. **Explanation of the meeting agenda**

    Purpose of the meeting

    - To gain an understanding of the *MCTT* program and the role of the site team
    - To confirm our commitment to the program and to the site team
    - To determine how we will implement *MCTT* at our center
    - To take on specific responsibilities for recruiting participants and implementing the *MCTT* program at our center

4. **Discussion of the *MCTT* program**
5. **Discussion of the site team**
6. **Development of a preliminary work plan**
7. **Discussion of *MCTT* partnerships and recruitment**
8. **Choice of a recruitment strategy**
9. **Next steps**
10. **Closing**

Expanded Agenda

More Is Caught Than Taught Program
Site Team Meeting

1. **Welcome**

2. **Introductions**

3. **Explanation of the meeting agenda**

    Purpose of the meeting

    - To gain an understanding of the MCTT program and the role of the site team
    - To confirm our commitment to the program and to the site team
    - To determine how we will implement MCTT at our center
    - To take on specific responsibilities for recruiting participants and implementing the MCTT program at our center

4. **Discussion of the MCTT program**
    - Share with participants your understanding of the MCTT program and why you want to implement it at the center.
    - Briefly go through the program, using the Program Talking Sheet, Program Blueprint, and Site Team Description forms as support materials
    - Discuss as a group some fundamental questions about MCTT and how the program will work at your center. Possible questions include:
        - What does the expression "more is caught than taught" actually mean?
        - What is an example of how children catch adult behavior in our own center, homes, and community?
        - What can the *More Is Caught Than Taught* program offer our center and our community?
        - What assumptions does this program make? Are they valid for our center and community?
        - What do we want to get out of this program? What do we expect to realistically get out of this program?
        - What are our reservations and/or concerns about this program?

- Discussion of the site team (possible questions to discuss):
  - How is the site team different from the rest of the *MCTT* group of participants?
  - What will be expected of site team members in terms of time and labor?
  - How will the site team members be partners with each other and with other *MCTT* participants?
  - What is exciting about being on the site team?
  - What are our reservations about being on the site team?

6. **Development of a preliminary work plan. Group and individual decisions and responsibilities include:**
   - Recruiting parents and community leaders–who will do it, how long will we spend on it?
   - Assembling materials and preparing for meetings–who will do it, what will we need?
   - Facilitating meetings–who will do it when, how will we prepare for it?
   - Documenting meetings–who will do it, what method will we choose, what materials will we need?
   - Doing follow-up to meetings–who will do it, what will we do?
   - Setting the initial schedule–how many meetings will we devote to each module, how often will we hold these meetings?
   - Is there anything else we need–equipment, supplies, resources, understanding of the program–before going ahead?

7. **Discussion of *MCTT* partnerships and recruitment**
   - Center staff will be instrumental in seeing the *MCTT* program through at the center and in enacting whatever changes result from the program. *MCTT* will provide them with an opportunity to be creative, to apply their knowledge of children in new ways, and to interact differently with each other and with the children in their care.
   - Parents are the first and most important educators of children, and *MCTT* is dedicated to supporting, enhancing, and augmenting that education by bringing parents into partnerships with the center and their community. Their experiences and perspectives are of vital importance to the *MCTT* process.
   - Community leaders play a vital role in the *MCTT* process by providing positive role models; by contributing their particular visions, energies, and knowledge; by being a resource that the center and parents can call on; and by being a bridge to the larger community.
   - All three groups are essential to the success of *MCTT*, and all will be full partners in this program at all levels. Parents and community leaders do not traditionally play

more than a supporting role in child care centers, however, and are rarely involved in decisions that affect how the center is run and what curriculum is used. Similarly, center staff are often not included in this type of decision-making at the center. For this reason, parents, community leaders, and staff may initially feel "unqualified" to participate.

- This is why it's important to recruit each person by emphasizing that *MCTT* is all about strengthening the child care center based on the vision, needs, and experiences of our particular community, and that each person's insight, knowledge, and experiences are crucial to this process.

8. **Choice of a recruitment strategy. Recruitment strategies include the following:**
    - Get as diverse a group as possible. Include grandparents, guardians, fathers, mothers, educators, health care workers, artists, business people, activists, "outside" child care providers, and others.
    - Talk with each person one-on-one and engage her/him on a personal level: talk about her/his children and what s/he wants for them, etc. Explain how this relates to *MCTT*.
    - Help each person make connections between her/his vision and goals for children and a strong partnership between parents, child care providers, and the community, and then tie this goal to *MCTT*.
    - Get together with them in person, not over the phone, and meet initially outside of the center.
    - Bring and use support materials that you can leave with them.
    - Be familiar with the *MCTT* process and give thought as to how you're going to present the program in an exciting way.
    - Think about the people you recruit and shape what you say to fit the individual listener's interests and strengths.
    - Be enthusiastic! Emphasize that *MCTT* is enjoyable.

9. **Next Steps**
    - Recruiting staff, parents, and community leaders individually
    - Recruiting staff, parents, and community leaders in groups if desired
    - Bringing all *MCTT* participants together for a full "Getting Started" meeting

10. **Closing**

Agenda

More Is Caught Than Taught Program
Recruitment Meeting for Staff

1. Welcome

2. Introductions

3. Explanation of the meeting agenda

    Purpose of the meeting

    - To gain an understanding of the *MCTT* program and the role of the center staff
    - To confirm our commitment to the program

4. Discussion of the *MCTT* program

5. Roles of *MCTT* participants and how we will "BE together"

6. Next Steps

7. Closing

Expanded Agenda

More Is Caught Than Taught Program
Recruitment Meeting for Staff

1. **Welcome**

2. **Introductions**

    Though staff will all know each other, this is nevertheless a valuable exercise. Perhaps each staff member could say a little bit here about her/his hopes and expectations for the *MCTT* program.

3. **Explanation of the meeting agenda**

    Purpose of the meeting

    - To gain an understanding of the *MCTT* program and the role of the center staff
    - To confirm our commitment to the program

4. **Discussion of the *MCTT* program**
    - Share with participants your understanding of the *MCTT* program and why you want to implement it at the center.
    - Briefly go through the program, using the Program Talking Sheet, Program Blueprint, and Site Team Description forms as support materials
    - Discuss as a group some fundamental questions about *MCTT* and how the program will work at your center. Possible questions include:
        - What do child care providers and parents have in common?
        - What roles do child care providers play in the lives of children?
        - What does "peerness" mean in a work setting?
        - What was the world like when we were children?
        - How has the world changed for children today?
        - What are the challenges we face as teachers that our teachers didn't face?
        - How will the *MCTT* program help the children in our care?
        - How will the *MCTT* program help us as child care providers?

5. **Roles of *MCTT* participants and how we will "BE together"**

    - Center staff will be instrumental in seeing the *MCTT* program through at the center and in enacting whatever changes result from the program. *MCTT* will provide staff with an opportunity to be creative, to apply their knowledge of children in new ways, and to interact differently with each other and with the children in their care. It is important to include all staff in the program, because everyone who interacts with children is a teacher of those children. Administrative staff, kitchen staff, bus drivers and others will be equal partners with the center director(s) and the classroom teachers in the *MCTT* program.

    - The *MCTT* site team is a group of people who are merely the primary facilitators and organizers of the *MCTT* program–they are not the "leaders" of the program.

    - Participants will come into the program with a wide array of experiences, beliefs, and priorities, and it is essential that each person's position be given respect. Participants are encouraged to share their hearts and minds openly and candidly; to listen to each other and give full consideration to each other's thoughts, feelings, and wishes; to try on new ideas and expand their thinking or views; and to take responsibility for helping to create an atmosphere of love, caring, sensitivity, and cooperation.

6. **Next Steps**

    - Bringing all *MCTT* participants–including the site team, staff, parents, and community leaders–together for a full "Getting Started" meeting

7. **Closing**

Agenda

More Is Caught Than Taught Program
Recruitment Meeting for Parents

1. **Welcome**

2. **Introductions**

3. **Explanation of the meeting agenda**

    Purpose of the meeting

    - To gain an understanding of the *MCTT* program and the role of parents, grandparents, and guardians
    - To confirm our commitment to the program

4. **Discussion of the *MCTT* program**

5. **Roles of *MCTT* participants and how we will "BE together"**

6. **Next Steps**

7. **Closing**

Expanded Agenda

More Is Caught Than Taught Program
Recruitment Meeting for Parents

1. **Welcome**

2. **Introductions**

   Though many parents may know each other, this is an important way of getting people to feel comfortable, introducing the site team members, and making sure that everyone is equally included. You might consider doing an ice-breaker exercise in addition to introductions.

3. **Explanation of the meeting agenda**

   Purpose of the meeting

   - To gain an understanding of the *MCTT* program and the role of parents, grandparents, and guardians
   - To confirm our commitment to the program

4. Discussion of the *MCTT* program

   - Share with participants your understanding of the *MCTT* program and why you want to implement it at the center.
   - Briefly go through the program, using the Program Talking Sheet and Program Blueprint as support materials.
   - Discuss as a group some fundamental questions about *MCTT* and how the program will work at your center. Possible questions include:
     - What do parents and child care providers have in common?
     - How are parents the primary teachers of their children?
     - What does "partnership" really mean? How is it important?
     - What was the world like when we were children?
     - How has the world changed for children today?
     - What are the challenges we face as parents that our parents didn't face?
     - How will the *MCTT* program help our children?

- How will the *MCTT* program help us as parents, grandparents, and guardians?

5. **Roles of *MCTT* participants and how we will "BE together"**

    - Parents are the first and most important educators of children, and *MCTT* is dedicated to supporting, enhancing, and augmenting that education by bringing parents into partnerships with the center and their community. Parents' experiences and perspectives are of vital importance to the *MCTT* process, and parents will be full partners in *MCTT* along with the center director, center staff, and community leaders.

    - The *MCTT* site team is a group of people who are merely the primary facilitators and organizers of the *MCTT* program–they are not the "leaders" of the program.

    - Participants will come into the program with a wide array of experiences, beliefs, and priorities, and it is essential that each person's position be given equal weight and respect. Participants are encouraged to share their hearts and minds openly and candidly; to listen to each other and give full consideration to each other's thoughts, feelings, and wishes; to try on new ideas and expand; and to take responsibility for helping to create an atmosphere of love, caring, sensitivity, and cooperation.

6. Next Steps

    - Bringing all *MCTT* participants–including the site team, staff, parents, and community leaders–together for a full "Getting Started" meeting

7. **Closing**

Agenda

More Is Caught Than Taught Program
Recruitment Meeting for Community Leaders

1. Welcome

2. Introductions

3. Explanation of the meeting agenda

4. Purpose of the meeting
   - To gain an understanding of the *MCTT* program and the role of community leaders
   - To confirm our commitment to the program

5. Discussion of the *MCTT* program

6. Roles of *MCTT* participants and how we will "BE together"

7. Next Steps

8. Closing

Agenda

More Is Caught Than Taught Program
Recruitment Meeting for Community Leaders

1. **Welcome**

2. **Introductions**
   This is an important way of getting people comfortable, introducing community leaders to each other and to the site team members, and making sure everyone is equally included. You might consider doing an ice-breaker exercise in addition to introductions

3. **Explanation of the meeting agenda**

   Purpose of the meeting
   - To gain an understanding of the *MCTT* program and the role of community leaders
   - To confirm our commitment to the program

4. **Discussion of the *MCTT* program**
   - Share with participants your understanding of the *MCTT* program and why you want to implement it at the center.
   - Briefly go through the program, using the Program Talking Sheet and Program Blueprint as support materials.
   - Discuss as a group some fundamental questions about *MCTT* and how the program will work at your center. Possible questions include:
     - What does the expression "It takes a whole village to raise a child" mean?
     - What is the role of the community in children's education?
     - What was the world like when we were children?
     - How has the world changed for children today?
     - What are the challenges we face as community leaders that are unique to today's world?
     - What is the role of community leaders today?
     - How do we reforge community connections that have broken down?

5. **Roles of *MCTT* participants and how we will "BE together"**

- It is vital to the success of the *MCTT* program to have full participation by community leaders. Community leaders provide positive role models for the children; they contribute their particular knowledge, energy, and vision; they are a resource that the center and families can call on; and they are a bridge to the larger community. Community leaders will be full partners in *MCTT* with center staff and parents.

- The *MCTT* site team is a group of people who merely are the primary facilitators and organizers of the *MCTT* program–they are not the "leaders" of the program.

- Participants will come into the program with a wide array of experiences, beliefs, and priorities, and it is essential that each person's position be given respect. Participants are encouraged to share their hearts and minds openly and candidly; to listen to each other and give full consideration to each other's thoughts, feelings, and wishes; to try on new ideas and expand; and to take responsibility for helping to create an atmosphere of love, caring, sensitivity, and cooperation.

6. **Next Steps**

    - Bringing all *MCTT* participants - including the site team, staff, parents, and community leaders - together for a full "Getting Started" meeting

6. **Closing**

Agenda

More Is Caught Than Taught Program
"Getting Started" Meeting

1. Welcome

2. Introductions

3. Explanation of the meeting agenda

   Purpose of the meeting
   - To review as a group our understanding of the *MCTT* program and the roles of participants
   - To confirm our commitment to the program

4. To establish a schedule for the next 4 or 5 meetings of the program

5. Discussion of the *MCTT* program

6. Roles of *MCTT* participants and how we will "BE together"

7. Scheduling upcoming meetings

8. Next steps

9. Closing

Expanded Agenda

More Is Caught Than Taught Program
"Getting Started" Meeting

1. **Welcome**

2. **Introductions**
   - This is the first meeting attended by all participants, and so it is a time both for celebration and for galvanizing the group. Therefore it is important that everyone get as comfortable and well acquainted with each other as possible.
   - In addition to introducing yourselves, participants might want to say at this point briefly why they are participating in the *MCTT* program and what elements of the program they find exciting and/or interesting.
   - Do at least one ice-breaker exercise.

3. **Explanation of the meeting agenda**

   Purpose of the meeting
   - To review as a group our understanding of the *MCTT* program and the roles of participants
   - To confirm our commitment to the program
   - To establish a schedule for the next 4 or 5 meetings of the program

4. **Discussion of the *MCTT* program**
   - Go through an overview of the *MCTT* program, using the Program Blueprint and any other support materials you'd like, and briefly discuss each module so participants will know what to expect.
   - Give participants a blank *MCTT* "Work Planning" sheet so they can write down ideas, concerns, and priorities as the program progresses.
   - Discuss as a group some fundamental questions about *MCTT* and the program at your center. Possible questions include:
     - What does the expression "more is caught than taught" actually mean?
     - What is an example of how children catch adult behavior in our own center, homes, and community?

- What can the *More Is Caught Than Taught* program offer our center and our community?
- What assumptions does this program have?
- Are these assumptions valid for our center and community?
- What do we want to get out of the *MCTT* program?
- What do we expect realistically to get out of the *MCTT* program?
- What are our reservations and/or concerns about this program?

5. **Roles of participants and how we will "BE together"**

   - It is vital to the success of the *MCTT* program to have full participation by parents, center staff, and community leaders. All three groups will be equal partners in *MCTT*.

   - Center staff will be instrumental in seeing the *MCTT* program through at the center and in enacting whatever changes result from the program. *MCTT* will provide them with an opportunity to be creative, to apply their knowledge of children in new ways, and to interact differently with each other and with the children in their care.

   - Parents are the first and most important educators of children, and *MCTT* is dedicated to supporting, enhancing, and augmenting that education by bringing parents into partnerships with the center and their community. Their experiences and perspectives are of vital importance to the *MCTT* process.

   - Community Leaders play an essential role in the *MCTT* process by providing positive role models; by contributing their particular visions, energies, and knowledge; by being a resource that the center and parents can call on; and by being a bridge to the larger community.

   - The *MCTT* site team is a group of people who are merely the primary facilitators and organizers of the *MCTT* program–they are not the "leaders" of the program.

   - Participants will come into the program with a wide array of experiences, beliefs, and priorities, and it is essential that each person's position be given equal weight and respect. Participants are encouraged to share their hearts and minds openly and candidly; to listen to each other and give full consideration to each other's thoughts, feelings, and wishes; to try on new ideas and expand; and to take responsibility for helping to create an atmosphere of love, caring, sensitivity, and cooperation.

6. **Setting a schedule for upcoming meetings**

   - Get as much of a consensus as possible about which day of the week and what times are best for participants, making sure they know that meetings will last 2 hours or more.

   - Set up 4 or 5 future meetings, trying to set them all for the same day of the week and time, which will help participants remember to attend.

7. **Next Steps**
   - The next module is the "Vision" module, when you will identify and develop a collective vision for the children in your care. In preparation for the "Vision" session, participants could think about the Biblical statement, "A people without vision will perish."

8. **Closing**

VISION MODULE

"A People Without Vision Will Perish"

– The Bible, Proverbs

What Is This Module?

The "Vision" module is perhaps the most vital module of *More Is Caught Than Taught*, because it is during this session(s) that you will establish a collective vision for children to serve as your foundation and road map for the rest of the program.

Your particular vision for children will be an expression of your love, hopes, and dreams for them, but it is much more than that. It is a celebration of your children's enormous potential. It is an affirmation of your power to actively influence and shape your children's lives in a positive way. Finally, it is a resource of incredible power that every person possesses. *MCTT* does not create this vision; it is a way of harnessing it.

Within all of us lies a great reserve of energy, and in the *MCTT* program you can open the door to that energy by exploring your vision and sharing it with others. Once this door is open, your capacity for building will be unlimited. Overcoming the material, economic, social, and spiritual barriers that prevent children from achieving their full potential is difficult for all families and extremely difficult for poor families. This goal is virtually impossible without energy, vision, motivation, and determination. In this module, the *MCTT* program both taps into these strengths and magnifies them by uniting the vision of parents, child care providers, and concerned community leaders.

In the "Vision" module we ask and answer the question: What kind of children do we want to grow? By asking this question, we are not looking to the people in power to tell us what our children need and should have. Instead, we are recognizing that we are the experts when it comes to the children of our own families and communities. We are the ones who know firsthand what their strengths and troubles are, what barriers lie before them, and what accomplishments they have made. By validating our role as experts, we affirm that our dreams for our children are both relevant and realizable, because they are grounded in the strength of our knowledge and experience.

In asking "What kind of children do we want to grow?," we are also assuming responsibility for the raising of our children. We recognize not only that we have enormous influence over how our children grow and who they become, but that this process involves decisions on our part. Are we choosing to grow children who will become leaders in tomorrow's world, or are we growing children who will simply be survivors in that world? Or, worse yet, are we raising children who will become casualties to violence, abuse, and spiritual bankruptcy?

If we want to grow leaders, we must instill in our children the skills, qualities, and characteristics that will enable them to overcome the barriers facing them. In this "Vision" module, we link our dreams for our children to the qualities which will enable them to fulfill these dreams. As a result, our vision becomes a call to action.

The "Vision Statement " which you create during this module will be your call to action. You will return to it again and again, during the *MCTT* program and after you have finished it. This is because the "Vision Statement" is the spiritual core of the program and it is also a tangible listing of your specific goals for your children. During the rest of the *MCTT* program you will be focusing on how to mold your child care/development program and curriculum to fit these goals.

Expected Outcomes

Participants will

- Expand your understanding and affirm your role in relation to children in your care.

- Develop a collective vision of the kind of family, community, and world you want to have.

- Identify and articulate barriers to achieving this vision.

- Develop a collective vision of the children you want to "grow" – a vision which includes the specific qualities, characteristics, knowledge, and skills they must have in

More Is *Caught* Than Taught　　　　　***Vision***　　　　　Page 43

order to overcome the barriers and become leaders in tomorrow's world.

- Emerge with a written vision statement that will guide the development and administration of programs at your center.

Preparing

Who will participate?

All members of the site team, staff, parents, and community leaders.

It's crucial that the person who will be the facilitator at this meeting be passionate about the importance and relevance of vision to this program and to the lives of participants and children. The facilitator must have real energy and commitment and must be able to convey these feelings to the other participants. Without the fire of a facilitator who feels and "lives" the session, the participants will come up short.

How long will it take?

The Vision session can take place in one meeting of two hours, but since the collective vision you develop here will be the cornerstone of the program, you are encouraged to devote as much time as you want and need to achieve that vision. Make sure you've got hold of that energy before moving on to the next module!

Where will it take place?

The "Vision" module is not site-specific. It can take place anywhere that is comfortable, convenient for participants, and free of noise and other distractions. A site where chairs can be freely moved about and where newsprint paper can be taped to the walls is an important consideration.

When will it take place?

You will have set the dates for this and future meetings in the "Getting Started" module, but you will want to send out a reminder to program participants including the date, time, and place of the session.

How will you document this module?

It is a good idea to touch base with the person who agreed during the "Getting Started" module to document the meeting to make sure s/he has all the necessary materials and equipment for the documentation method that you have selected (audio taping, video

> Up to 25 years ago, people didn't have a vision for organizing, putting something together for their children. Instead they were taking them to the fields and having them sit at the end of the row while they chopped cotton or whatever. In those days, they didn't think, "Well, maybe one person can organize and take care of all our children while we work."
>
> –Mary Jones, Director, Kiddy Land Child Development Center

taping, making photographs, and taking good notes are some of the options).

What will you need to bring to the session?

Some suggestions:

- Blank newsprint paper. This works very well in this session; creating a banner-sized "Vision Statement" with the articulated vision of participants written large for all to see really gives momentum to the process and makes the "Vision Statement" a powerful, common property.
- Markers
- Loose paper
- Pencils or pens
- Masking tape
- Documentation materials and equipment
- Attendance sheet
- Agendas
- Food and drinks for meal or snack

Other possible materials include:

- Photos of participants' children or children close to them
- Photos of women and men of vision

What else?

Is there anything else you need to do to prepare for the "Vision" module?

Challenges of this Module

The "Vision" module is empowering and exciting for participants. It can also be intimidating at first. We are accustomed to "experts" telling us what is right for us and our children without asking for our input or acknowledging our role as the primary teachers of children. Participants may have never before been asked seriously what they want for themselves and for children. As a result, they may have difficulty believing that their vision is important, that it is powerful, and that it will really be used in guiding the *MCTT* program and the future of the center. To counteract this, it is essential to validate the role and vision of each participant, and to affirm the importance and strength of the "Vision Statement" you will create. A key thing to remember is that this vision is deeply spiritual.

Putting this Module into Action

The "Vision" Session

The facilitator will lead the session by introducing exercises, establishing times for each exercise, and, most importantly, creating a fun, energetic, and connected environment for the session.

Basic approach:

1. **Identify what "Vision" is and what role it plays in people's lives.**

   - Discuss in small groups the Biblical statement, "A people without vision will perish." Then share ideas among the groups.

2. **Identify the world your children will inherit in 15-20 years in terms of social, economic, political, and spiritual conditions.**

   - Think individually about what the world will be like in 15-20 years.

   - Share individual thoughts in small groups, making sure someone in each group is writing down what's said.

   - Come together as a full group to call out ideas to two participants at the front of the room who will write them on newsprint.

How the World Will Possibly Be in 15-20 Years:

An example from Joyland, Kiddy Land, and Miller's Centers

Parents will lose control	‣ Self-destruction	‣ Breakup of families
‣ More gangs, more drugs	‣ Black-on-Black crime	‣ Total automation
‣ More crime	‣ More homelessness	‣ Better conditions for African-Americans
‣ Lack of leadership	‣ Wider gap between haves and have nots	‣ Fewer governmental programs
‣ Breakdown in moral standards	‣ Increased need for a sense of community and family	‣ Increased pollution of the environment

1. **Identify the world you would like to have in 15-20 years.**

    - Think individually about what world you would build if you had all the resources and the power.

    - Feel and see yourself in an ideal community. What does it look like?

    - Share your vision of an ideal community and world with small groups. Come together as a full group to call out ideas to two participants at the front of the room who will write them on newsprint paper.

Vision of How We Would Like the World To Be:

An example from Joyland, Kiddy Land, and Miller's Centers

‣ Love	‣ Individual responsibility	‣ Unity
‣ Honesty	‣ More self-love	‣ No drugs
‣ Respect for parents	‣ Sharing	‣ No violence
‣ Value the environment	‣ Safe communities, neighborhoods looking	‣ Clean, healthy environment
‣ Abolish racism, classism, sexism	‣ Kids can be kids	‣ Communities raising children

1. **Identify the barriers to your vision and reflect on the material and non-material nature of these barriers.**

    - Discuss in small groups what keeps you from having this ideal world, what the barriers are.

    - Come together as a full group to call out ideas to two participants at the front of the room who will write them on newsprint.

5. **Identify the attributes your children will have to possess in order to lead the world towards your vision.**

    - Discuss in small groups what qualities, characteristics, skills, and knowledge your children will need to possess in order to overcome these barriers and create the world of your vision.

    - Come together as a full group to call out ideas to two participants at the front of the room who will write them on newsprint.

Qualities, Characteristics, Knowledge and Skills Our Children Must Have to Bring About Our Vision:

An example from Joyland, Kiddy Land, and Miller's Centers

1. **Affirm the "Vision Statement" created in the session and agree to base the rest of the *MCTT* program on this vision.**

   - Look at the final section of your newsprint. This is your "Vision Statement." These are your unique priorities, goals, and requirements for the children in your care. Everything in the *MCTT* program will come back to this document.

7. **Discuss next steps.**

   - The facilitator should tie the "Vision" module to the rest of the program. If you're going on to the "Environment" module next, let participants know how vision leads to environment: "If we want to build these children, what environment do we want them to have? What environment must we create in order to 'grow' the children of our vision?"

8 **Evaluate the session using evaluation forms.**

Additional options:

   a. Use photos of participants' children or children close to them. When they arrive, participants could tape photos to a blank piece of paper on an easel and write the child's name above it. Then these would be a reference point in the room that would make the discussion of children more grounded, less abstract. The facilitator could point to the photos and mention children by name throughout the session to make it more personal. Another option along the same lines would be for participants to bring in something special relating to their child: a toy, something the child has made, and so on.

   b. Ask participants to identify all of the steps in creating a perfect vegetable garden, then ask them to define the steps involved in "growing" the children in their care. Make reflections on the process of each activity and the need to be at least as proficient in growing children as we are in growing vegetables. Then follow with steps 2-8 above.

   c. The "Vision" module offers a wealth of opportunities for discussion that can be very deep, educational, philosophical, and spiritually bonding. Consider taking the time needed to explore some of the following questions:

- How is vision different from hope?
- What is the significance of the fact that the elements of the vision are primarily non-material?
- If the "Vision" and the barriers to it are mostly spiritual, does this tend to level the field between "powerless" and powerful people?
- How does the vision of your group compare with the vision of national and international leaders?
- Can the vision of the group be achieved without personal transformation?
- What are the implications if the entire world shared the vision of your group?
- If "*More Is Caught Than Taught*," then what vision are children likely to "catch" from you?
- Is a person without vision in effect making the statement: Please lead me, regardless of where you're taking me?
- What is your vision for yourself?
- Other options for increasing the power of the "Vision" module might include viewing videos; reading excerpts, papers, and articles; and attending lectures on a relevant subject before the Vision Session.

> I am a working mother with a number of children and I started this business not knowing anything about business practices, but being willing to learn and read. I'm hoping that this program will give the parents that I'm serving some incentive to work and make life better where they are right now, because each year can bring about a change if you work towards that change. Nobody ever has to be in one place and stay there unless you have no motivation to move. So I hope that I will able, as I have in the past, to touch the lives of some of these young women to do something with their lives.
>
> –Clara Card, Director, Joyland Child Development Center

Follow-up

Bring the site team together to do a group evaluation of the first meeting and to add relevant ideas to the "Vision" section of the work plan.

Write up all the lists you generated during the meeting and send copies to all *MCTT* participants or distribute them at the next meeting.

More Is *Caught* Than Taught — Vision — Page 49

Resources

Books:

- *Black in Selma,* J.L. Chestnut, Jr.
- *A Black Parent's Handbook,* Baruti K. Kafele
- *Different and Wonderful: Raising Black Children in a Race-Conscious Society,* Dr. Darlene Hopson, Dr. Derek Hopson
- *Empowering African American Males to Succeed: A Ten-Step Approach for Parents and Teachers,* Mychal Wynn
- *How to Generate Values in Young Children: Integrity, Honesty, Individuality, Self-Confidence, and Wisdom,* S.S. Riley
- *In My Place,* Charlayne Hunter-Gault
- *The Measure of Our Success: A Letter to My Children and Yours,* Marian Wright Edelman
- *The Promised Land,* Nicholas Lemann

Catalogs:

- *Beyond the Stereotypes: A Guide to Resources for Black Girls and Young Women*
- *In Her Own Image*
- *A Reality Check on the American Dream*
- *Women Make Movies*
- *Videotapes*
- *One Woman, One Vote*
- *The Promised Land*

Support Materials

- Agenda for all *MCTT* participants at the "Vision" session(s).
- Expanded Agenda for members of the *MCTT* site team. This expanded agenda will provide you with helpful information as you go through the module.
- Documents resulting from the "Vision" sessions at Joyland, Kiddy Land, and Miller's Child Care programs. These are included to give you a sense of what to expect. It's a good idea to share these with the facilitator and the site team but not the whole group, because they might influence this Work.

Agenda

More Is Caught Than Taught Program
Vision Session

1. Welcome

2. Introductions

3. Explanation of the meeting agenda

4. **Purpose of the meeting**
   - To develop a collective vision which will guide the development and administration of programs for the care and development of children at this center

5. Vision exercises

6. Next Steps

7. Closing

Expanded Agenda

More Is Caught Than Taught Program
"Vision" Session

1. Welcome

2. Introductions

3. Explanation of the meeting agenda

   Purpose of the meeting
   - To develop a collective vision which will guide the development and administration of programs for the care and development of children at this center

4. "Vision" exercises
   - Introduce the "Vision" module by reviewing the purpose of the *MCTT* program.
     - The *More Is Caught Than Taught* program is built around a partnership among parents, community leaders, and child care providers. During the program you will develop a vision for your children and work toward building a curriculum that reflects your vision. In this module you will define and establish your group's vision for children.
   - Identify what "vision" is, what role it plays in people's lives.
     - Discuss in small groups the Biblical statement, "A people without vision shall perish." Then share ideas among the groups.
   - Identify the world your children will inherit in 15-20 years in terms of social, economic, political, and spiritual conditions.
     - Think individually at first and then share ideas in small groups.
     - Come together as a full group to call out ideas to two participants at the front of the room who will write them on newsprint paper.
   - Identify the world you would like to have in 15-20 years.
     - Think individually at first and then share ideas in small groups.
     - Come together as a full group and have two participants write ideas up on newsprint.

- Identify the barriers to your vision and reflect on the material and non-material nature of these barriers.
    - Discuss in small group what keeps you from having this ideal world, what the barriers are to having it.
    - Come together as a full group and have two participants write up ideas on newsprint.
- Identify the attributes your children will need to possess in order to lead the world towards your vision.
    - Discuss in small groups the qualities, characteristics, skills, and knowledge your children are going to need in order to overcome these barriers and create the world of your vision.
    - Come together as a full group and have two participants write up ideas on newsprint.
- Affirm the "Vision Statement" created in the session and agree to base the rest of the *MCTT* program on this vision.
    - Look at the final section of your newsprint. This is your "Vision Statement." These are your unique priorities, goals, and requirements for the children in your care. Everything in the *MCTT* program will come back to this document.

5. **Next Steps**
    - If you choose to do the program as it's laid out, the next module is the "Environment" module. In these sessions you will be looking at the material and non-material environment – how it affects children, and how it ties in to your vision. Encourage participants to start thinking now about their definition of environment and the effect it has on them and their children. "If we want to build these children of our vision, what environment will we need to create?"

6. **Closing**
    - Fill out evaluation forms
    - Review the date and time for the next meeting
    - Express appreciation and affirmation of the meeting and participants

VISION

I. How the world will be 15-20 years from now (the world our children will inherit)

- Parents will lose control
- More gangs
- More crime
- Better conditions for African-Americans
- Fewer governmental programs
- A social revolution
- More impersonal
- Total automation
- More elderly, and no one to care for them
- Move toward religion
- Poor rearing of male children
- More hi-tech
- Increased need for a sense of community and family
- Self-destruction
- Abuse of the justice system
- Black-on-Black crime
- Child abuse
- Domestic violence
- More diseases
- Breakdown in moral standards
- Deterioration of the political structure
- Discrimination against women
- Fewer males
- More homelessness
- Wider gap between haves and have-nots
- Choice between mean-spiritedness and community
- More drugs
- More unemployment
- Pollution of the environment
- Changing educational system
- Overpopulation
- Fewer jobs for low-income folks
- Discrimination against African-Americans
- Lack of money and resources
- Breakup of families
- Lack of spirituality
- Overcrowded jails
- No change in values
- Lack of discipline
- Disrespect for one another and ourselves
- Not facing up to responsibilities
- Apathy
- No motivation
- No ambition
- Lack of leadership

"Vision" Statements were created by MCTT participants from Joyland, Kiddy Land, and Miller's Centers

VISION

II. Vision of How We Would Like the World to Be

- Love
- Honesty
- Respect parents
- Value the environment
- Individual responsibility
- Communities raising children
- Safe, neighborhoods and people looking out for each other
- Clean, healthy environment
- No drugs
- No violence
- Unity
- No hatred
- Even distribution of wealth
- Peace
- Hope
- Solid values
- All basic needs (food, medical, clothing, housing) met
- Free to be yourself
- Self-sufficiency
- Respecting other cultures
- All people able to reach full potential
- Access to technology for all
- Black role models and leaders
- Quality time for children
- Respecting and valuing all work
- Everyone has a job
- Sharing
- Kids can be kids
- More self-love
- Abolish racism, classism, sexism
- Spirituality
- More parks
- Parents who love and care for children and have the support they need
- Better manners
- Partnership between husband and wife
- No guns
- Laughter
- Good education for all
- Valuing of children as people
- Dream of M.L. King
- Passion and compassion
- Justice
- Diverse people working together
- No discrimination
- Respect and revere the elders
- Honest and fair political system
- Families that are financially stable
- Celebrating and appreciating diversity
- Flowers and gardens
- Involving and integrating the elderly
- Equal opportunity
- Enjoyment and fun

VISION

III. Barriers to Our Vision

- Selfishness
- Greed
- No self-respect
- Fear
- Lack of trust
- Complacency
- Egos
- Misplaced priorities
- Bad government
- False pride
- Jealousy
- Lack of love
- Ignorance
- No vision
- Lack of spirituality
- Lack of funds
- Racial discrimination
- Economic injustice
- Lack of unity
- Desertion of culture and community by Blacks
- Lack of good parenting
- Pulling each other down
- Lack of good public officials and leaders who are honest and caring

VISION

IV. Qualities, Characteristics, Knowledge and Skills Our Children Must Have To Bring About Our Vision

- Love
- Hopefulness
- Ability to adapt
- Understanding and diplomacy
- Courage to be different
- Conviction
- Self-determination
- Self-confidence
- Self-control
- Innovativeness
- Academic skills and people skills
- Honesty
- Courtesy
- Discipline
- Assertiveness
- Responsibility for actions
- Creativity
- Flexibility
- Spirituality
- Optimism and resiliency
- Knowledge of parenting
- Sense of responsibility and getting involved
- Respect
- Positiveness about others
- Feeling for people/sensitivity/empathy
- Tolerance
- Resourcefulness
- Knowledge of history, culture, and heritage
- Wisdom
- Independence, self-sufficiency
- Joy
- Technological skills
- Common sense
- Child-like trust and wonder
- Concern for fellow man
- Generous, ability to share
- Trustworthy
- Self-respect
- Respect for others
- Cleanliness
- Ability to learn and think fast
- Education–more than a GED
- Job training
- Ability to communicate
- Know what is expected of them by family, community, and the world
- Know what to expect of others
- Determination
- Know right from wrong
- Strong self-esteem
- Skills in public speaking

ENVIRONMENT MODULE

*"Take care of our children
Take care of what they hear
Take care of what they see
Take care of what they feel.
For how the children grow so will be the shape of Aotearoa."*

– Dame Whina Cooper, Maori Kuia (Elder)

What Is This Module?

"Environment" has an enormous impact on all of us, every day. It affects us both spiritually and physically, but we are not always aware of this. Because the environment is all around us, we often don't examine it or think about it; we simply accept it as it is.

In the Environment module of *MCTT*, you will explore what "environment" means, and you will examine different environments for children in your community. By consciously focusing on the material and spiritual surroundings that influence children, you will highlight the "messages" that your children are receiving from the environment. Finally, you will determine what environment can best support your vision by sending messages that will most effectively promote the attributes, characteristics, and knowledge you are seeking for your children.

Children are like little scientists, learning about their world by performing experiments, by observing things and making rules based on their discoveries. They learn about heat by touching something that is hot; they learn about sweetness by tasting something with sugar in it. In fact, children are constantly testing their environment–picking things up, putting things in their mouths, throwing things, breaking things, watching things. This is part of their job as scientists, their task of growing and learning.

In learning from the environment, however, children do not just learn about shape, taste, and other physical things. They also absorb attitudes about love, about anger, and about safety and danger. They receive constant spiritual information from their surroundings, and they assemble a set rules about these things, too. Such rules–the way children make sense of the information all around them–will play an important role in defining who they are, because as they explain their world they are also explaining themselves in that world.

Children do not learn only from "learning" environments such as the child care center or school. They learn primarily from their home environment, and they also gain impressions from their neighborhood, from their place of worship, from stores, from friends, from television, from books, from toys.

In thinking about environment, then, we must consider everything that our children come into contact with, and we must think about the messages these things are sending our children. Are our children receiving messages that will cause them to define themselves as happy, as confident, as strong, as intelligent? Or are they receiving messages that undercut their strength and self-confidence?

Because environment is so important to children's development, many curriculum guides contain chapters on how to set up a child care center so as to create the best learning environment. Most of these guides, however, base their recommendations on what the children are supposedly learning and what their parents, teachers, and community want them to learn. These assumptions can be based on a substantial amount of knowledge, but they're still assumptions.

With *MCTT*, you make the connections between your children's environment and your goals for them. During the "Vision" module, you established your vision for the children of your center and your community. Now you will evaluate your environment based on that vision. What elements of the environment are sending messages that support your vision? What elements of the environment are sending messages that are contrary to your vision? By making connections between your children's environment and your "Vision" Statement–your tangible list of goals for them–you will be able to define and begin to establish the environment that will be the most supportive, and the most nurturing, of the children you want to grow.

Expected Outcomes

Participants will:

- Define what is meant, physically and spiritually, by "environment"

- Examine the effect environment has on children and all people

- Identify elements of the environment that support your vision for children

- Visit a variety of environments where children receive care and examine these environments through the lens of your vision

- Define the environment that is most supportive of your vision for children

Preparing

Who will participate?

All members of the site team, staff, parents, and community leaders.

How long will it take?

The Environment module is meant to be spread over two meetings (or more) with site visits in between. It is important to allow time for the site visits, with each participant making 2-3 visits, if possible.

Where will it take place?

The two or more meetings of the "Environment" module can take place anywhere you will feel comfortable, that is convenient for participants, and that will be free of noise and other distractions. A site where chairs can be freely moved about and where newsprint paper can be taped to the walls is an important consideration. The site visits will take place at child care centers, schools, playgrounds, homes, and other environments where children learn.

When will it take place?

You will have set the dates for this and future meetings in the "Getting Started" module, but you will want to send out a reminder to program participants including the date, time, and place of the "Environment" meetings.

How will you document this module?

It is a good idea to touch base with the person who agreed during the "Getting Started" module to document the meetings so as to make sure s/he has all the necessary materials and equipment for the documentation method that you have chosen (audio taping, video taping, making photographs, and taking good notes are some of the options).

What will you need to bring to the session?

Some suggestions:

- Your "Vision Statement"
- Newsprint
- Markers
- Loose paper
- Pencils or pens
- Masking tape
- Documentation materials and equipment
- Attendance sheet
- Agendas
- Handouts
- Evaluation forms
- Food and drinks for meal or snack

Other possible materials include:

- Photos of different environments
- Drawings by children of their environments
- A large-scale version of your "Vision Statement"

> If you want to see yourself, go watch your children playing house. They put their hands on their hip just like you, they raise their voices just like you, they try to be just like you.
>
> –Patricia Aaron, *More Is Caught Than Taught* Resource Advisory Committee

What else?

Is there anything else you need to do to prepare for the "Environment" module?

Challenges of this Module

One of the most difficult things about the "Environment" module is trying to wrap your mind around what "environment" really means. We are so used to hearing about "the environment," meaning our physical surroundings, or "the learning environment," meaning the classroom, that it can be tempting to fall back on these definitions. Dealing with the whole environment that affects children can seem like an overwhelming task: too big and too slippery.

But our experience has taught us that the most important elements of the environment, the things that have the most impact on us, are those intangible, spiritual elements that at first seem so difficult to label. This is why it's crucial to tie these spiritual elements to concrete exercises, so as to allow participants to make this connection for themselves. It is equally important to look at the environment in relation to your own "Vision Statement." This will provide a useful structure for bringing the concept of environment to a manageable size. It will also ensure that you are designing a new environment based on your own goals and definitions.

Another challenge of this module is the fact that people will bring differences to these meetings. Not everyone agrees on what environment is best for children: some may set an early bedtime, some may let their children stay up late; some may correct their children when they make mistakes, some may let their children figure out mistakes on their own; some may like Sunday School, and others may prefer other means of inculcating moral values.

The fact is, we have a wide range of diversity in likes and dislikes, in upbringing and culture, in values and customs. This complexity is a wonderfully rich resource that will benefit you and the children in your care. But with this diversity comes a need to examine and work through these differences. Later modules of *MCTT*–"Internalized Oppression" and "How to BE Together"–are dedicated to this process. During the "Environment" module, the essential thing is to recognize that various positions by participants can be valid, and that you should not assume that your views, regardless of how "right" they maybe, will win the support of everyone. It is important to reaffirm the notion that a conflict of ideas is valued and expected.

A final challenge to this module is that of not putting center staff, parents, and community leaders in a position where they will feel defensive. This is the first module in which you will examine the child care center and home, and there is a risk that the discussion could turn into criticism or be perceived as criticism. This doesn't mean that you shouldn't be honest about your feelings, but it does mean that you should be aware of the feelings of others.

Putting this Module into Action

"Environment" Meeting #1

The facilitator will lead the session by introducing exercises, establishing times for each exercise, and, most importantly, creating a fun, energetic, and connected atmosphere for the session.

Basic approach:

1. **Introduce the "Environment" module by connecting it to the rest of the *MCTT* program and your vision for children.**

   - Hand out copies of your "Vision Statement" and briefly review the qualities, characteristics, skills and knowledge your children must have to be leaders in the world. The question and challenge for this meeting is: If these are the attributes we want children to have, what kind of environment must we create in order to provide the best chance of developing these characteristics? What kind of environment in the community, center, and home must be created in order to build children who look like this?

2. **Identify what environment is, what role it plays in our lives.**

   - "What makes up the environment?" Answer this as a group by calling out ideas to two participants at the front of the room who will write them on newsprint.

   - Distribute the first handout, "A Store Environment," and use it to help individuals focus on a specific environment. If you were able to go to only one store, what store would you choose? Why would you choose that store—what is there about that store that makes you choose it? Think about one store you would not like to go back to—what are the things you don't like about it?

- Break into small groups to discuss what stores you've chosen and why.

- In your small groups, identify five things in the stores you like that make you feel good—what things in the environment do you all respond to in a positive way? Make sure someone is writing down what's said.

- Come together as a full group to call out each group's five identified things to two participants at the front of the room who will write them on newsprint.

- Determine as a full group what the most important element of the store environments is, and then discuss what that element means to you. Two participants will write ideas on newsprint.

- Look again at your list of elements of the environment. Is there anything you want to add?

- Go over your list of environmental elements as a full group and identify which elements are physical and which are non-physical, or spiritual. Discuss what the difference is between the physical and the spiritual elements and the ways that each of these affect us and our children.

3. **Make connections between the environment and your vision for children.**

    - Think individually about five items on your "Vision Statement" that are important to you. Write these items on the second handout, "Connecting Environment to "Vision," and then look at your list of environmental elements. Write down which elements of the environment will best support each of your five vision items and how.

    - Share individual thoughts in small groups, making sure someone in each group is writing down what's said.

    - Come together as a full group to call out ideas to two participants at the front of the room who will write them on newsprint.

> The teacher we talked to had been at the center for twenty-four years. She had taught generations of children there. I liked the atmosphere; it was calm, peaceful. If I was a little kid I would say, "Oh, I love this place." The kids were very respectful of the teachers.
>
> –Phillis Hodge, Parent, Joyland Child Development Center

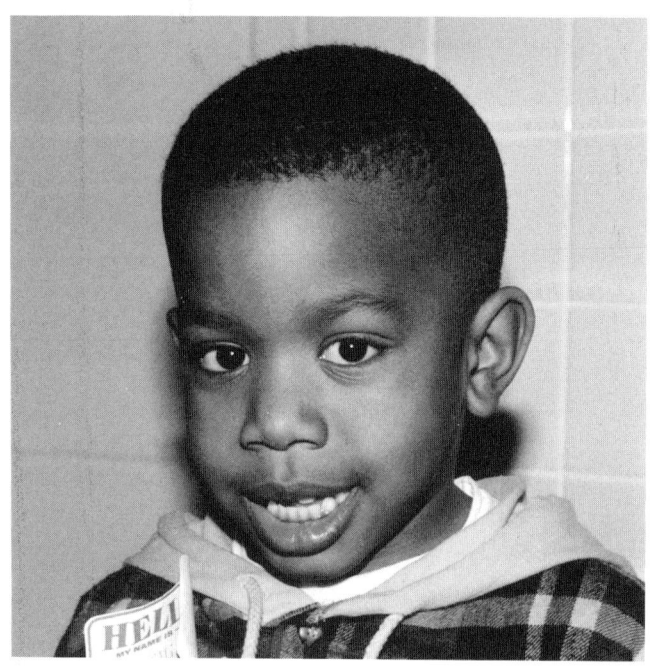

- (Be sure to keep these handouts, because you'll fill in the rest during the next "Environment" meeting.)

4. **Schedule visits to children's environments.**

    - In order to learn about the environment, we want to visit some environments where children spend time. Discuss as a full group what these environments are in your community. Some of these will likely be homes, day-care centers, churches, schools, family day-care homes, and community centers.

    - Write up a list of the children-related environments you'd like to visit and determine who will visit which site. Participants can visit sites in small groups, and each participant should try to visit two to three sites. (Note: Visiting a home may be difficult to arrange, but it's very important.) A site visit to your center by the full group should be the first part of the next "Environment" module meeting.

5. **Discuss next steps.**

    - The next part of the "Environment" module will be the site visits. These visits will provide you with concrete information about different environments for children, and you will examine them with a new focus as a result of this meeting. The site visits will also give you some common experiences so that as you consult you will be able to call upon shared knowledge and experiences. At the next "Environment" meeting, you will discuss the site visits and what environmental elements you will choose in order to produce the children of your vision.

6. **Evaluate the session using evaluation forms.**

Additional options:

    i. Use photographs of different environments taped to the wall. These could be a family reunion, a farm, a prison, a schoolroom, a bus full of people, a city block, and so on. Discuss how each environment makes you feel and why. Make a list of the elements of each environment, both physical and spiritual, and discuss how these elements contribute to the way you feel about that environment.

ii. Use drawings of the environment by children at the center, taped to the wall. Discuss how the drawings convey the children's feelings about their environment: are they happy, sad, scared, proud? Discuss what elements of the environment they have chosen to portray in their drawings. Discuss what elements of the environment they have left out of their drawings.

iii. Use a large-scale version of your "Vision Statement" taped to the wall in addition to handing out copies to each participant. This will help keep participants focused on your vision and will make it easier to connect vision to environment.

iv. Other options for increasing the power of the "Environment" module might include viewing videos; reading book excerpts, papers, and articles; and attending lectures on a relevant subject before the initial environment meeting.

Follow-up to Meeting #1

- Bring the site team together to do a group evaluation of the first meeting and to add relevant ideas to the "Environment" section of the work plan.

- Write up all the lists you generated during the meeting and send copies to all *MCTT* participants.

- Contact the various sites you wish to visit and set up appointments.

- Send a schedule of site visits to all *MCTT* participants as a reminder with as much advance notice as possible. Also remind them when the second "Environment" meeting will take place.

Environment Site Visits

Take your "Vision Statements" with you on the site visits. While you're there, try to differentiate between the physical and spiritual elements of that particular environment, and think about the different messages that these elements are sending to you and to the children there.

- Take notes during your visits: write down what you like, what you don't like, and especially which elements of the environment are most supportive of your *MCTT* group's "Vision Statement."

"Environment" Meeting #2

The facilitator will lead the session by introducing exercises, establishing times for each exercise and, most importantly, creating a fun, energetic, and connected atmosphere for the session.

Basic approach:

1. **Review the importance of the "Environment" module by connecting it to the rest of the *MCTT* program and your vision for children.**

    - Briefly review your "Vision Statement" as well as your list of environmental elements. During the last meeting, you made connections between vision and environment by identifying physical and spiritual elements of the environment and by exploring which of these elements were sending "messages" that were the most supportive of your vision for children.

    - The site visits gave you the opportunity to apply this new focus to environments where children are in your community. The site visits also gave you some common experiences that you will draw on during this meeting.

    - The purpose of this meeting is to discuss the site visits and then, based on this experience and your understanding of the environment, to define an environment that will best support your vision.

2. **Discuss and Process the Site Visits.**

    - Go around the room and invite each person to share her or his experiences of the site visits. Some questions you might want to consider are:
        ○ What did you notice about each setting?
        ○ What did you like? Why?
        ○ What did you not like? Why?
        ○ What "messages" were being sent to children at each site?

    - Discuss the group visit to your center.

> Children learn from everything that happens during the day. A curriculum is not just lesson plans, it's everything that happens to children during the day. The child is a whole being: intellectual, social, etc.
>
> –Otis Houser, Teacher, Kiddy Land Child Development Center

More Is *Caught* Than Taught *Environment* Page 69

- What are some environmental elements that your center shares with other places you have visited?

- What are some environmental elements that are different at your center and at the other sites?

3. **Define the environment that is most supportive of your vision for children.**

    - Look individually at your "Connecting Environment to Vision" handout from the last session. Think about the environmental elements you wrote down and, based on your experience from the site visits, write down as many specific examples as you can for five of the environmental elements on your sheet.

        One group, for example, wrote "warmth" as an environmental element supporting their vision for "love." In what ways can "warmth" be present and be fostered in the environment? Some reinforcements might be bright colors, good-morning hugs, singing together, rugs on the floor, smiles, photos on the walls, and other positive signals.

    - Discuss in small groups what you've written down. Then, as a group, develop a list of the environmental elements, both general and specific, that will contribute most to nurturing and growing the children of your vision.

    - Come together as a full group to call out ideas to two participants at the front of the room who will write them on newsprint.

4. **Discuss Next Steps.**

    - The facilitator should tie the "Environment" module to the rest of the program. If you're ready to finish the "Environment" module and are going on to the "Internalized Oppression" module next, let participants know how these modules are connected. We want to create this ideal environment so as to grow the children of our vision, but much of this environment concerns feelings, behaviors, and attitudes that we cannot simply change with the snap of our fingers. In the "Internalized Oppression" module, you will look at some of the "caught" and "taught" roles that affect all of us. These roles affect who we are, how we interact, and how we teach our children.

5. **Review your schedule and establish or affirm dates for the "Internalized Oppression" session and future meetings.**

- In the "Getting Started" module you established a schedule for the first few meetings of the *MCTT* program. This is a good point to review that schedule and to add further meeting dates if you need to do so.

  The "Internalized Oppression" module is an intense but exciting experience for participants. Because it is such a charged topic, it takes people a while both to become involved and then to let go out of the session. There is also a video included as part of the meeting. For all these reasons, this session will take longer than the others. We suggest a meeting of 4-5 hours, perhaps scheduled on a Saturday or Sunday.

6. **Evaluate the session using evaluation forms.**

Additional Options:

1. **Devote a session to looking at the environment of a child care center as it relates to the staff. Here are some questions you could explore:**

   - Does each staff member have a vision for children that matches the vision of the program?

   - What are the personal aspirations of each staff member? Are their aspirations good models for children?

- What activities are staff persons voluntarily pursuing to develop their knowledge and skills relative to care and early childhood development?

- Do staff members treat themselves and their fellow workers in keeping with how the vision of the program would have children treated?

2. **Devote a session to looking at the environment of a child care center as it relates to the administration. Some questions you could explore are:**

   - Does the style of administrators reflect qualities such as respect, openness, honesty, caring, "peerness," cooperation, and love?

   - Is there an administrative program or plan that works to monitor and improve the social climate of the program?

   - Does the administration regularly invite the staff to discuss the intent and impact of the administrative style as well as specific administrative policies?

3. **Devote a session to looking at the environment of a child care center as it relates to parents. Certain questions deserve exploring:**

   - Is the program "parent friendly"? What evidence is there to support the answer to this question?

   - What roles are defined for parents? Are these meaningful roles?

   - Does the program offer support services to families?

   - How often are parents invited to comment and make recommendations on the policies and operation of the program? Is there a formal evaluation program that includes parents?

   - Are parents visited in their homes and other settings?

Follow-up to Meeting #2

- Bring the site team together to do a group evaluation of the second meeting and to add relevant ideas to the "Environment" section of the work plan.

- Write up the list you generated during the meeting and send copies to all *MCTT* participants or distribute them at the next session.

Preparation for the "Internalized Oppression" module

Copy the materials in Appendix B and ask participants to read the materials in preparation for the "Internalized Oppression" module. Site team members may have additional materials that can inform and expand the discussions in the "Internalized Oppression" module. Encourage this sharing, as it can increase participation in the next module.

Books:

- *Different and Wonderful: Raising Black Children in a Race-Conscious Society*, Dr. Darlene Hopson and Dr. Derek Hopson
- *Helping Young Children Understand Peace, War, and the Nuclear Threat*, Nancy Carlsson-Paige
- *How to Generate Values in Young Children: Integrity, Honesty, Individuality, Self-Confidence, and Wisdom*, S.S. Riley
- *How to Talk so Kids Will Listen and Listen so Kids Will Talk*, Adele Faber and Elaine Mazlish
- *Learning Centers for Young Children*, Georgia Bradley Houle
- *Learning Environments for Children*, Henry Sanoff and Joan Sanoff
- *Principles of Parenting*, H. Wallace Goddard
- *Stories in the Classroom: Storytelling, Reading Aloud, and Roleplaying with Children*, Bob Barton and David Booth

Catalogs:

- *Beyond the Stereotypes: A Guide to Resources for Black Girls and Young Women*
- *In Her Own Image*
- *A Reality Check on the American Dream*
- *The Video Project: Films and Videos for a Safe and Sustainable World*
- *Women Make Movies*

> You got to watch the moves you make. Just check yourself in front of them because they're picking up on it and they'll take it to another child. A lot of what is picked up on comes from home and children bring it to school, teach it to other children, and they'll take it and teach it to somebody else. You know it's going to go further and as they get older, they're going to take it to another school, and, before you know it, it's like the big thing, spread out, like gangs, for example. I think gangs are something that started out real small and in the bigger cities. Maybe some of them moved here, and you see the TV advertisements with gangs and the head scarves and the signs. I even see little children doing it, and I think that's bad.
>
> –Aurelia Martin, Parent, Miller's Toulminville Day Care Center

Videotapes

- *The Killing Culture*

Support Materials

- Agendas for all *MCTT* participants at the Environment sessions
- Expanded Agendas for members of the *MCTT* site team. These expanded agendas will provide you with helpful information as you go through the meetings.
- "A Store Environment" handout
- "Connecting Environment to Vision" handout
- Newsprint paper

Agenda

More Is Caught Than Taught Program
"Environment" Meeting #1

1. Welcome

2. Introductions

3. Explanation of the meeting agenda

    Purpose of the meeting
    - To define what is meant, physically and spiritually, by "environment"
    - To examine the effect environment has on children and all people
    - To identify elements of the environment that support one's vision for children
    - To schedule visits to children's environments

4. Environment exercises with handouts

5. Scheduling site visits to children's environments

6. Next Steps

7. Closing

Expanded Agenda

More Is Caught Than Taught Program
"Environment" Meeting #1

1. **Welcome**

2. **Introductions**

3. **Explanation of the meeting agenda**

   Purpose of the meeting

   - To define what is meant, physically and spiritually, by "environment"
   - To examine the effect environment has on children and all people
   - To identify elements of the environment that support one's vision for children
   - To schedule visits to children's environments

4. **Environment exercises with handouts**

   - Introduce the "Environment" module by connecting it to the rest of the *MCTT* program and your vision for children.
     - Use copies of your "Vision Statement" and briefly review the qualities, characteristics, skills, and knowledge your children must have to be leaders in the world. The question and challenge for this meeting are vital: If these are the attributes we want children to have, what kind of environment must we create in order to have the best chance of developing these characteristics? What kind of environment in the community, center, and home must be created in order to build children who look like this?
   - Identify what environment is, what role it plays in our lives.
     - As a group, answer these question: What makes up the environment? Write the list up on newsprint.
     - Use the handout "A Store Environment" to explore how environment affects us and to identify which elements of an environment affirm us and which do not.
     - Identify which elements from the environment list are physical and which are non-physical, or spiritual.
   - Make connections between the environment and your vision for children.

- Use the handout "Connecting Environment to Vision" to choose which elements of your environment list will best support and nurture five qualities, characteristics, skills, or areas of knowledge from your "Vision" Statement.

5. **Scheduling site visits to children's environments**

    - Discuss the environments in your community inhabited by children and where they receive care.

    - Schedule visits to these environments by *MCTT* participants in small groups. Note: it is important to visit at least one home environment. Each participant should try to visit two or more sites.

6. **Next Steps**

    - The next part of this module is the site visits. These visits will provide you with concrete information about different environments for children, and you will examine them with a new focus as a result of this meeting. They will also give you common experiences to draw upon in the next meeting. During the next "Environment" meeting, you will discuss the site visits and what environmental elements you will choose in order to build the children of your vision.

7. **Closing**

    - Fill out evaluation forms.

    - Review the date and time for the next meeting. (Note: a group site visit to your center should be scheduled prior to the meeting.)

    - Express appreciation and affirmation of the meeting and the participants.

Agenda

More Is Caught Than Taught Program
Environment Meeting #2

1. Welcome

2. Introductions

3. Explanation of the meeting agenda

    Purpose of the meeting
    - To share and process experiences from the site visits
    - To define the environment that is most supportive of your vision for children

4. **Discussion of the "Environment" module**

5. **Discussion of the site visits**

6. **Environment exercises with handout**

7. **Next Steps**

8. **Review and renew the schedule for upcoming meetings**

9. **Closing**

Expanded Agenda

More Is Caught Than Taught Program
"Environment" Meeting #2

1. Welcome

2. Introductions

3. Explanation of the meeting agenda

    Purpose of the meeting
    - To share and process experiences from the site visits
    - To define the environment that is most supportive of your vision for children

4. Discussion of the "Environment" module
    - Re-introduce the "Environment" module by connecting it to the rest of the *MCTT* program and your vision for children. Briefly review your "Vision Statement" as well as your list of environmental elements from the first meeting of the "Environment" module. During the last meeting, you made connections between vision and environment by identifying physical and spiritual elements of the environment and by exploring which of these elements were sending "messages" that were the most supportive of your vision for children.

        The site visits gave you the opportunity to apply this new focus to environments where children spend time in your community. The site visits also gave you some common experiences that you can draw on during this meeting.

5. Discussion of the site visits
    - Go around the room and invite each person to share her or his experiences during the site visits. These are some questions you might want to consider:
        - What did you notice about each setting?
        - What did you like? Why?
        - What did you dislike? Why?
        - What "messages" were being sent to children at each site?
    - Discuss the group visit to your center. Here are some questions you might want to consider:

- What are some environmental elements that your center shares with other places you have visited?
- What are some environmental elements that are different at your center and at the other sites?

6. **Environment exercises with handout**
   - Use your "Connecting Environment to Vision" handout from the last meeting to further the environment that will best support your vision for children. Do this by writing down as many specific examples as you can, based on your experience from the site visits and elsewhere, for five of the environmental elements on your sheet.

7. **Next Steps**
   - If you're ready to finish the "Environment" module and are going on to the "Internalized Oppression" module next, explain to participants how these modules are connected. We want to create this ideal environment so as to produce the children of our vision, but much of the environment concerns feelings, behaviors, and attitudes that we cannot simply change by snapping our fingers. In the "Internalized Oppression" module, you will look at some of the "caught and taught" roles that influence all of us in the ways we interact and teach our children.

   Copy the materials in Appendix B and ask participants to read them in preparation for the "Internalized Oppression" module. Site team members may have additional materials that can inform and expand the discussions in the "Internalized Oppression" module. Encourage this sharing, as it can increase excitement and involvement in the next module.

8. **Review and renew the schedule for upcoming meetings**
   - In the "Getting Started" module you established a schedule for the first few meetings of the *MCTT* program. This is a good point to review that schedule and add further meeting dates if you need to do so.
   - The "Internalized Oppression" module is an intense but exciting experience for participants. Because it is such a charged topic, it takes people a while both to become involved in and then to let go of the session. There is also a video included as part of the meeting. For all these reasons, this session will take longer than the others. We suggest a meeting of 4-5 hours, perhaps scheduled on a Saturday or Sunday.

9. **Closing**
   - Fill out evaluation forms
   - Express appreciation and affirmation of the meeting and the participants

A Store Environment
MCTT Environment Handout

A store that I enjoy shopping in is:	look, feel, people, colors, temperature, lighting, sounds
A store that I do not like shopping in is:	look, feel, people, colors, temperature, lighting, sounds

Connecting Environment to Vision
MCTT **Environment Handout**

Elements of our vision	(Examples: love hopefulness, self-control, etc.)				
Elements of the environment that support our vision **(Meeting 1)**					
Examples of an environment that will produce the children of our vision **(Meeting 2)**					

More Is *Caught* Than Taught

Environment

INTERNALIZED OPPRESSION MODULE

"Everywhere I look it's a mirror, I look at a bad reflection. It's hard, man! It's like, What the hell did I do, and you're always feeling guilty and stuff. And after a while you just get so much rage from all that confusion that the rage just says, OK, you are bad so be a part of it."

–Shank, a gang member, from Maria Hinojosa's book, <u>Crews</u>

What Is This Module?

Remembering our exploration of the "Environment" module of *More Is Caught Than Taught*, we are reminded that we are all constantly receiving messages from the people and things around us. These messages help us to make sense of ourselves and our world. They also convey our assigned "place" in society.

The fact is, American society is divided along many lines, including race, class, gender, age, and others. We cannot ignore these divisions, nor can we ignore the fact that they affect all of us. Sometimes their manifestations are stark and obvious (physical attacks, denials of jobs and housing, unearned privileges, abusive remarks), but less easily identifiable signs of prejudice and division also assault us each day.

Indeed, all the messages arising out of these divisions tell us not only what side of the line we are on (if we're black or white, male or female, etc.) but they also tell us which side is "better." They tell us that it's better to be young than old, that it's better to have light skin than dark skin, that it's better to be a doctor than a nurse, that it's better to be a man than a woman.

Because these notions of superiority and inferiority are so pervasive and sometimes so subtle, they are messages that we catch and internalize even when we consciously disagree with them. Having internalized them, we then use these messages against ourselves and, as a result, they become self-fulfilling prophesies. We become caught up in maintaining our own oppression. ("Internalized Oppression is a phenomenon that happens when people are bombarded with gross misinformation and mistreatment over a period of time. Members of the targeted group internalize the misinformation and the hurtful behavior and turn upon themselves, their family members, and other people of their group." See Appendix B, <u>Healing Racism</u>).

In this module, you will examine the system of supposed inherent superiority and inherent inferiority that gives rise to and supports these destructive messages. You will look at the thoughts, feelings, and behaviors that are generated as a result of this system and are reinforced through internalized oppression. And you will consider the effect these thoughts, feelings, and behaviors have on children and on your work with children.

Many different aspects of racism, classism, sexism, and other forms of prejudice exist, and they all affect society and our work. In this module, we are choosing to focus on internalized oppression not because it is the only destructive aspect or the most important aspect. The attitude of inherent superiority known as Unconscious Racism also has a very powerful and negative impact; but the exploration and eradication of this attitude must be done by those who have been placed by society into the "superior" position. (Unconscious Racism in the United States is rooted in misinformation about "people of color": it is internalized in such a way that the "white" person who carries the misinformation is not conscious that the misinformation is even there. Unconscious Racism is one of the most difficult and insidious forms of racism, simply because it is unconscious and often the intentions of its perpetrators are good - Healing Racism).

We have chosen to focus on internalized oppression because it is the aspect of the superiority and inferiority system that has the greatest impact on the "caught" messages that we who are the targets of oppression teach our children. As African-Americans, as low-income people, as women, we are on the receiving end of many negative messages. When we internalize them, they become barriers to our on empowerment and our ability to grow the children of our vision.

The Internalized Oppression module is an opportunity to get the facts, think about systems, look at your own thinking and feelings, and make new decisions about what bias is and what it does. By consciously focusing on internalized oppression and the systems that create it, you are invited to bring your own negative "caught" messages into awareness and begin or continue the process of altering them.

Because this is such a charged issue and understanding it is so important to the *More Is Caught Than Taught* program and to fulfilling our vision for children, we have included in this manual three essays on internalized oppression (Appendix B). We hope they will help you in defining internalized oppression and in seeing how and why this module lies at the heart of the *MCTT* program.

Expected Outcomes

Participants will:

- Examine the system of supposed inherent superiority and inherent inferiority (S/I system) and the consequences of this system on individuals, groups, and society as a whole

- Speculate about the particular impact the S/I system has on children

- Explore the alternative to the S/I system and investigate the consequences of this alternative on individuals, groups, and society as a whole

- Consider how the S/I system channels our feelings

- Acquire skills to manage our feelings outside of the S/I system

Preparing

Who will participate?

All members of the site team, staff, parents, and community leaders.

Because this meeting is dealing with issues that are so charged with sadness, guilt, anger, and fear, it is essential that the facilitator take as much time as needed to prepare for the session. We strongly recommend that the program director, the facilitator, and other members of the site team carefully read all related materials and envision outcomes for the Internalized Oppression module and discuss strategies to achieve outcomes. They should review the suggested videos, especially A Class Divided, and the accompanying study sheet. They should also read the essays of Appendix B and develop discussion questions. Finally, they should review the *Session*

Guidelines (page 114) and develop strategies to implement guidelines for discussions.

How long will it take?

The "Internalized Oppression" module should be covered in one meeting, but because it is both exciting and controversial, it will take longer than many of the other meetings. It will take time for participants both to get in and to get out of it, and we suggest the use of the video, A Class Divided, for this session. We recommend a meeting of 4 to 5 hours, perhaps scheduled on a Saturday or Sunday.

Where will it take place?

The "Internalized Oppression" module can take place anywhere you will feel comfortable, that is convenient for participants, and that will be free of noise and other distractions. A site where chairs can be freely moved about and where newsprint can be taped to the walls is an important consideration. You will also need access to a VCR and television set during this session.

When will it take place?

You will have set the dates for this and future meetings in the "Internalized Oppression" module, but you will want to send out a reminder to program participants including the date, time, and place of the Internalized Oppression meeting and reminding them that this session is especially important.

How will you document this module?

It is a good idea to touch base with the person who agreed during the "Getting Started" module to document the meetings so as to make sure s/he has all the necessary materials and equipment for the documentation method that you have chosen (audio taping, video taping, taking photographs, and taking good notes are some of the options). How you decide to document *MCTT* at your program will, of course, depend on the equipment to which you have access, as well as which methods you prefer. Before ruling out any method due to lack of equipment, ask yourselves if there is anyone who might lend or otherwise provide you with the materials you seek.

What will you need to bring to these meetings?

Some suggestions:

- A Class Divided videotape and study guide
- A VCR

More Is *Caught* Than Taught — *Internalized Oppression* — Page 87

- A television set
- The three essays on internalized oppression from this manual
- Your "Vision Statement"
- Session Guidelines
- Newsprint
- Markers
- Loose paper
- Pencils or pens
- Masking tape
- Documentation materials and equipment
- Attendance sheet
- Agendas
- Handouts
- Evaluation forms
- Food and drinks for meal or snack

Other possible materials include:

- Other articles or books on internalized oppression
- The Color of Fear videotape

What else?

Is there anything else you need to do to prepare for the "Internalized Oppression" module?

Challenges of this Module

The Internalized Oppression module is a wonderful, exciting experience. It is also very draining and very scary because it invites participants to share from their places of greatest vulnerability. This is one of the most explosive, difficult, fear-laden and guilt-laden topics in American society and, to some degree, we have all been conditioned to deal with it through blaming others and/or blaming ourselves.

By its very nature, however, the system of supposed inherent superiority and inherent inferiority victimizes all members of American society: white people as well as people of color, men as well as women, rich people as well as low-income people. It is important that all participants become aware of this and realize that the purpose of this module is to explore and expose the system, not to point fingers or assign blame.

Equally important, there is no legitimate place for guilt, blame, and shame about one's own feelings or one's own response or participation in the S/I system. Though an important part of this module involves recognizing how we unconsciously contribute to maintaining this system, it is equally true that we all work, to greater and lesser degrees, toward countering its destructive effects.

It is essential, therefore, to affirm that all participants come into the discussion from where they are and as who they are. We cannot help who we are–this is a given, and this is OK. If people don't feel safe being who they are, they cannot be expected to participate freely.

The ultimate challenge of this module, then, is to recognize and affirm that there are ways to examine this system and participants' own responses to it that do not involve guilt, blame, or shame. Instead, by sharing openly and honestly from a place of safety and by recognizing that we are all victims of the S/I system, participants will challenge themselves and others in a way that fosters and supports the dignity and self-esteem of all people.

Another challenge of this module is that of helping people to see the relevance of this work to the *MCTT* program before the session. Participants may not see initially how this module ties in to a revitalization of your child care program. It is important to make these connections so that participants will be interested in and committed to attending the session. However, it is not important that participants grasp or "agree" with the concept of internalized oppression before the meeting–this is part of the process they and you will go through during the module.

A final challenge of this module is that of being its facilitator. Because of the nature of this material, it is vital that the facilitator be just that–a facilitator, not a teacher, instructor, or judge. The facilitator must be a full, equal member of the discussion, committed to sharing from the same place of honesty and vulnerability as all the other participants.

> Working and watching the children, we experience those things they go through as a result of being categorized and separated because of who they are and because of experiences that they've had, sometimes for which they are not responsible but for which they have been penalized. This work helps us to know how fragile the sense of self is, that sense of self-esteem is, and how quickly we can deteriorate an individual, cause a person to feel alone, to feel different, to feel anger and sadness--all of those things that are not productive for our children.
>
> --Ethel White, Community Leader, Joyland Child Development Center

Putting this Module into Action

Internalized Oppression Session

The facilitator will lead the session by introducing exercises, establishing times for each exercise, and, most important, creating a fun, energetic, and connected atmosphere for the session.

Basic approach:

Because this module may be the most difficult to administer, each of 10 primary activities is described in greater detail. The recommended exercises have proven to be very effective tools to examine the S/I belief system. Although the exercises are rather straightforward, their full power can be easily missed or lost. Therefore, we suggest careful study of this module, and we recommend that activities of this module follow the order in which they are presented here.

Activities

Activity 1 - Welcome participants
warmly and express appreciation for the following:

    a. coming to the session

    b. giving a day to the subject

    c. studying the assigned readings

    d. being willing and courageous enough to address the issues of internalized inferiority and superiority

    e. showing general cooperation and support of the program and the *MCTT* process

Activity 2 - Check-in

Check-in is an activity designed to: i) release energy; ii) bring persons to the here-and-now; iii) account for the persons' moods, feelings, attitudes, etc.; iv) build connections, empathy, rapport; v) support connections between an individual's tasks/work life and her or his feelings/being; vi) stress the value of the "whole" person; vii) reduce conflict between the focus of the session and other agendas; and viii) help keep communications clear by providing more information about the thinking and emotional states of participants.

The focus of Check-in is on i) significant activities and events that have happened to individuals (since they were last together); and

ii) sharing of work activities only as they relate to stored energy (such as sadness, gladness, fear, anger).

    a. Assemble participants in a circle with no tables or other obstructions between people.

    b. Target a time limit for check-in (about 1 to 3 minutes per person).

    c. Check-in works better when, instead of being asked to speak in a definite order, persons are given the option of sharing "as the spirit moves them."

    d. Ask individuals to assess where their energies are at the moment. Some responses might be: "I am thinking about my children missing me on a Saturday" or "I am anxious about how this day will go when we talk about these issues" or "My sister and her family are coming to visit and I have not finished cleaning the house" or "I worked very late last night and I am a little out of it."

    e. Thank participants for their candid sharing and assure them that they are OK wherever their energies are. As the session goes on, they are likely to get fully involved.

Activity 3 - Vision for the session and expected outcomes

Remind participants of the purpose of the "Internalized Oppression" Module:

    a. Examine the system of supposed inherent superiority and inherent inferiority (S/I system) and the consequences of this system on individuals, groups, and society as a whole

    b. Determine the particular impact the S/I system has on children

    c. Explore the alternative to the S/I system and investigate the consequences of this alternative on individuals, groups, and society as a whole

    d. Consider how the S/I system channels our feelings

    e. Suggest ways to acquire skills to manage our feelings outside of the S/I system

    f. Connect insights, discoveries, thoughts, experiences, and knowledge to the vision and mission of the program

Add the following hopes and wishes for the session:

1. Individuals will learn things about themselves and others that will be valuable in other areas of their lives

2. The group will grow closer together and become more understanding of differences

3. Individuals will increase their valuing of differentness and people who are culturally different

   Introduction of facilitator

   - Give some professional and personal background information about the facilitator.

   - Explain the role of the facilitator as helping the group accomplish its goals by keeping a focus on the process or the way discussion flows as well as on the content of discussions.

   - Invite the facilitator to express her/his motivation, including joy and excitement, about being with the group and about the subject of their session.

Activity 4 - Presentation of Session Guidelines for participants and facilitators

   - Make individual copies of the Session Contract and/or write the contract on a flip chart

   - Discuss each item of the contract as thoroughly as necessary for all to agree or disagree with the contract

   - (See page 114 For Session Guidelines)

   - (See page 116 For Facilitator Guidelines)

   a. After presentation and discussion of the Session Guidelines, the group is asked to express (with a show of hands or verbally) a willingness to abide by the guidelines to the best of their ability. (This is a social contract that all participants are expected to take seriously.)

   The facilitator will explicitly agree to the terms of her/his contract and ask the group for support to i) keep discussions on track; ii) keep up with time and facilitate renegotiation of time if/when necessary; iii) steer folks back to "I" statements and self-focus; iv) interrupt clashes of personalities rather than differences of opinion; v) support individuals who exhibit shy behavior and do not speak up; vi) remind the outspoken to share "air time" and vii) call time for process when deemed necessary by the facilitator or a member of the group.

Activity 5 - S/I exercise

The "S/I Line" and the Okay Corral are tools that will be used for discussion to examine approaches, rules and principles for enabling people to work and associate in harmony across lines of diversity. Participants will examine theories, principles, and techniques related to communicating and associating with others. The discussion should be conducted in a spirit of examination and exploration. Any attempt to define or label individuals must not be allowed. Encourage individuals to keep a self-focus and look for their own "caught" and "taught" patterns of thinking, feeling, and behavior. Discourage participants from trying to define or establish universal truth about which should govern, describe or measure the experiences, values, and world views of others.

The "S/I Line" exercise is designed to stimulate and guide critical analysis of belief systems (large group session). The S/I exercise is designed to work somewhat as a game.

A. Arrange the group in a semicircle facing the flip chart or simply have participants gather in front of the flip chart.

B. Invite participants to "join in a little exercise to see what we come up with." The facilitator draws a line across the chart (example below). At the beginning of the line an "S" is placed above and an "I" is placed below. The facilitator begins the process and sets the pattern by adding letters to the line and explaining that each letter represents a word. For example: ("D" = Doctor), ("P" = Patient), ("T" = Teacher), ("S" = Student), ("P" = Parent),

("C" = Child), ("P" = Preacher), and ("C = Congregation).

C. The participants are encouraged to continue the association. If asked about the S and I that begin each line, the facilitator should ask permission to explain a little later. Depending upon the facilitator's style, she might simply claim ignorance or, in a playful way, ask the participants to follow orders. It is very important that the discussion not center on the "S" and the "I" at this point. It is also important that the facilitator write the offerings of the group on the line <u>as they are lived out</u> in society, not as

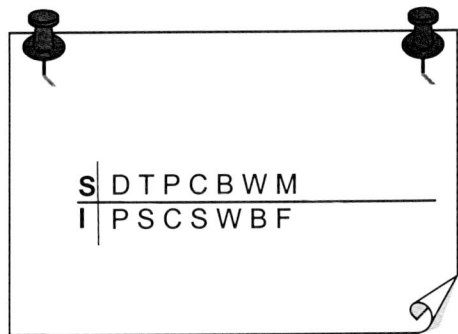

they <u>should be</u>. For example, if someone offers "men" and "women," the facilitator would put "M" for men on the top of the line and "W" for women beneath "M" on the line. And if "rich" and "poor" are offered, the facilitator should put "R" for rich on the top of the line and "P" for poor on the bottom of the line and so forth. The facilitator should encourage participants not to think too deeply and not to work too hard on their offerings. Participants should simply report the first things that come to their minds, such as Boss-Worker, Sister-Brother, Rich-Poor, Blonds-Brunets, etc.

D. As the facilitator obviously changes the offerings of the group and as participants begin to see a pattern, some individuals will focus on the placement of the letters on the line and want them to be placed as they "should" be placed. Some persons will likely resist the placement because it does not reflect their values. At this point explain that the placement reflects how things <u>are</u> in society and not how they might or should be. Encourage participants to reflect on the notions that reflect existing and established patterns of society, even though these patterns may be changing. Other persons in the group might begin to focus on the "S" and the "I" at the beginning of the line and want to know what they represent. The facilitator should ask the group to guess the meaning of the "S" and the "I." The group is likely to guess the right answer, but if they do not, the facilitator should offer clues until they arrive at the answer.

It is very important that the discussion not bog down on whether or not "the line is absolutely true." Emphasize the objective of getting a general picture of American society or Western society. If individuals are "heard" and feel free of being labeled personally by the line, discussion is more likely to proceed with support and involvement of all participants.

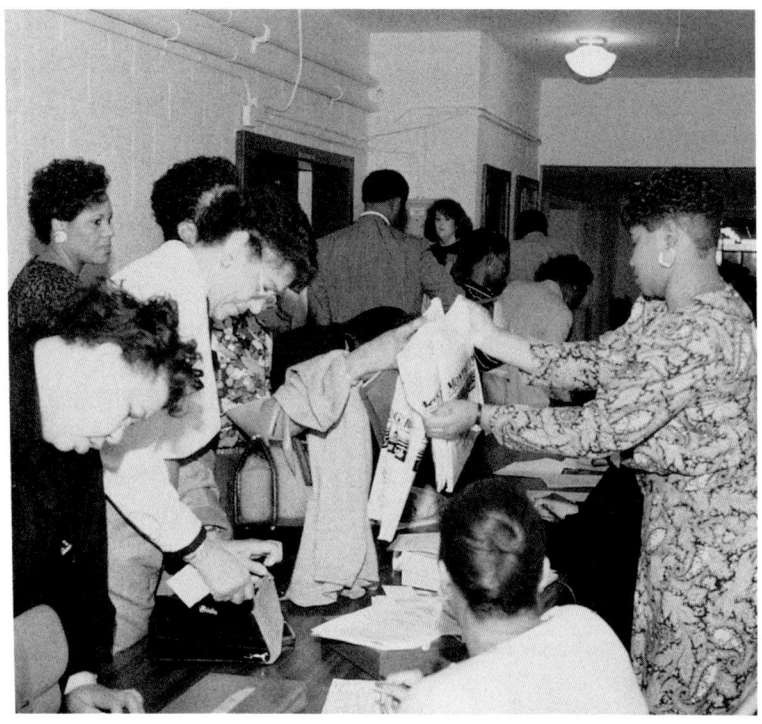

The facilitator should point out that the "S" and "I" stand for "inherent superiority" and "inherent inferiority." That is to say, the system assumes that some people, simply because they are male, rich, adult, white, educated, etc., are inherently better than others who are female, poor, "young," black, and uneducated.

Offer a few examples (such as women and the right to vote, blacks who were categorized as three-fifths human by the United States government, and the treatment of Native Americans by the U.S. government).

E. Once several lines have been filled in and there is general agreement on the picture and what it represents, reflections on the system can begin.

F. This exercise opens discussions on the questions and issues listed below. In order to help participants enter the discussion fully energized, you might underscore your beliefs a) that you love and care for America, b) that examining and constructively criticizing America is not for you a negative act but rather a responsible and caring act, c) etc.

Framework for discussion

Note: If time and group size are factors that limit discussion, consider dividing the group into pairs or triads. In addition, small groups can be given individual questions for discussion and can report their conclusions to the large group.

Question - Does the line represent America?

Point - People on the bottom of the line (such as women, the poor, the physically challenged, ethnic minorities, etc.) would tend to agree that the line is valid.

Point - The line represents the structure of most Western societies and probably of most societies generally.

Question - Which group (the "S's" or "I's") has the greatest investment not just in moving people around on the line, but in eradicating the line?

Point - Both the "S's" and the "I's" have a vested interest in maintaining the line. Note that changing positions and "tinkering" with the line is not the same as eradicating the system.

Point - Many groups and individuals want to see people moved around on the line but do not want to destroy an entire system that suggests that some people are inherently superior and others inherently inferior.

Point - Both groups, inside and outside of conscious awareness, actually work to keep the line in place. What are some of the behaviors of each group that preserve the status quo?

Question - Is the relationship symbiotic in nature? (Symbiosis = a dependent relationship that is beneficial to both members; includes parasitism, a relationship in which the parasite depends on and may injure its host; helotism, a master-slave relationship found in some societies; a system that requires cooperation of both the "S's" and the "I's" to exist).

Question - Do all members of society experience the dynamics of both the "S" and "I" position?

Point - All members of society likely experience both the "S" position and the "I" position during life, although age, class, race, profession, etc., in various

> Just like the body dies from lack of use--if you don't use your muscles, they will atrophy and die; if you don't use your mind, it gets slow on you--and if you don't have any reason to use your body or your mind in that you cannot define a vision or a place that you want to go, then as a person you begin to deteriorate, if you don't have anything to look forward to.
>
> --Hattie Myles, Community Leader, Miller's Toulminville Day Care Center

configurations cause most of us to experience either the "S" or the "I" as a dominant position (the place of our psychological identity). Give some examples.

Question - Is it true that the average child, by the age of six, has already learned how to think, feel, and behave relative to the positions on the line?

Point - If a group of 100 randomly selected children were to be approached individually a) by a man who drove a battered old pickup truck and wore dirty work clothes, and then b) by the same man, this time driving a shiny new car, wearing a suit, and carrying an attaché case, would we see a pattern of behavior in the children that was different towards the man? If so, what would be some of the differences and what might cause the differences in feeling, thinking, and behavior?

Question - How, specifically, is the S/I belief system passed from generation to generation?

Point - Parents and family are the primary teachers of children.

More is "caught" from the primary teachers than is "taught." This fact means that attitudes and out-of-awareness feelings and motivations "caught" by children are internalized in their life's work of "making sense" of everything and becoming.

The "S/I Line" exercise is followed by an exercise aimed at the examination of thinking, feeling, and behavior produced by the S/I belief system.

G. Divide participants into small groups (consisting or 3 to 5 persons) and invite them to identify, share, and write (mostly one-word) descriptions of thinking, feelings, and behavior that accompany the S & I positions. Underscore the need to share their thinking as they write their responses, and remind them that everyone has experienced life on both sides of the line. The handout (page 20) can be used to help participants categorize their responses. Encourage participants to make an effort to label their offerings as "thinking," "feeling" and "behavior," but the focus of discussions should not shift to whether responses are, in fact, thinking, feeling, or behavior. Point out the fact that some responses will fit equally well in different boxes.

H. Reassemble the group for large discussion. Have individuals call out the responses recorded on their papers (and additional ones spontaneously) and write these responses on chart paper. Organize and label their responses as they appear on the handout.

Framework for discussion

Question - Who is victimized by the line?

Point - When consideration is given to issues like quality of human relationships, personal safety, quality of work relationships, sharing resources, building communities, peaceful coexistence, productivity and spiritual health, we find that all members of society are victimized by the line.

Question - Can significant inferences be drawn given the fact that the great majority of us possess a very refined understanding of the system (as evidenced by the ease with which the thinking, feeling and behavior of both sides are identified)?

Question - Can the S/I belief system exist without the outcomes, thinking, feelings, and behaviors that participants identified in small groups?

Point - When individuals or groups of people believe and act towards others as though they are superior, understandable and predictable reactions by others will result. The same is true for individuals or groups of people who believe and act as though they are inferior.

Question - Can the vision (refer to the statement generated in the Vision module) of participants be achieved within the S/I belief system? If so, how? If not, why not?

At this point in the examination of the S/I belief system, participants may be anxious and ready to move on to solutions. The next exercise is a transition to the exploration of alternatives to the S/I belief system. The "OK Corral" (taken from Transaction Analysis) is the focus of this large group exercise (page 20).

Activity 6 - The OKAY CORRAL

A powerful tool for building I'm OK You're OK relationships is the Cooperative Mode. This concept is also

from Transaction Analysis. The Cooperative Mode can be used as a contract for "being together," and a framework for reexamination of values, styles, relationships and the administrations that cover and bind our programs together.

Explanation of the Okay Corral and points for discussion

The Okay Corral exercise is designed to stimulate and guide critical analysis of belief systems and patterns of thinking, feeling, and behaving (large group session).

A. Arrange the group in a semicircle facing the flip chart or simply have participants gather in front of the flip chart.

B. Invite participants to explore the Okay Corral and examine their own primary and secondary life positions.

Framework for discussion

The Okay Corral suggests that there are four fundamental positions that an individual might assume as ways of BEING in the world. These positions are not static. That is to say an individual will migrate to a "favorite" or familiar position at which they will spend most of their time. Life will, the theory suggests, enabling the individual to experience all the positions, thus causing each of us to become familiar with the thinking, feelings and behaviors of each place in the Okay Corral.

- The first position, "I'm Okay; You are Okay," or the plus plus position is the goal of personal development and leads to peace, joy, love, empowerment, fulfillment, etc.

- The second, "I'm Okay; You're Not Okay," or the plus minus position, finds its social expression in "getting rid of" behaviors; the ultimate expression is to kill or get rid of the other.

- The third position, "I'm Not Okay; You are Okay," or the minus plus position is expressed in "getting rid of self" behaviors and is ultimately expressed in suicide.

- The fourth position, "I'm Not Okay; You're Not Okay," or the minus minus position is expressed in "getting away from" behavior with insanity the ultimate social expression.

Points for discussion

Point - The social expression of the + -, - +, and - - positions should be seen as being on a continuum. For example, the plus minus position would have at one end prejudice and subtle discrimination and have ethnic cleansing and genocide on the opposite end of the continuum. All along the continuum are varying degrees of the two extremes. Some examples might be found in written and unwritten social laws and policies that relate to the way society deals with minorities, women, the homeless, non-English speakers, non-Christians, etc.

Point - Except for the plus plus place, invite participants to reflect upon the "S/I Line" and identify positions along a continuum for the remaining three positions.

Question - Can the I'm OK You're OK position not coexist with the S/I belief system?

Point - The I'm OK You're OK position has never existed in recorded history with <u>significant</u> numbers of different peoples for a <u>significant</u> period of time.

Question - The I'm OK You're OK position is new and radically different from the S/I belief system: how does the plus plus position place those who pursue it at odds with the S/I belief system which permeates present-day society?

Question - Only the I'm OK You're OK position can lead to achieving the vision of the participants: why?

Activity 7 - View and discuss the video <u>A Class Divided</u>

Points for discussion

Encourage the participants to be aware of both their thinking and their feelings. A strategy that can be used to bring diversity to the group process for this discussion is to divide the group into three sub groups and ask each group to focus on the children who have collars, the children without collars, or Jane Elliot, as the authority figure.

Framework for discussion

Process the general thinking and feeling responses first with questions such as these: What are some of the thoughts that came to your mind first? What were some of your feelings? Why?

Question - What did the children learn from the experience?

Question - What did the children already know about discrimination?

Question - What were physical responses to messages?

Question - What were the messages sent by authority figures (such as Jane Elliot)?

Question - What is to be learned from how fast the children internalized the messages from Jane Elliot?

Question - Discuss how powerful the opinion of a loved and respected person is.

Question - How did the children call upon what they already knew to support the messages?

Question - Discuss the process of translating the name "brown eyes" to negative.

Question - How long did it take for the messages to take effect?

Question - What happened to the thinking process because of the collar?

Question - Discuss the findings that the children's achievement scores changed.

> Modeling is going to be there whether we acknowledge it or not. Kids are going to pattern themselves after somebody. Hopefully, with the awareness that modeling is taking place, we're more cognizant of what we do and the activities and behaviors we exhibit. Not just when we want the kids to see us do good things, but by taking that on as a part of our everyday behavior, so that kids see us do what we say, and not do one thing and say another. By doing this, we actually empower our kids to take on those behaviors that will be successful for them in life.
>
> --Constance Hendricks, Community Leader, Joyland Child Development Center

Question - One child focused rage on the object, the collar. Were there other outlets for such anger?

Question - Discuss the ability of the children to make the connections between what they experienced and learned and other situations and experiences.

Activity 8 - Discuss Internalized Oppression Articles (Appendix C)

- Thank participants for doing their reading assignment and express "OKness" for those who did not do the assignment.

- Explain that the readings will be processed and drawn upon later in the session.

Framework for discussion

Organize participants into small groups.

Process the general thinking and feeling responses first with questions such as these: What were some of the thoughts that came to your mind first? What were some of your feelings? Why?

Question - How would you describe internalized oppression and its effects?

Question - In what life situations will a person manifest internalized attitudes and behavior?

Question - Is it likely that any individual groups targeted in American society (women, blacks, Native Americans, the poor, etc.) are completely free of internalized oppression?

Question - What factors motivate individuals to fight to keep themselves in the negative/powerless position defined by the society?

Activity 9 - Early experiences with the "other(s)"

Framework for discussion

This discussion will allow participants to personalize the exploration of internalized oppression by reflecting upon their own early experiences and relating them to the material presented and previous discussions.

Divide the participants into sub-groups of 5 or 6 and remind them of the contract for no guilt, blame, or shame.

> How does a child catalog this discrimination in his mind? What does this do to him for next year when this has happened to him this year and then he has to go back and face that system? Our children need a lot of teaching about how to get along where they're going after they leave us.
>
> --Clara Card, Director, Joyland Child Development Center

Ask participants to recall and share their earliest encounter with the "other," be they whites, blacks, Native Americans, Jews, or others.

Question - Was it a positive and/or negative experience?

Question - What were the basic feelings (sadness, gladness, fear, anger) that accompanied the experience?

Question - What decisions did you make, or what decisions were you "invited" to make?

Question - What information did you not have (as a child) and/or what information would you like to have had?

Question - Have you revised the early decisions? If so, how?

Activity 10 - Making Connections generally and specifically for the program

Framework for discussion

At this point you will want the participants to pull it all together by reflecting and drawing upon what they have learned and what has been reaffirmed for them. They might also have very penetrating and perplexing questions.

Keep the focus of the discussion "in the room" and keep the point of authority focused on the wisdom, experiences, needs, concerns, insights and feelings of participants. Encourage them to embrace the notion that this experience is for them in their "real" lives in their "real" world. Remind them that the aim of the session is not to find "ultimate truth," to change anyone else, or to make grandiose statements. Rather, the aim of the session is for the participants to clarify their understanding of the power and impact of oppression in all of its forms with special emphasis on the more virulent forms such as racism, classism, and sexism; to help participants consult and make the most powerful and relevant decisions regarding the care and development of children in this program; and to help individuals move closer to becoming that ideal model for children who will "catch" health and power from them.

Question - What feelings have you experienced and what were the stimuli for your feelings?

Question - What insights have you gained and/or what doors have been opened for you?

Question - Do you have unresolved or troubling questions? If so, what are they? And how would you like to go about finding answers?

Question - Is it appropriate to integrate the "caught" attitudes of teachers, parents, and others into the core development program of our child care program?

Question - What ideas, approaches and strategies would you offer to build resistance to internalized oppression and unconscious "isms" – racism, classism and sexism, etc.?

Question - What lessons have you learned that you might take out into the community?

Discuss next steps.

- The next module in this manual is "How to BE Together," and while the order of other modules is not of crucial importance, it is essential that the "How to BE Together" module follow the "Internalized Oppression" module, because the work continues from one to the other.

    The great strengths of your program, and of the *MCTT* process, include the diversity of experiences and expectations among participants. Tapping that richness and potential automatically brings a clash of ideas. The "How to BE Together" module addresses how to stimulate, encourage, support, and manage that clash of ideas. During the "Internalized Oppression" module you demonstrated that you can talk about and deal with tough issues as a group. This experience will help prepare you to discuss and manage differences among you.

Evaluate the session using evaluation forms.

Additional options:

Other options for increasing the effectiveness of the "Internalized Oppression" module might include viewing videos; reading book excerpts, papers, and articles; and attending lectures on a relevant subject before the meeting. Other exercises might include Trust Walks, "Fish Bowl" discussions with participants divided by race, gender, age or other significant differences as they talk about things that they like and dislike about their cultural heritage, including lesser-known benefits and handicaps associated with their culture.

Follow-up

- Bring the site team together to do a group evaluation of the session and to add relevant ideas to the "Internalized Oppression" section of the work plan.

- Write up all the lists you generated during the meeting and send copies to all *MCTT* participants or bring them to the next meeting.

Resources

Books:

- *Beginnings: The Social and Affective Development of Black Children*, Margaret B. Spencer

- *Black Children: Their Roots, Culture, and Learning Styles*, Janice E. Hale-Benson

- *Crews: Gang Members Talk to Maria Hinojosa*, Maria Hinojosa

- *Developmental Psychology of the Black Child*, A.N. Wilson

- *Dialogue: Racism, the Monster in Our Midst*, Rita Starr

- *Different and Wonderful: Raising Black Children in a Race-Conscious Society*, Darlene Hopson, Derek Hopson

- *Diversity in the Classroom*, Frances Kendall

- *Testing African American Students*, Asa G. Hilliard III

- *Valuing Diversity: The Primary Years*, Janet Brown McCracken

Catalogues:

- *Beyond the Stereotypes: A Guide to Resources for Black Girls and Young Women*

- *In Her Own Image*

- *A Reality Check on the American Dream*

- *Women Make Movies*

Videotapes

- *A Class Divided*

- *Color Adjustment*
- *The Color of Fear*
- *Ethnic Notions*

Support Materials

- Agendas for all *MCTT* participants

- Expanded Agendas for members of the *MCTT* Site Team. These expanded agendas will provide you with helpful information as you proceed with the session.

- Three essays on internalized oppression

- Training Session Contract

- Group affinity sheet

- Handout on vision and barriers

- Handout on thinking, feeling, and behavior

- Documents resulting from the Internalized Oppression session with participants from Joyland, Kiddy Land, and Miller's. These are included to give you a sense of what to expect. It's a good idea to share these with the facilitator and the Site Team but not with the whole group, because they might influence your own work.

Agenda

More Is Caught Than Taught Program

Internalized Oppression

1. Welcome

2. Introductions

3. Explanation of the meeting agenda

   Purpose of the meeting
   - To examine the system of supposed inherent superiority and inherent inferiority (S/I system) and the consequences of this system on individuals, groups, and society as a whole
   - To examine the particular impact the S/I system has on children
   - To explore the alternative to the S/I system and examine the consequences of this alternative on individuals, groups, and society as a whole
   - To explore how the S/I system channels our feelings
   - To acquire skills to manage our feelings outside of the S/I system

4. Internalized Oppression exercises with handouts

5. Next Steps

6. Closing

Expanded Agenda

More Is Caught Than Taught Program

Internalized Oppression

1. **Welcome**

2. **Introductions**

3. **Explanation of the meeting agenda**

   Purpose of the meeting

   - To examine the system of supposed inherent superiority and inherent inferiority (S/I system) and the consequences of this system on individuals, groups, and society as a whole

   - To examine the particular impact the S/I system has on children

   - To explore the alternative to the S/I system and examine the consequences of this alternative on individuals, groups, and society as a whole

   - To explore how the S/I system channels our feelings

   - To acquire skills to manage our feelings outside of the S/I system

4. **Internalized Oppression exercises with handouts, Refer to the Facilitator's Guide in the Introduction for additional comments.**

   - Review the "Vision Statements." If there is a significant number of persons who did not participate in the Visions Session, this is a good place to repeat the visioning exercise.

   - Put the S/I line on newsprint and lead participants into discussions.

   - Put the OK Corral on newsprint and lead discussions.

   - View and discuss <u>A Class Divided</u>.

5. **Next Steps**

   - The next module is the "How to BE Together" module. It is important that you do this one next because the work you've done in the "Internalized Oppression" module will help you as you address the diversity of your group in the "How To BE Together" module. Everyone brings their own ideas, experiences, and expectations into their work, and this diversity is extremely rich and powerful. It also causes a clash of ideas. "The How To BE Together" module addresses how to stimulate, encourage, support, and manage that clash of ideas.

- Fill out evaluation forms
- Review the date and time for the next meeting
- Express appreciation and affirmation of the meeting and participants

6. Closing

More Is *Caught* Than Taught — Internalized Oppression — Page 109

Vision	Barriers

How the System of Inherent Superiority/Inherent Inferiority Is Revealed in Thoughts, Feelings, and Behavior

Superior Thinking	Inferior Thinking
Superior Feeling	**Inferior Feeling**
Superior Behavior	**Inferior Behavior**

The Okay Corral

Four possible ways of BEING in society

I'M OK, YOU'RE OK	I'M OK, YOU'RE NOT OK
+ +	**+ -**
Ultimate expressions of this way: Peace Joy Love Sisterhood Brotherhood	Ultimate expressions of this way: Holocaust, Ethnic cleansing, Murder **Lesser degrees:** Forced segregation Helping you kill yourselves through drugs and guns Denying you jobs Denying you housing
I'M NOT OK, YOU'RE OK	**I'M NOT OK, YOU'RE NOT OK**
- +	**- -**
Ultimate expression of this way: Suicide **Lesser degrees:** Black on Black crime Drugs Jailing myself Sense that "I need to be removed"	Ultimate expression of this way: Insanity **Lesser degrees:** Despair Checking out; Drugs

How the System of Inherent Superiority/Inherent Inferiority is Revealed in Thoughts, Feelings, and Behavior

Superior Thinking
- Important
- Better than
- Always right
- Because I said so
- You bow down at my feet
- We're decision makers
- They can't do without me
- Supposed to be listened to
- I'm a contributor

Inferior Thinking
- Unsure
- Doubtful
- Don't matter
- It doesn't matter what I think
- Others know best
- I don't have anything to give

Superior Feeling

• Self-righteous	• Powerful
• I'm important	• Assertive
• Sense of control	• Threatened by others
• Arrogant	• Stingy
• Secure	• Feel good
• Happy	• Intolerant
• Suspicious	• Confident
• Impatient	• Generous/benevolent

Inferior Feeling

• Angry, mad	• Hopeless
• Victim (blaming)	• Lack of faith
• Inadequate	• Feel bad
• Insecure	• Low self-esteem
• Distrustful	• Humble
• Resentful	• Ugly
• Unimportant	• Guilty
• Scared	• Nervous
• Powerless	• Unloved
• Uncertain	• Unappreciated
• Self-doubt	• Stingy
• Ashamed	•

Superior Behavior

• Arrogant	• Ambitious
• Aggressive	• Do it when I get ready
• Making eye contact	• Call others by first name
• Intimidating	• Initiator
• Dominating	•
• Face to face	•
• In your face	•
• Take charge	•

Inferior Behavior

• Timid	• No eye contact
• Indecisive	• Laziness
• Shy	• Destructive
• Don't socialize	• Doing wrong
• Wait for others to take charge	• Acting out
• Rebelling	• Procrastination
• Apologetic	• Fighting
• Talk fast and softly	• Nonchalant

Created by *MCTT* Participants from Joyland Child Development Center, Kiddy Land Child Development Center, and Miller's Toulminville Day Care Center.

Relationships Established Under the System of Inherent Superiority/Inherent Inferiority

S	Dr	T	P	B	L	H	R	W	M	Y	E
I	P	S	C	E	C	W	P	B	W	O	Un

S	E	T	Bl	R	A	P	T	PCo	R	Us
I	U	F	Br	L	D	U	S	Non	W	T

Dr. Doctor Patient	Employed Unemployed
Teacher Student	Thin **Fat**
Parent Child	Blond Brown
Boss Employee	Right Left
Lawyer Client	Able **D**isabled
Husband Wife	Pretty Ugly
Rich Poor	Tall Short
White Black	**PC o**wner **Non** PCNon-owner
Man Woman	Right Wrong
Young Old	Us Them

Session Guidelines for <u>Participants</u>

a. Participants will assume responsibility for their own learning.

- Encourage participants to be active and ask for what they want and claim time for amplification of concerns they have.

- Remind participants not to expect that the facilitator or others can and will know their needs, concerns, and desires or address them.

- Advise participants not to wait until the end of the session to express feelings and wishes.

b. Urge participants to speak their reality when moved.

- Encourage participants to be in touch with their own feelings and thoughts and not to wait for validation or permission of others to express them.

- Affirm that each individual's reality is as valuable and necessary as the reality of any other person in the group.

c. Advise participants to respect the need and rights of others to speak about their reality.

- Remind participants that just as each individual is encouraged to know and speak about her/his own reality, each person should value and support this same opportunity for others in the group regardless of position, rank, etc.

d. Encourage participants to ask felt questions.

- Underscore the fact that questions are valued, expected, and appreciated.

- Encourage individuals not to censor themselves or their questions, for their questions are likely doorways for all group members to refine their individual understanding and expand their personal knowledge.

e. Ask participants to be aware of their needs and represent them.

- Assure participants that their job is to know and represent their own needs, from the temperature in the room to the need for breaks to a change in the agenda.

- Invite participants to consider their individual needs as valid and equal to those of all others.

f. Encourage participants to consider taking risks and being vulnerable.

- Support participants in **not doing anything that they really do not want to do**, but at the same time encourage them to "try on" new thinking and feelings and to practice new behaviors during the session.

- Stress that being candid, taking risks, and being vulnerable are powerful instruments of discovery.

g. Invite participants to use "I" statements primarily vs. general or global terms (such as "we," "everybody," "you all," "no one").

- Remind participants that the norm of the session will be for individuals to speak for themselves rather than attempting to represent "everybody," such as women, whites, blacks, the poor, etc.).

- Ask participants, in their discussions, to experiment with the power of their views, wishes, opinions and experiences (as opposed to merely echoing popular opinion, authoritative sources, research, etc.).

h. Advise participants to agree to disagree with each other and affirm each others, thoughts and ideas.

i. Remind participants that conflicts between ideas, experiences, values, and world views are expected and that many similarities are also expected.

- Tell participants that individuals are expected to agree and disagree with each other's thoughts and ideas as they explore issues and options.

j. Point out to participants that from the natural clash of differing ideas and feelings insight can emerge if guilt, blame, and shame are not elements of the discussion. Therefore, participants will be discouraged from resorting to guilt, blame, or shame at any level.

- Finally, urge participants to find and express humor as a vital part of examining and learning about issues of such great importance to the program as children, families, and communities.

Session Guidelines for <u>Facilitators</u>

a. The facilitator will, with the cooperation of the group, build and maintain an atmosphere that is safe and conducive to exploring new thoughts, feelings, and behaviors.

- Point out that the facilitator can achieve very little without the understanding and support of the group.

- Explain that fostering the safety in the group for each individual to express her/his own reality without punishment or embarrassment is the chief responsibility of the facilitator.

b. The facilitator will be honest and truthful in all matters addressed in the training session.

- When the facilitator is baffled s/he will say "I don't know," and that response will be OK.

- The facilitator will not misrepresent her/his feeling and will explain her/his actions and motivations when asked.

c. The facilitator will respect the thoughts, feelings, and needs of each individual and will treat all participants with equity and fairness.

- The facilitator will strive to be fair, and if unfairness is suspected by a group member the facilitator will address the concern without being punitive.

d. The facilitator will act as a peer to session participants and acknowledge feelings, needs, and wishes as appropriate to the objectives of the training session.

- The facilitator will not set her/himself apart as an expert, authority, or emotionally disconnected part of the group.

e. The facilitator will have fun.

- Like participants, the facilitator will also seek to find and express humor.

After presentation and discussion of the Session Guidelines, the group is asked to express (with a show of hands or verbally) a willingness to abide by the guidelines to the best of their ability. (This is a social contract that all participants are expected to take seriously.)

The facilitator will explicitly agree to the terms of her/his contract and ask the group for support to i) keep discussion on track; ii) keep up with time and facilitate renegotiation of time if/when necessary; iii) steer folks back to "I" statements and self-focus; iv) interrupt clashes of personalities rather than differences of opinion; v) support individuals who exhibit shy behavior and do not speak up; vi) remind the outspoken to share "air time"; and vii) call time for process when deemed necessary by the facilitator or a member of the group.

HOW TO BE TOGETHER MODULE

"In our every deliberation, we must consider the impact of our decisions on the next seven generation."

— The Great Law of the Six Nations of the Iroquois Confederacy

What Is This Module?

Every person is different, and we all bring our differences to our interactions with others. We bring our difference in heritage, in gender, in culture, in upbringing, in education, in work, and in all those things that have shaped who we are, what our outlook is on life and the world around us, and what our goals are for ourselves and our children.

There are some large areas of difference in American society as a whole. These include ethnic background, level of wealth, and gender. But there are also innumerable smaller areas of difference: where we come from, how big our family is, how old we are, whether we prefer to read or watch television. Regardless of whether your group of *MCTT* participants is all of the same race, gender, or income bracket, there is a great deal of diversity among you.

This diversity is a wonderful resource for your *MCTT* group, your child care program, and American society in general; the more viewpoints and experiences that are incorporated into programs, the stronger they become. Diversity provides an opportunity to present your outlook and also to hear and learn about the perspectives of others.

However, this diversity also creates disagreement and a conflict of ideas. It may mean that a parent's view of how to raise her or his child is dramatically different from the view of the child's teacher. It may mean that the opinion of a community leader regarding what the child care program needs varies distinctly from what the staff feels is needed. It may mean that teachers have divergent ideas as to how music should be used in a classroom, what is clutter and what is beauty, how children should be comforted when they're sad, or how rules should be enforced.

Because we have been taught that the best thing is to "get along," our tendency often is to minimize difference or to accept the prevailing point of view. But our difference is a strength, not something to be hidden. It is also something that we cannot change simply because we want to agree with others or because we want others to agree with us. By not acknowledging our difference or the conflict that it creates, we allow the formation and persistence of dynamics that are unhealthy for everyone involved.

In order to tap into the strength of our diversity, then, we must acknowledge and appreciate it. And we must also be able to listen to and accommodate the experiences, beliefs, and priorities of others.

In the "How To BE Together" module of *More Is Caught Than Taught*, you will review the system of supposed inherent superiority and inherent inferiority and assess its possible impact on the care of children in the program and relationships between parents, teachers, and children. You will also explore the diversity in your group, and you will look at how the S/I model affects how you interact with each other. Through the "Cooperative_Mode," you will gain access to new tools for communicating about and managing differences and conflict. (You will find a discussion of the "Cooperative Mode" in Appendix C, page 227. It is essential that this document be studied before this session). Finally, this module will help you develop a specific contract for how you will be together for the rest of the *MCTT* program and beyond.

The "How To BE Together" module will invite you to increase your strength as a group. It will also prepare you to take full advantage of the diversity of your group and thereby build a stronger curriculum. As you proceed with the *MCTT* program, your decisions will become more difficult as the issues grow more difficult and complex. What early childhood theories or what beliefs, principles, and values will frame and guide the growth and development of children in the program, and why? What approaches and strategies or what curriculum will be used to plan daily activities and evaluate the development of children? What standards will be used to used to hire and terminate workers in the program, and to fashion staff and board development programs? What will your priorities be for continually improving your program?

These are the kinds of very complex questions that your group will address as you get into the "Early Childhood Theorist"; "Curriculum, Lesson-Planning and Assessment"; and "Work Planning" modules. Discussing and reaching agreement on these questions and issues is formidable and made even more challenging as most

people come into discussions about the well-being of children with strong ideas, wishes, and opinions and are deeply attached to them. "Hearing" others, giving consideration to their experiences and opinions, and being flexible on these issues require communication skills, mental discipline, and a love of differentness that cannot be taken for granted regardless of the background of the individual. It is suggested that you acknowledge, affirm, and struggle with difference rather than deny or discount its significance in age, education, income, race, gender and other cultural realities.

This "How To BE Together" module will culminate in a social contract. Your group will work towards identifying specific behavior that individuals will follow and behavior that will be avoided in their relationships with each other. You will define "how to be together" free of prejudices and feelings, thoughts and behaviors that are born out of notions of inherent superiority and inferiority among human beings. In ridding your group of these destructive aspects and taking advantage of the strength of your diversity, this module will prepare you to create a curriculum that reflects your vision for children.

Expected Outcomes

Participants will:

- Explore specific ways that the S/I system and internalized oppression affect relationships
- Increase appreciation for the challenges of working with people who are different
- Cultivate approaches, skills, and knowledge that will facilitate working together
- Develop a specific contract for "How To BE Together"

Preparing

Who will participate?

All members of the site team, staff, parents, and community leaders.

How long will it take?

The "How To BE Together" module is time-consuming but very valuable. Allow at least six to eight hours. You are encouraged to study this module carefully and plan well. Any extra time or resources that you allocate to this module will be helpful in achieving the contract and the understanding that you are seeking.

Where will it take place?

In addition to a place where you will feel comfortable and that is convenient for participants, you should choose a place that feels private, where participants will have the freedom freely to express their emotions. A site where chairs can be freely moved about and where newsprint paper can be taped to the walls is an important consideration.

When will it take place?

You will have already set the dates for this and future meetings, but you will want to send out a reminder to program participants including the date, time, and place of the "How To BE Together" session.

How will you document this module?

It is a good idea to touch base with the person who agreed during the "Getting Started" module to document the meeting so as to make sure s/he has all the necessary materials and equipment for the documentation method that you have chosen (audio taping, video taping, taking photographs, and taking good notes are some of the options).

What will you need to bring to the session?

Some suggestions:

- Your "Vision Statement"
- Your chart from the "Internalized Oppression" module on how the S/I system reveals itself in thoughts, feelings, and behavior
- Newsprint
- Markers

- Loose paper
- Pencils or pens
- Masking tape
- Documentation materials and equipment
- Attendance sheet
- Agendas
- Copies of the "Cooperative Mode"
- Evaluation forms
- Food and drinks for meal or snack

What else?

Is there anything else you need to do to prepare for the "How To BE Together" module?

Challenges of This Module

The biggest challenge of this module is that of getting over the notion that difference is bad and conflict should be avoided. When faced with a difference of opinion, people tend either to discount what the other person is saying or discount their own experience and perspective. It is important to counteract this tendency by stressing to each participant that her or his perspective is a vital,

valuable resource to the group which she or he should both represent and advocate.

Because of this desire to avoid conflict, participants may also lean toward generalities or toward focusing the conversation on others outside the immediate group. The purpose of this module, however, is to explore and manage the diversity among you. This means grounding the conversation in the here and now, looking honestly at yourselves, and revealing the dynamics behind your interactions.

These dynamics can be hard to confront and even harder to discuss, because our culture has given us little training in how to deal with conflict other than through either accusations or silence. Therefore, in order to feel safe, participants will need assurance that there are tools such as the "Cooperative Mode" (Appendix C) and the Sessions Guidelines (page 114) which can aid communications, smooth interaction around differences, and help people to be respectful of each other.

Putting This Module into Action

"How To BE Together" Session

The facilitator will lead the session by introducing exercises, establishing times for each exercise, and, most importantly, creating a fun, energetic, and connected atmosphere for the session.

Basic approach:

1. **Introduce the "How To BE Together" module by connecting it to "Internalized Oppression," the other modules of the *MCTT* program, and the work with children.**

   - Briefly review the chart you created in the "Internalized Oppression" module showing how the system of inherent superiority and inherent inferiority reveals itself in thoughts, feelings, and behavior. In the "Internalized Oppression" module you explored the destructive dynamics of the S/I system and the internalized oppression that results from it. Now you will use your heightened awareness as you examine the dynamics of your *MCTT* group and your child care program. This module will provide you with tools which will help you ask and answer the question: How can we be together in a way that respects, affirms, and supports our differences?

2. **Explore how the system of inherent superiority and inherent inferiority, which was examined in the "Internalized**

> The conversation brought feelings of anger and deep sadness to me, brought to the surface some things we think we've repressed but which can be immediately brought back as if they were yesterday.
>
> –Ethel White, Community Leader, Joyland Child Development Center

Oppression" module, might be manifested in the child care programs.

- Break into small groups and discuss how the S/I system affects child care programs in one or more of the following categories:
  - the relationship between the staff and children and the behavior of children in the program
  - the administration of the center
  - the relationships between parents and the center
  - the community's relationship to the center
  - the program's curriculum, lesson plans, and assessments

- Each topic should be covered by at least one group. In discussing these topics, another helpful way of thinking of it might be: What are the things that can and must be changed? Be sure to have one person in your group capturing ideas on paper.

- Come together as a full group to call out ideas to two participants at the front of the room who will write them on newsprint.

- Discuss and process your ideas as a full group.

- Some questions you might want to consider:
  - What came up in common among the different categories?
  - Was the impact of the S/I system greatest, or most visible, in any one particular category?
  - If you had to identify one element in each category as the greatest problem, what one would that be?

3. **Introduce the "Cooperative Mode" as a tool for interacting.**

The objective of the Cooperative Mode exercise is to acquaint participants with the Cooperative Mode so that they can decide if they do or do not want to apply the "Cooperative Mode" to the child care program. On the surface, the "Cooperative Mode" might seem simplistic. But to the contrary, the "Cooperative Mode" is a very powerful foundation on which cooperative rather than competitive relationships can be built. The "Cooperative Mode" invites one to examine fundamental ways of "BEING" with others

and points to options that empower the individual and lead to healthier and more positive group dynamics. Putting the "Cooperative Mode" into action is a process, the benefits of which increase over time. Two questions are before the group: Is the "Cooperative Mode" an approach that is beneficial, and is the group willing to put forth the effort to learn about the "Cooperative Mode" and put it into practice? The following exercises will enable participants to reach a level of understanding such that they can make a basic decision about the "Cooperative Mode."

Participants will find that they are familiar with the concepts and elements of the "Cooperative Mode." It is just the organization of those elements that makes the "Cooperative Mode" unique. The knowledge and experiences of participants are vital for discovering the potential of the "Cooperative Mode." The exercises invite participants to call upon their knowledge and experiences to identify examples of "power plays," strokes, paranoid fantasies, and other elements of the "Cooperative Mode." A major objective of the exercise is to define the terms used in the "Cooperative Mode." You are encouraged to give participants freedom to be flexible with the "labels" but not the concepts. Safety is very important to the success of this exercise. Explain that participants will be asked to identify behavior and experiences that they learned in early childhood and that may be dysfunctional at this point in their lives. One of the underlying assumptions of the exercise is that all of us think, feel, and behave in ways that that could be improved. Another assumption is that outmoded thinking, feeling, and behavior are altered when we are able to isolate, examine, and clearly understand the consequences or benefits of changing our ways.

Keep discussions light, remembering that the objective is to define the meaning of terms and explore concepts so that decisions can be made about whether to use the "Cooperative Mode." Be aware that some individuals will insist on the facilitator "explaining" the terms before they start small group discussions. Encourage participants to trust themselves and the group to discover the "right" meanings of the terms and concepts of the "Cooperative Mode" through discussion. Remind individuals that the objective is not to label individuals, point fingers, instruct, or correct others. Personal experiences and reflections on self are only used to frame these discussions because personal examples tend to expedite examination of the "Cooperative Mode" as opposed to bogging down in abstract concepts.

4. **Explore the "Cooperative Mode."**

   - Break into groups of four or five people and begin the exploration by reading the statement on cooperation vs. competition and inviting participants to discuss these concepts. Here are possible discussion points to include:

     - The goal is not competition OR cooperation but rather competition AND cooperation. Competition is valuable at times and should be supported. At other times cooperation works better.

     - Competition often retards and confuses the building of intimate relationships.

     - The "Cooperative Mode" is firmly built on the notion that cooperation is preferred (most of the time) to competition in the development and maintenance of personal relationships.

       ○ What would be gained by creating an environment that is permeated by the notion of abundance (abundance of energy, affirmation/strokes, recognition, love, contact, time, attention, caring, etc.)?

       ○ What happens (how do people think, feel and behave) when the environment is permeated by a sense of scarcity?

   - Summarize the discussion and introduce the next discussion by inviting someone to read the statement on "No power plays." Emphasize: A power play is a way of structuring time, and everybody engages in power plays at one level or other. Discuss the notion that power plays are behaviors we likely learned in early childhood as a way of coping with the big, powerful people in our lives. They might be viewed as a survival strategy devised by a little, young, and powerless person in response to the unique styles and characteristics of mother or father.

     For the purposes of this exercise, power plays are not to be viewed as "wrong" or "bad" but as "taught" or "caught" behavior that participants might want to isolate, examine, and then decide to keep or reject.

- Discuss **"Power Plays,"** beginning with the question: What is your "favorite" power play? Subsequent amplifying questions could be:
  - How did you go about getting your way when you were a child? What did you have to do to get attention?
  - When under pressure, what behavior today are you likely to resort to in order to get your way?
  - How might you use power plays in the workplace or early childhood program?
  - Some typical responses might be: using guilt, crying, threatening violence to self or them, withdrawing, manipulating them, out talking them, sweet talking them, pleading, yelling, being sick, etc.

- Summarize the discussion by asking participants as a full group to share key learnings, affirmations, and questions. Check to see if there is general agreement on the definition of power plays. Offer participants the option of sharing any decisions that they have made or are considering making relative to the use of power plays. Emphasize that the Cooperative Mode calls for negotiation for what one wants rather than using power plays.

- Invite someone to read the statement on **"No Rescues"** and then discuss rescues, emphasizing that the three main elements of the definition of rescuing are: 1) doing for others what they can do for themselves; 2) doing more than your "50% share"; and 3) doing what you have not been asked to do. Being nice and helpful to others is not a

- As participants remain in their small groups, invite them to identify an interaction with another person(s) where they think they rescued or attempted to rescue others. Participants may also identify interactions where others attempted to rescue them. Reinforce the contract of no guilt, blame, or shame, especially for oneself.

- Summarize the discussion by asking participants as a full group to share key discoveries, affirmations and questions. Check to see if there is general agreement on the definition of rescues. Offer participants the option of sharing any decisions that they have made or are considering making relative to rescuing others.

I think there's been a change in me from the day I heard the MCTT concept. It was like a knock up side the head almost. "Yes, you're right, more is caught than taught." It brought home a lot of stuff and brought to mind some of the kinds of things that children really do get from us. It makes me aware not just on the job but also with my own daughter.

–Carol Samuel, Teacher, Joyland Child Development Center

- Introduce the next section by inviting someone to read the statement on "**No Secrets or Lies**." Point out that the emphasis is on misrepresenting or hiding one's feelings rather than the traditional definition. Ask the group to identify examples of this behavior. Offer the following example for clarification:

    - Rob is sitting at his desk looking rather forlorn and unhappy. Clara comes over and says, "How are you doing, Rob; are you OK?" Rob says, "Oh, I'm OK." Clara says, "Gee, Rob, you just look rather down." "No, Clara, I am really all right."

    - At this point Clara has to decide whether her intuition is really off or Rob is not "telling the truth" and representing his true feelings.

    - If Clara's intuition is right, an option for Rob is to say, "Yes Clara, I am a little off today. Thanks for asking, but I really don't want to talk right now." This accounts for Clara's intuition and concern, while also protecting Rob's boundaries.

- Summarize the discussion by asking participants as a full group to share key discoveries, affirmations, and questions. Check to see if there is general agreement on the definition of rescues. Offer participants the option of sharing any decisions that they have made or are considering making relative to "secrets" and "lies." Emphasize that most of the time people around us seek to know where we are emotionally because of genuine concern, and we honor them when we share truthfully. This enriching of relationships is not diminished when we set boundaries on how much of our emotions we want to share. As a matter of fact, it is likely to build trust.

Note: Skip the section on "**Giving of Strokes**" and save it for last, because giving strokes is the most important and comprehensive concept of the Cooperative Mode, and because the exercises which support the examination of strokes are more involved.

- Continue the pattern of introducing the elements of the "Cooperative Mode" by inviting someone to read the statement on "**Checking Our Paranoid Fantasies**." Then invite participants to find real-life examples (full groups), drawing conclusions, checking for discoveries, affirmations, and questions (large groups) – remembering that you are seeking to understand what the "Cooperative Mode" has to offer. Discussion points for this section are:

- Checking out paranoid fantasies is a way of asking, not accusing.

- Checking out paranoid fantasies works better when anger, sadness, fear, and even joy are set aside. This gives the other person more emotional space to hear your paranoid fantasy and acknowledge her or his actions and motivations. Another way of thinking about managing feelings as you are checking out paranoid fantasies is to give the other person the benefit of the doubt. Share your paranoid fantasy from a place that says, "I really don't know. Will you share with me what, why you did/said . . ."

- Asking the other person to hear your paranoid fantasy is an essential step in the process which helps to create an atmosphere of trust and honesty, which, in turn, increases the likelihood of getting a truthful response.

- Ask participant to role-play the process based on real experiences.

- Ask participants to reflect upon their feelings and their thinking as they practiced checking out paranoid fantasies.

- Summarize this discussion as you did others.

- Continue discussion by inviting another person to read the statement on "**Offering Resentments**." Offering resentments is very similar to checking out paranoid fantasies. Asking the person if they will hear the resentment is key. Keeping emotions under control is important, as it helps those who are receiving the resentment to hear it and take it in. Explain that those hearing the resentment need not respond any more than to acknowledge that they heard the resentment. Resentments are shared so that one may let go of feelings and move on to a happier relationship.

- Ask participants to practice hearing and offering resentments. They may choose to base their practice on real feeling that they have or had with fellow workers or family members.

- Ask participants to reflect upon their feelings and their thinking as they practiced offering and hearing resentments.

- Summarize the discussion as you did others.

- Invite someone to read the statement on **"Confidentiality"** as the discussion of the "Cooperative Mode" continues. Remind participants that the "Cooperative Mode" invites individuals to examine their thinking, feelings, and behavior and invites them to change for their own benefit and the benefit of the group. The operative word is CHANGE. This means individuals must experience high levels of trust, love, and support. Your *MCTT* meetings can become a laboratory for discovery and change. These sessions will provide a safer place to practice new behavior if the members contract not to share the positions and experiences of others outside their laboratory.

- After the discussion, invite participants to construct and enter into a social contract for confidentiality.

- Returning to the section on **"Giving of strokes,"** invite someone to read the statement on strokes. Make an effort to approach the exploring of strokes in the spirit of fun and games. It is important that participants allow themselves to feel and experience giving and receiving strokes. Much is missed if discussions remain in the realm of "thinking" rather than "experiencing" and then discussing. We suggest that the stroke handout (page x) be passed out after the first two stroke exercises. This will help keep the focus on experience and feelings.

    - Define a stroke as a single unit of recognition. Or as one isolated interaction of one person to another. Examples of a stroke would be a smile, a spoken word, or a touch.

- Explain that the objective of the following exercise is to find labels and ways of talking about strokes, the unit of recognition. While they are in their small groups, ask participants to offer what they would guess to be an unconditional positive stroke. Invite them to "do" it rather than merely discuss the task.

- Process the experience with these and other questions:
  - How did you feel giving strokes?
  - How did you feel receiving strokes?
  - What are some of your observations?

- Explain that there are four categories of strokes:

  1. unconditional positive - strokes for being: you are beautiful, I love being around you, hug, kiss (stroke is an unconditional affirmation of the receiver's being)

  2. conditional positive - strokes for having and/or doing: you *have* well-behaved children, you *have* a good attitude about . . ., you *did* a great job (stroke is related to a specific condition)

  3. conditional negative strokes for having and/or doing: you *have* a very junky car, you nit-pick all the time, you *did* a lousy job on that report (stroke is related to a specific condition)

  4. unconditional negative: you are no good, I wish you were never born, I hate you, slap or blow, curse (stroke is unconditional and goes against the receiver's being). There is never a just cause for these strokes, as they are damaging to the receiver and the giver.

- Ask participants to reflect on the strokes that they gave and received and attempt to identify them as one of the four types of strokes.

- Summarize the discussion by asking for observations and insights.

- Ask participants to do the following three-steps exercise exactly:
  - Step one - The giver of the stroke (Mary) will turn to a member of the group and make a statement like the following: "(John), I really like the way you encourage people in our little group to speak out."

- Step two - The receiver of the stroke (John) will receive the stroke and repeat the stroke exactly, "Thank you (Mary), I really like the way I encourage the members of our group to speak out also.

- Step three - The receiver of the stroke (John) adds a statement like the following, "Furthermore I like my ability to connect with people." (This is called a self-stroke.)

• Have participants continue this pattern by choosing someone and offering a stroke. The second person receives the stroke, repeats the stroke verbatim, and adds a statement that says "and furthermore what I like about myself is," giving themselves a deep and powerful stroke. Be aware that this exercise is very powerful and can enable participants to become aware of many confusing and conflicting feelings as well as joyful and confirming feelings relative to the way they give and receive strokes. Discourage participants from simply making a game out of the task and not letting themselves struggle with their true feelings.

• Ask participants to share their experiences in the large group. Help them keep in touch with the fact that giving and receiving strokes is learned and that different cultures and families within cultures use strokes differently.

• Process the experiences of individuals with questions like the following:

    - What were your overall feelings?

    - What steps were easiest and what steps were most difficult?

    - What are some of the things that you were told about strokes in early childhood?

• Pass out the stroke handout (page 140) and continue to discuss the four kinds of strokes and the five things that one can do with strokes: give, receive, reject, ask for, and self-stroke.

• Process the experience with these and other questions:

    - Why is stroking more difficult as you move down the list?

    - Does age or gender make a difference?

    - Why are children able to stroke more freely?

- Think of the total process of giving and receiving strokes in a group, family, or organization as the "stroke economy." What might an ideal stroke economy (subjective) look like?

- What are some dysfunctional things that were "taught" or were "caught" about giving and receiving strokes?

- How can the stroke economy of the *MCTT* group and the child care program be improved? (Be specific.)

• Summarize the discussion of strokes by asking about insights, observations, learnings, affirmations, and commitments to try out new behavior.

• Summarize the discussion of the "Cooperative Mode" similarly.

• Discuss the adoption or use of the "Cooperative Mode" in the program.

5. Develop an informal social contract for being together.

In our examination of the "Cooperative Mode," you looked at how the *MCTT* group <u>might</u> "BE together." The next task is to define how the site team <u>will</u> "BE together." Can the experience of your *MCTT* group be a model for how parents will BE with children, administrators will BE with staff, teachers will BE with children, teachers will BE with parents, and so on? In other words, you will create a model for how you want people in the program to associate with each other as a model for children to catch.

• Break into small groups and make lists of the "dos" and "don'ts" of how to "BE together." What are the attitudes and behaviors that support the S/I system that we want to change? What are the attitudes and behaviors that break the S/I system that we want to promote?

• Come together as a full group to call out ideas to two participants at the front of the room who will write them on newsprint.

• Discuss the "How To BE Together" "do" list as a full group. If we had to choose five most important elements, what would they be? Are there parts of this list that you can't do, or that you will feel uncomfortable saying you will do, or will try to do?

- Ask participants to affirm this list or those parts of the list that they're willing to establish as a guide to their own behavior. Whatever you choose to affirm from this list will become your informal social contract and will guide how you will be together for the rest of the *MCTT* program and beyond.

6. **Discuss next steps.**

The facilitator should tie the "How To BE Together" module to the rest of the program. If you're going on to the "Early Childhood Theory" module next, let participants know how the work you've done at this session will help you in evaluating and exploring various early childhood theories. Now that you have reached this point and have developed a vision for children, considered the physical and spiritual environments surrounding them, and examined your own interactions with children and each other, you are ready to go into the theories that will guide your work on your curriculum.

7. **Evaluate the session using evaluation forms.**

Additional options:

1. Have participants go on a Trust Walk. This exercise quickly gets individuals to become intimate and raises the level of sharing fears and expectations. This exercise is done by having each participant choose a partner who is culturally different. One of the partners will blindfold the other and the two of them walk outside for about 20 minutes. Upon the command of the facilitator, the partners will exchange places and continue walking and talking for another 20 minutes. At the end the facilitator will process the experience.

2. Other options for increasing the power of the "How To BE Together" module might include viewing videos; reading book excerpts, papers, and articles; and attending lectures on a relevant subject before the "How To BE Together" meeting.

Follow-up:

Bring the site team together to do a group evaluation of the meeting and to add relevant ideas to the "How To BE Together" section of the work plan.

Write up all the lists you generated during the meeting and send copies to all *MCTT* participants or bring them to the next session.

Make a poster-sized list of your contract for being together and bring it with you to future meetings.

Resources:

Books:

- *Alike and Different: Exploring Our Humanity with Young Children,* ed. Bonnie Neugebauer
- *Black and White Styles in Conflict*, Tom Kochman
- *Developing Cross-cultural Competence: A Guide for Working with Young Children and their Families*, E.W. Lynch and M.J. Hanson
- *Enabling and Empowering Families: Principles and Guidelines for Practice*, Carol Dunst, Carol Trivette and Angela Deal
- *Families and Early Childhood Programs*, Douglas R. Powell
- *A Great Place to Work*, Paula Jorde Bloom
- *How to Talk So Kids Will Listen and Listen So Kids Will Talk*, Adele Faber and Elaine Mazlish
- *Parents Unite! The Complete Guide for Shaking Up Your Children's School*, Philip and Susan Jones
- *Teacher-Parent Relationships*, Jeanette Stone
- *Valuing Diversity: The Primary Years*, Janet McCracken Brown

Support Materials:

- Agendas for all *MCTT* participants
- Expanded Agendas for members of the *MCTT* site team. These expanded agendas will provide you with helpful information as you go through the meetings.
- The Cooperative Mode handout
- Documents resulting from the "How To BE Together" session conducted by Kiddy Land, Joyland, and Miller's child care programs. These are included to give you a sense of what to expect. It's a good idea to share these only after you are already well into the discussion, as otherwise they might influence the work of the group.

My conception of the *More Is Caught Than Taught* Program is that it is a working curriculum format for community involvement, parent involvement, and staff involvement, to give the community some kind of hands-on experiences working together so we can claim the children as ours. If the children see these things happening with the community, the parents, and the staff–people getting along and caring about each other and caring about them–then they will catch some of this and become more productive, caring people themselves.

–Clara Card, Director, Joyland Child Development Center

Agenda

More Is Caught Than Taught Program

"How To BE Together"

1. **Welcome**

2. **Introductions**

3. **Explanation of the meeting agenda**

   Purpose of the meeting
   - To explore specific ways that internalized oppression affects relationships
   - To increase our appreciation for the challenges of working with people who are different from us
   - To develop approaches, skills, and knowledge that will facilitate working together
   - To develop a specific contract for "How To BE Together"

4. **"How To BE Together" exercises with handouts**

5. **Next Steps**

6. **Closing**

Expanded Agenda
More Is Caught Than Taught Program
"How To BE Together"

1. **Welcome**

2. **Introductions**

3. **Explanation of the meeting agenda**

   Purpose of the meeting

   - To explore specific ways that internalized oppression affects relationships

   - To increase our appreciation for the challenges of working with people who are different from us

   - To develop approaches, skills, and knowledge that will facilitate working together

   - To develop a specific contract for "How To BE Together"

4. **"How To BE Together" exercises with handouts**

   - Introduce the "How To BE Together" module by connecting it to the "Internalized Oppression" module and the rest of the *MCTT* Program

     ○ Briefly review the chart you created in the "Internalized Oppression" module showing how the system of inherent superiority and inherent inferiority reveals itself in thoughts, feelings, and behavior. In the "Internalized Oppression" module, you explored the destructive dynamics of the S/I system and the internalized oppression that results from it. Now you will use your heightened awareness as you examine the dynamics of your *MCTT* group and your child care program. This module will provide you with tools which will help you ask and answer the question: How can we be together in a way that respects, affirms, and encourages our difference?

   - Explore how the system of inherent superiority and inherent inferiority is manifested in child care programs

     ○ In small groups, discuss how the S/I system affects child care programs in one or more of the following areas: the relationships between the staff, children, and center; and the program's curriculum, lesson plans, and assessments. A helpful way of guiding these discussions might be to ask: What are the things that can and must be changed?

- Write your ideas up on newsprint and then discuss and process them as a full group
- Introduce the "Cooperative Mode" as a way of interacting and do Cooperative Mode exercises
    - Discuss each element of the "Cooperative Mode."
    - Invite participants to identify and share their own manifestation of elements of the "Cooperative Mode." For example, "What is your favorite power play?" "When and how are you likely to rescue someone?"
    - Practice giving and receiving strokes.
- Develop an informal social contract for being together
    - In small groups, make lists of the "dos" and "don'ts" of being together. What are the attitudes and behaviors that support the S/I system that we want to change? What are the ones that break the S/I system that we want to promote?
    - As a full group, write your ideas up on newsprint and discuss the "do" list. Are there parts of this list that individuals feel they can't do or feel uncomfortable saying they will try to do?
    - Ask participants to affirm this list or those parts of the list that they're willing to establish as a guide to their own behavior. The result will be your informal social contract which will guide how you will be together for the rest of the *MCTT* program and beyond.

5. **Next Steps**
   - If you're ready to finish the "How To BE Together" module, the next module of the *MCTT* program is the "Early Childhood Theory" module. Now that you have reached this point and have developed a vision for children, considered the physical and spiritual environments surrounding them, and examined your own interactions with children and each other, you are ready to go into the theories that will guide your curriculum.

6. **Closing**
   - Fill out evaluation forms
   - Review the date and time for the next meeting
   - Express appreciation for and affirmation of the meeting participants.

Stroke = Unit of Recognition

	Positive	Negative
Doing (Conditional)	"Great Job." "You really pulled that one out." "Here is your paycheck."	"You didn't get that report in on time." "Don't park in my space, stupid."
Being (Unconditional)	"Hello." "I like your style "You are beautiful." "I love you."	"Gee, I am Stupid." "Drop dead." "I wish you were never born."

Stroke Economy - We do FIVE things with strokes:

Give
Receive
Reject
Ask for
Self-stroke

In a health environment we can do all of these freely. However, there are myths that we grew up with which constrict and direct our personal use of strokes.

The Cooperative Mode

The Cooperative Mode is based on the assumption of <u>abundance</u> as opposed to <u>scarcity</u>, and <u>cooperation</u> as opposed to <u>competition</u>.

1. **No power plays:** a power play is defined as attempting to force someone to do something they basically don't want to do, whether subtly and covertly or openly and abusively.

2. **No rescues:** a rescue is doing something for someone which they can do for themselves, doing something without being asked, or doing more than one's 50% share of the interaction.

3. **No secrets or lies:** defined as withholding or misrepresenting one's feelings, motives, or position. This is detrimental in that it discounts and discredits the intuition of others who may have guessed the truth of the situation.

4. **Giving of strokes:** acting out on the assumption of an abundance of strokes and giving and receiving freely.

5. **Checking out paranoid fantasies:** the assumption that there is often a "grain" of truth in every paranoid fantasy. Paranoid fantasies should only be offered if the other person agrees explicitly to hear or receive them.

    Example: Pat: "Mildred, I have a paranoid fantasy. Would you like to hear it?" Mildred: "Yes, Pat, I would." Pat: "When I was talking about my low self-image, you were smiling. My paranoid fantasy is that you were making fun of me. Were you?" Mildred: "It is true that I was smiling, but actually because you made me think of myself. I guess I was amused at the both of us for the way we behave."

6. **Offering resentments:** like paranoid fantasies, resentments should also be shared only if the other person agrees to hear them. The individual to whom the resentment is being offered does not have to respond; s/he has only agreed to hear the resentment.

7. **Confidentiality:** offers protection that the revelation of real feelings will not be used in the future in any way without the expressed consent of the individuals involved.

"HOW TO "BE" TOGETHER"
"Dos":

- Accept change
- Affirm others
- Allow people to be responsible for themselves
- Appreciate others
- Ask for clarity regarding anything you're unsure about
- Be considerate
- Be honest
- Be natural
- Be open to learning new things and thinking new ways
- Be open to constructive criticism
- Be patient
- Be polite
- Be real
- Be sensitive to cultural differences
- Be willing to accept the group's decision
- Be yourself
- Check out, rather than assuming, bad intentions by someone else
- Compliment people when they have a good idea
- Divide all benefits equally
- Do unto others as you would have them do unto you
- Encourage others
- Focus on process
- Give positive reinforcement when needed
- Have and show integrity
- Keep a balance between work relationships and friendships with colleagues, and be able to separate them when necessary
- Keep an open mind
- Know that actions speak louder than words (example: rolling your eyes, looking off into space)
- Listen to each other

Created by MCTT participants from Joyland, Kiddy Land, and Miller's Centers

- Look for and acknowledge the position of others
- Look for others' strengths
- Look for things to appreciate
- Recognize that everyone else's views, feelings, etc., are as valid as your own
- Recognize and accept other ways of doing things
- Respect diversity
- Respect yourself and others
- Share ideas and encourage each other
- Share responsibility for what affects all of us
- Speak your own reality
- Stay focused
- Support others
- Take risks
- Treat each other as peers and equals
- Trust
- Try to have fun
- Value and respect individual differences and opinions
- Value the experiences of others

"HOW TO "BE" TOGETHER"
Don'ts:

- Always take charge—give others an opportunity
- Assume everyone else knows less than you
- Assume you know what someone else is thinking or feeling
- Be a "last word" person
- Be afraid to ask and answer questions
- Be afraid to make a mistake
- Be afraid to voice your opinion
- Be chauvinistic
- Be demanding
- Be disrespectful
- Be envious
- Be narrow-minded
- Be impolite
- Belittle others or their comments
- Carry excess baggage or grudges
- Categorize
- Criticize
- Cut people off
- Diagnose
- Do for others what they can do for themselves
- Dominate
- Exalt yourself
- Focus on the negative

Created by MCTT participants from Joyland, Kiddy Land, and Miller's Centers

More Is *Caught* Than Taught

- Give anyone preferential treatment
- Have a chip on your shoulder
- Hold others back
- Intimidate another person
- Isolate or reject
- Look for faults
- Make decisions for other people
- Make life a system of rights and wrongs
- Put anybody on a pedestal
- Put down
- (Dysfunctionally) rescue others
- Talk at once
- Take charge of the responsibilities of others
- Tear down
- Think for others
- Think you have nothing to say
- Try to suppress anyone
- Try to impress others with your knowledge and big words

EARLY CHILDHOOD THEORY MODULE

"Had she paints, or clay, or knew the discipline of dance, or strings: had she anything to engage her tremendous curiosity and her gift for metaphor, she might have exchanged the restlessness and preoccupation with whim for any activity that provided her with all she yearned for. And like any artist with no art form, she became dangerous.

Toni Morrison

What Is This Module?

We all carry with us a philosophy, or theory, of how young children grow and what influences their development. This philosophy is made up of things we have learned through experience with children, things we have been taught by our parents or elders in our community, things we have learned through study, and things we have learned from society at large. In a formal or informal way, our philosophy directs our decisions, guides our actions, underlies our curricula, and influences the way we organize child care programs.

In the "Early Childhood Theory" module of *MCTT*, you will explore the philosophy guiding your center and identify those ideas, principles, and practices related to early childhood development which are most supportive of your vision for children. You will do this by examining your own "caught" and "taught" theories and by becoming familiar with and evaluating the work of established early childhood theorists.

Our early childhood philosophies are actually made up of two different, sometimes complementary and sometimes contradictory, bodies of knowledge and series of responses. These are our "caught" philosophies–those ideas, principles, and practices we have picked up from observing how mother got treated and how dad got treated, how girls got their way and what was expected of boys, what was said about those who were different as opposed to what we said about "us." We observed the big people around us as well as the small and tried to "make sense" of all of their behavior, their relationships, their feelings, and their attitudes. Our "taught" messages are those that parents and others around us explicitly told us. Again, sometimes the messages agreed and sometimes they did not. For example, a child might be taught that "you should never hit anyone in anger." What a female child might "catch" from observing how every once in a while Mommy comes up with bruises and acts angry towards dad is that you must suffer hitting and never let on to anyone how you feel. Remember that this is the logic of a four-year-old who must make sense of what she sees without the benefit of wisdom and facts. Most of what rules our lives and influences our feelings and behavior are the "caught" messages. Learning is even more powerful when the "caught" messages and the "taught" messages are the same. Thus, bringing parents, teachers and significant others together to thoughtfully and explicitly identify the messages and the methods of communicating messages that children will use to construct themselves is essential to creating an optimum environment that will enable children to develop to their fullest potential.

Often we are guided by our "caught" philosophies without stopping to reflect on the reason behind them; we act on them simply because we believe "that's the way it's done." This can cause us to be driven by theories that sometimes are based on tradition and nothing else, and it can also block us from being open to different approaches. Many of our "caught" philosophies, however, have been passed along to us because they are tried and true, or because they address our children's development in a way that is overlooked by the prevailing "taught" theories.

Similarly, we often accept a "taught" philosophy as true because it comes from an "expert," even if it goes against what we know about children. Just like "caught" theories, "taught" theories can sometimes be grounded in ideas and information that are not the most helpful to our children's development. Yet many "taught" theories contain insight, wisdom, and experience that prove invaluable for good child care.

Both our "caught" and "taught" philosophies influence how we respond to children, so if these philosophies are not integrated, we are sending children mixed messages. More importantly, we are primarily communicating our internal philosophy, often unintentionally. For example, when a child misbehaves, if a teacher suggests a "talk" to work it out but underneath he or she really wants to slap the child, the child will likely pick up on that unspoken message and respond to it, not to the invitation to work through the problem.

This module helps you explore what "caught" and "taught" philosophies you hold and why. It encourages you to look at the areas where your "caught" beliefs and your "taught" beliefs coincide and where they contradict each other. And this process allows you to more clearly define and integrate your own beliefs and principles about raising children.

In this module you will also examine the prevailing "taught" theories of early childhood education so as to gain a fuller understanding of the ideas that are shaping early childhood practices and to determine the relevance of these ideas to the children of your community and your vision for them.

Not everyone is familiar with the work of Piaget, Montessori, Freud, and Erikson, but everyone who has worked in a child care setting or has raised children has been affected by the ideas of these and other early childhood theorists. They are conveyed when we talk about stages of development, or when we analyze a child's anger, or even when we explain a child's bedwetting.

By isolating these theories and evaluating them against each other and against your own philosophies, you will be able to distinguish them from a general body of knowledge and recognize them for what they are: theories, not facts, of child development that you have the right to accept or reject as valid for your children.

As you break these theories down into their various parts, you will also be able to determine what elements of different theories are supportive of your vision. And, ultimately, as you define a working list of guiding philosophical principles for your child care-program, you will be able to incorporate those elements of various established theorists that are supportive of your vision and discard those that are not. By doing this, you will be both focusing and strengthening your center's philosophy and also firmly linking your philosophy to your vision.

The working philosophy you develop during this session will serve, along with your "Vision Statement," as your foundation for the next stage of MCTT, when you will concentrate on building a curriculum that will best promote the skills, knowledge, and attributes of the children of your vision.

Expected Outcomes

Participants will:
- Make connections between "caught" and learned philosophies

- Reconsider the theories presently guiding and directing your child care program

- Examine and demystify prevailing early childhood theories to the extent that you are comfortable selecting those things that are supportive of your vision for children and rejecting those things that are not

- Develop a working philosophy for your child care program that represents the early childhood theories of *MCTT* participants and your vision for children

Preparing

Who will participate?

All members of the site team, staff, parents, and community leaders

How long will it take?

The "Early Childhood Theory" module can take place in two meetings of two hours each, but you are encouraged to devote as much time and energy as you need to accomplish this module.

Where will it take place?

The "Early Childhood Theory" module can take place anywhere you will feel comfortable, that is convenient for participants, and that will be free of noise and other distractions. A site where chairs can be freely moved about and where newsprint can be taped to the walls is an important consideration.

When will it take place?

You will have already set the dates for this and future meetings, but you will want to send out a reminder to program participants including the dates, time, and place of the Early Childhood Theory sessions.

How will you document this module?

It is a good idea to touch base with the person who agreed during the "Getting Started" module to document the meetings so as to make sure s/he has all the necessary materials and equipment for the documentation method that you have chosen (audio taping, video taping, taking photographs and taking good notes are some of the options).

What will you need to bring to these meetings?

Some suggestions:

- Your "Vision Statement"
- Copies of your curriculum, lesson plans, assessment tools, and other things associated with the curriculum (enough for all participants)
- The mission statement of the program, if you have one
- Newsprint
- Markers
- Loose paper
- Pencils or pens
- Masking tape
- Documentation materials and equipment
- Attendance sheet
- Agendas
- Handouts
- Evaluation forms
- Food and drinks for meal or snack

What else?

Is there anything else you need to think about or map out in your mind before going ahead?

Challenges of This Module

Everyone has his or her own ideas about the best way to raise children. These ideas are both valid and valuable. The purpose of this module, however, is not only to define and examine your personal ideas, but also to be open to the ideas of others. This will require setting aside biases toward those theories or theorists you favor and really looking for new ideas that will support, or add to, your philosophy.

Another challenge of this module will be that of shedding the tendency to defer to the "experts." The names Freud, Montessori, Piaget, etc., can be intimidating, but their theories are simply ideas that, like any others, can be evaluated, dissected, challenged, and improved. Participants may feel that they need to accept or reject theories wholesale, so they should be affirmed in their right and their ability to choose only those elements of different theories that support your program's vision.

Finally, bringing one's own "caught" philosophy regarding early childhood development into awareness and distinguishing it from a "taught" philosophy can be extremely challenging. "Caught" responses can be buried deep inside us, and they can also be in direct contradiction to our "taught" responses. Integrating these "caught" and "taught" theories is essential if we are to avoid sending children confusing, mixed messages, but this integration is a struggle and it can sometimes challenge long-held beliefs. For this reason, it is important that participants feel they can share in an environment that is free of criticism and judgment as to the validity or appropriateness of certain ideas or attitudes.

Putting This Module into Action

Early Childhood Theory Meeting #1

The facilitator will lead the session by introducing exercises, establishing times for each exercise, and, most importantly, creating a fun, energetic, and connected atmosphere for the session.

Basic approach:

1. **Introduce the "Early Childhood Theory" module by connecting it to the rest of the *MCTT* program and to your vision for children.**

    - Up to this point in the *MCTT* program, you have defined your vision for the children you want to grow, defined the environment that will be most supportive of your vision, examined internalized oppression as a barrier to fulfilling your vision, and developed a contract for being together within the context of the *MCTT* program and the child care center. In this module, you will consider various theories, your own and those of well-established "experts," as a way of answering the question: What ideas, principles, and practices concerning early childhood development are most supportive of our vision for children?

2. **Explore your "caught" and "taught" early childhood theories.**

   - Use the handout "Caught and Taught Responses" to help participants discover how they respond to various situations. Write down the answers to the examples given and then come up with additional situations.

   - Get together in small groups to discuss what you wrote on your handouts. Then widen the discussion to "taught" and "caught" early childhood philosophies in general. What are your "caught" philosophies–those practices, beliefs, and convictions you hold about raising children that have come from your family, your community, and your culture? What are your ""taught"" philosophies, those you have learned from books, school, etc.? Write down a list each for "caught" and "taught" philosophies.

   - Come together as a full group to call out ideas to two participants at the front of the room who will write them on newsprint. Then process this information as a large group. Here are some possible questions to discuss:

     ○ What "caught" philosophies do people hold in common?

     ○ Are your "caught" and "taught" philosophies generally in sync with each other or generally in contradiction to each other? Why might this be?

     ○ Have you modified your earlier position; why or why not?

     ○ What is the power of your "caught" philosophy in relation to your "taught" philosophy?

     ○ Which philosophy are you likely to use when under stress?

     ○ What messages are lived out in the program?

3. **Determine the philosophy guiding the operation of your center.**

    - On an individual basis, examine the curriculum, lesson plans, and other materials from the center. Make notes about what you think the philosophy behind these materials is and what you like and don't like about them.

        Have one person present the center's mission statement or statement of guiding principles. If you do not have a mission statement or a philosophy already written down, develop one with the group as a whole. Using the handout "Our Early Childhood Theory," write down the principles and values that guide the operation of the center and influence major decisions and procedures. You will use the resulting document in the next meeting as a way of comparing your philosophy to that of recognized early childhood theorists.

4. **Discuss next steps.**

    - In the next meeting of the "Early Childhood Theory" module you will examine the theories of several recognized "experts" on early childhood theory, and you will develop or choose a theory that best suits your guiding principles and your vision for children.

5. **Evaluate the session using evaluation forms.**

Follow-up to Meeting #1

- Bring the site team together to do a group evaluation of the first meeting and to add relevant ideas to the "Early Childhood Theory" section of the work plan.

- Write up all the lists you generated during the meeting and send copies to all *MCTT* participants or bring them to the next meeting.

Early Childhood Theory Meeting #2

The facilitator will lead the session by introducing exercises, establishing times for each exercise, and, most importantly, creating a fun, energetic, and connected atmosphere for the session.

Basic approach:

1. **Review what the "Early Childhood Theory" module is and how it fits into the MCTT program and into your vision for children**

    - The "Early Childhood Theory" module is the time for examining, developing, and strengthening the philosophy which guides your day-care program. In the last meeting, you looked at your own "caught" and "taught" theories of early childhood development as well as the stated and untested theories currently in use at your center. In this meeting, you will explore the work of respected early childhood theorists and select from their theories those elements that are supportive of your vision for children.

2. **Examine the ideas of recognized early childhood theorists.**

    - Break into small groups and, using the handout "Early Childhood Theorists," have each group choose an equal number of theorists to examine. It is fine for a theorist to be covered by more than one group as long as each theorist is covered at least once.

    - Read the statements about your group's theorists individually and rank them according to the philosophies and theories you like best. Number one should be the highest ranking.

    - Discuss ideas in your group and rank your theorists as a group.

    - Present your group's ranking and the reasons behind it to the other groups. Then discuss as a full group why certain elements work well and why others don't, and why some theorists' statements ring more true than others. Each person is encouraged to contribute her or his own ideas and preferences as well as those of the group. During this conversation, all participants should write down ideas and concepts that they like from all of the different theorists.

    - Using your notes from the previous discussion, develop a list of various elements that you like from all the different theorists by calling out ideas to two participants at the front of the room who will write them on newsprint.

- Discuss as a full group what elements you've chosen and why. Some questions you might want to consider are these:

    o Did any one of the theories work completely for us?

    o What does it mean when we accept some elements of these theories and reject others?

    o Could this mean that we have theories of our own that are equal in importance to those we are examining?

    o Were there general themes of the theorist that you liked or disliked?

    o Did any views of the theorist speak to the spiritual elements of your beliefs or the vision for children?

3. **Develop a working philosophy that represents the early childhood theories of *MCTT* participants.**

- Review as a full group your mission or philosophy statement from the last session and compare it to the theories you have just examined. Some questions you might want to consider include these:

    o Are our guiding principles wholly grounded in any one of these specific theories?

    o What elements of different theories are apparent in our guiding principles?

    o What do we have in our guiding principles that is missing from these theorists' work?

    o Is there anything in our list of guiding principles that we think differently about now?

- Develop a new list which combines your guiding principles or mission statement from the last session with the theoretical elements you liked from this session. This list will serve as your working philosophy and will help guide you as you examine and build your curriculum in the next module.

4. **Discuss next steps**

   - The next module of the *MCTT* program is the "Curriculum, Lesson Planning, and Assessment" module. During these sessions, you will be putting all of the knowledge you have gained so far–about environment, internalized oppression, being together, and early childhood theory–into developing a curriculum that will build the skills, qualities, characteristics, and knowledge of the children of your vision.

     Because the "Curriculum, Lesson-Planning, and Assessment" module is so important and so potentially time-consuming, it is a good idea to be well-prepared beforehand. Toward this goal, all participants should take home copies of the current curriculum, lesson plans, assessment tools, etc., and should go through them as thoroughly as possible before the first meeting.

5. **Evaluate the session using prepared forms.**

Additional Options:

   i. Bring in an "expert" from a university or elsewhere to present the various early childhood theories for meeting #2. This can serve as a replacement for the "Early Childhood Theorists" handout as a basis for a discussion of various theorists.

   ii. Play a guessing game as a part of exploring early childhood theories in meeting #2. Assign different participants roles as various theorists and then ask them to respond to situations based on that person's theory. An example: "You're Piaget. I want to enhance a child's self-esteem. What should I do?" Ask the same question of all the "actors" and then discuss the difference in responses. Some questions you might consider are these:

      - I want to enhance a child's sense of self-esteem. What should I do?

      - This child does not share well with others. What should I do?

      - This child is very shy and I want her/him to be more outgoing. What should I do?

- This child hits and bites. What should I do?

iii. Examine the perspectives of Black, women, or other minority writers and theorists concerning early childhood education. What do they believe about the prevalent theories? What alternate theories do they propose? You might want to consider the work of Janice E. Hale-Benson, Amos Wilson, Carol Gilligan, and James Comer, among others.

iv. Other options for increasing the impact of the "Early Childhood Theory" module might include reading excerpts, papers, and articles and attending lectures on a relevant subject before the sessions.

Follow-up to Meeting #2

- Bring the site team together to do a group evaluation of the second meeting and to add relevant ideas to the "Early Childhood Theory" section of the work plan.

- Write up the list you generated during the meeting and send copies to all *MCTT* participants or distribute them at the next meeting.

Resources

Books:

- *Ages and Stages*, Karen Miller
- *Approaches to Preschool Curriculum*, Michael Anziano, et. al.
- *Beginnings: The Social and Affective Development of Black Children*, Margaret B. Spencer, et. al.
- *Beyond Self-Esteem: Developing a Genuine Sense of Human Value*, N.E Curry and C.N. Johnson
- *Black Children: Their Roots, Culture and Learning Styles*, Janice E. Hale-Benson
- *Child Development, Teacher's Annotated Edition*
- *Childhood and Society*, Erik Erikson
- *The Developmental Psychology of the Black Child*, Amos N. Wilson
- *Developmentally Appropriate Practices in Early Childhood Program: Serving Children from Birth through Age 8*, Sue Bredekamp

- *Growing Pains: Helping Children Deal with Everyday Problems through Reading*, Maureen Caddigan and Mary Beth Hanson
- *In a Different Voice*, Carol Gilligan
- *Infants and Toddlers: Curriculum and Teaching*, LaVisa Cam Wilson
- *Maria Montessori: Dr. Montessori's Own Handbook, A Short Guide to her Ideas and Materials*, Maria Montessori
- *The Piaget Handbook for Teachers and Parents*, Rosemary Peterson and Victoria Felton-Collins
- *Principles of Parenting*, H. Wallace Goddard
- *Reconceptualizing the Early Childhood Curriculum: Beginning the Dialogue*, Shirley A. Kessler and Beth Blue Swadener
- *Training Teachers: A Harvest of Theory and Practice*, Margie Carter and Deb Curtis

Support Materials

- Agendas for all *MCTT* participants at the Early Childhood Theory sessions
- Expanded Agendas for members of the *MCTT* site team. These expanded agendas will provide you with helpful information as you go through the meetings.
- "Caught and Taught Responses" handout
- "Our Early Childhood Theory" handout
- "Early Childhood Theorists" handout

Agenda

More Is Caught Than Taught Program
"Early Childhood Theory" Meeting #1

1. Welcome

2. Introductions

3. Explanation of the meeting agenda

   Purpose of the meeting

   - To examine and make connections between "caught" and learned theories of early childhood development

   - To understand the philosophy guiding the child care program

   - To share or develop a written statement of philosophy or mission for the child care program

4. **Early childhood theory exercises with handouts**

5. Next Steps

6. Closing

Expanded Agenda

More Is Caught Than Taught Program
"Early Childhood Theory" Meeting #1

1. Welcome

2. Introductions

3. Explanation of the meeting agenda

   Purpose of the meeting

   - To examine and make connections between "caught" and learned theories of early childhood development

   - To understand the philosophy guiding the child care program

   - To share or develop a written statement of philosophy or mission for the child care program

     ○ Introduce the "Early Childhood Theory" module by connecting it to the rest of the *MCTT* program and your vision for children.

       - Up to this point in the *MCTT* program, you have defined your vision for the children you want to grow; described the environment that will be most supportive of your vision; examined internalized oppression as a barrier to fulfilling your vision; and developed a contract for "being together" within the context of the *MCTT* program and the child care center. In this module, you will consider various theories, your own and those of well-established "experts," as a way of answering the question: What ideas, principles, and practices concerning early childhood development are most supportive of our vision for children?

     ○ Explore your "taught" and "caught" early childhood theories.

       - Use the handout "Taught and Caught Responses" to think individually about how you respond to various situations. Write down your answers to the examples given and then come up with a few examples of your own.

       - Discuss your ideas in small groups and develop a list of "caught" and "taught" early childhood philosophies.

       - Write the lists up on newsprint and process the ideas as a full group.

4. **Early childhood theory exercises with handouts**

5. **Next steps**

    - In the next meeting of this module, you will examine the theories of several recognized "experts" on early childhood theory, and you will develop or choose a theory that best suits your guiding principles and your vision for children.

6. **Closing**

    - Fill out evaluation forms.

    - Review the date and time for the next meeting.

    - Express appreciation for and affirmation of the meeting participants.

Agenda

More Is Caught Than Taught Program
"Early Childhood Theory" Meeting # 2

1. **Welcome**

2. **Introductions**

3. **Explanation of the meeting agenda**

   Purpose of the meeting

   - To examine and demystify prevailing early childhood theories
   - To evaluate prevailing early childhood theories against our vision for children and affirm those elements that support our vision
   - To develop a working philosophy for the child care program that reflects the early childhood principles of *MCTT* participants and our vision for children

4. **Early childhood theory exercises with handouts**

5. **Next Steps**

6. **Closing**

Expanded Agenda

More Is Caught Than Taught Program
"Early Childhood Theory" Meeting #2

1. Welcome

2. Introductions

3. Explanation of the meeting agenda

   Purpose of the meeting

   - To examine and demystify prevailing early childhood theories

   - To evaluate prevailing early childhood theories against our vision for children and affirm those elements that support our vision

   - To develop a working philosophy for the child care program that reflects the early childhood principles of *MCTT* participants and our vision for children

4. **Early childhood theory exercises with handouts**

   - Reintroduce the "Early Childhood Theory" module by connecting it to the rest of the *MCTT* program and your vision for children

     ○ This module is when you examine, develop, and strengthen the philosophy which guides your child care program. In the last meeting, you looked at your own "caught" and "taught" theories of early childhood development, as well as the written and unwritten theories currently in use at your center. In this meeting, you will explore the work of respected early childhood theorists and select from their theories those elements that are supportive of your vision for children.

   - Examine the theories of recognized early childhood theorists

     ○ In small groups, use the handout "Early Childhood Theory" and have each group choose an equal number of theorists to consider. Read the synopses and rank them on an individual basis and then as a group.

     ○ Invite groups to present their theorists and rankings to each other, then process group and individual ideas. Write down notes about what you like about different theorists' work.

- Write up on newsprint a list of various elements that you like from the different theories and discuss what elements you've chosen and why. What supports your vision for children?

- Develop a working philosophy that represents the early childhood theories of *MCTT* participants and your vision for children.

  - Review as a group your mission or guiding principles statement from the last meeting and compare it to the theories you have just examined.

  - Develop a new list combining your philosophy from the last session and the elements of other theories that support your vision for children. This list will serve as your working philosophy and will help guide you as you examine and build your curriculum in the next module.

5. Next Steps

- If you're ready to finish the "Early Childhood Theory" module, the next module of the *MCTT* program is the "Curriculum, Lesson Planning, and Assessment" module. During this module, you will be putting all of the knowledge and experience you have gained so far into developing a curriculum that will build the skills, qualities, characteristics, and knowledge of the children of your vision.

  Because the next module is so important and so potentially time-consuming, it is a good idea to be well prepared beforehand. Toward this goal, all participants should take home copies of the current curriculum, lesson plans, assessment tools, etc., and go through them as thoroughly as possible before the next meeting.

6. Closing

- Fill out evaluation forms.
- Review the date and time for the next meeting.
- Express appreciation for and affirmation of the meeting participants.

MCTT "Early Childhood" Handout

Situation	"Caught" Response	"Taught" Response
A child uses bad language		
A child is "playing with himself" sexually or with another child		
A child shares with you a story about her parents fighting		
Other situations:		

"Early Childhood Theory"

MCTT Handout

What do we believe about children and learning?

What influences learning the most?

How is moral and intellectual capacity developed?

What is the influence of play?

What is the influence of parents?

What is the influence of siblings?

What is the influence of setting boundaries?

What is the influence of the child's observation?

What is the influence of reinforcement?

Early Childhood Theorists

MCTT Handout

Socialization: a process which occurs as young children interact intimately with parents and other members of a "primary reference group"

Children gradually become members of a particular social group as they learn language and other shared symbols with which to communicate. Various social scientists have theorized about the relationship between what is inherent and what is acquired in the process of socialization, sometimes referred to as the "nature vs. nurture" issue. The following represent some of the most well-known socialization theorists:

Freud: concerned mainly with the interplay of the conscious and the unconscious (ego and superego) and unconscious (the id, or libidinal energy) personality; developed a psycho-sexual theory. He suggested that as children become aware of societal rules and boundaries they gradually inhibit their sexual impulses and consequentially develop the power of abstract thought– "symbolic thought," such as language, art, sciences, etc.

Erikson: concerned with the psycho-social development of the human reality through the resolution of a specific crisis at each of seven stages of life. Each crisis is precipitated by one's physical and emotional maturation from one stage to another and can be resolved either positively or negatively, culminating in either "ego integrity" or "despair" later in life.

Piaget: concerned primarily with the relationship between a child's ability to move from an egocentric to an empathic outlook – and the resulting development in a child's moral and intellectual capacities. Piaget traced the socialization process from infancy through adolescence and identified stages that children pass through in their comprehension of their social and physical environments. Piaget's work is often used as a foundation for the development of math and science curricula for elementary children.

Montessori: concerned with the development of a child's growing capacity for concentration and work appropriate to the stage of development – and with creating child-scaled, stimulating environments. Montessori believed children pass through "sensitive periods" when they are ready to learn certain concepts better than other times in their lives. She also felt passionately that when all children are given the opportunity to develop their potential, war will stop.

Skinner & Watson: concerned with the shaping of children's behavior and personality through rewarding desirable, and ignoring undesirable, behaviors. Watson claimed that he could make a child into any kind of adult, with any occupation, through this method. Behavioral theorists regard even variations in achievement as the result of some form of behavioral modification process through which children are rewarded for different behavior. The education system in general subscribes to this theory.

Bandura: concerned with the application of behavioral theory to a child's tendency to acquire behaviors through observing relevant others engaging in behaviors which are either rewarded or ignored. This "social learning" theory has particular implications for the ability of a child to learn both desirable and undesirable behaviors, such as violence, moral laxity, and discrimination through television, videos, video games, comics, and books. However, it also applies to learning through peer group behavior.

Cooley & Mead: concerned with the development of self-concept through a social looking-glass process, in which a child forms a social identity as parents and significant others reflect back to the child certain attributes, beliefs, and values shared by other members of the family or social group. A child then learns to appraise himself or herself accordingly, adjusting behavior or appearances to fit more closely the social model. Every social interaction with the primary reference group then reinforces the "looking glass self." These theorists are convinced that a person cannot evolve a self-concept without contact with other human beings. The nature of the self-concept, however, depends entirely on the social mirror reflected to the child during the socialization process. Mead identified stages marking the development of a child's ability to internalize the various roles within a social system.

Whitehead & Jordan: concerned with the nature of the human potential, such as psychomotor, affective, volition, cognitive, intuitional, and spiritual. Each area of potential is stimulated through different interactions with the physical, social, and spiritual environments. Children need to be seen as endowed with unlimited human potential, activated and realized through guided interactions toward specified goals and ideals. Potential is released through synchronized development of one's knowing and loving capacities.

Gardnes & Lazear: concerned with recognizing that humans are endowed with capacities for multiple intelligences. Through recognizing at least seven kinds of intelligence, such as interpersonal, body/kinesthetic, musical/rhythmic, visual/spatial, in addition to the more traditional intelligences - verbal/linguistic and logical/mathematical - parents and teachers learn how to value and stimulate the development of each intelligence. Multiple intelligences theory helps us appreciate more deeply the concept of diversity.

Compiled by:
Dr. Anne R. Breneman

CURRICULUM MODULE

"The A Curriculum is like a road map: the philosophy is the landscape; the goals are the destination, the activities are the vehicles, but, as in reality, the trip is filled with bumps, curves, detours and may or may not closely resemble the actual plan"

— *MCTT* Participants

What Is this Module?

The most casual examination of early childhood development theory and practice reveals contradictions in our understanding of the processes of human learning, the nature of human development and the best way to approach early childhood development. However, recent study of the brain has further unraveled some of the mystery of how we human beings function, and some of these discoveries are profound and wondrous indeed.

The human brain is the most complex organ that is known to human kind. The human mind, which is somehow linked to the brain, is a faculty that is complex beyond most of our imaginations.

Regardless of what is not known, understood or agreed upon, there is some common ground upon which most scientists and students of human development agree. It is agreed that during the earliest years of life the human brain develops at a phenomenal rate that is unmatched at any other time in life. There is general agreement that the actual mental capacity of the individual can be dramatically and permanently increased or retarded by the quantity and quality of nutrition and social interaction given in early childhood.

As you address the need for a curriculum, a plan, to guide your work with young children, it seems noteworthy that you are joining a legion of scientist, educators, philosophers, and caregivers who are seeking to better understand learning and development in early childhood and who are crafting and refining plans, approaches, methodologies, theories and curricula.

The stakes are very high, for now we know that the quality of life of every village, city and nation will be fashioned by today's children. In the child care community, we affirm this belief and advocate for quality development opportunities for all children "so that the next Martin Luther King, Elizabeth Cady Stanton, or Barbara

Charline Jordan will not slip through the fingers of society" for lack of providing them every opportunity to fully develop their human potential.

Your curriculum can be likened unto maps of the early seafarers. The maps, the best to be had at the time, combined all that was known and believed about a world acknowledged to be very large and not well understood. With each exploratory voyage, new knowledge was gained and the maps were revised. Likewise, your curriculum should combine the best that is known in the field of early childhood development at this time and be viewed as a work in progress. As you learn more from study and informed reflection on your experience, you will revise your curriculum to reflect your new knowledge.

Another dimension of early childhood curricula is its development. Creating a business plan for a center-based or home-based child care program that would pass the scrutiny of a bank loan officer would be a daunting task for many directors. A good business plan would require detailed analysis of location, facility, staffing, potential market, program, promotion of the business, fire and other safety regulations, insurance, and financial operations, just to name a few of many considerations. Very often, operators of small business (which the child care program is) simply do not develop a comprehensive business plan, but elect to rely on short term planning based on whatever experience, knowledge and instincts they possess. Some combination of not seeing the value of a comprehensive business plan, not having the where-with to develop one, or simply not having to develop one causes most community-based programs to operate without a sound business plan. This is not to say that a "formal" business plan in-and-of-itself makes a child care program more or less sound.

Child care providers, for the most part, accept the notion that having a curriculum is good and necessary, and virtually all programs have a curriculum in one form or other. Additionally, most programs that are regulated by state or federal agencies don't have the option of not having a curriculum. This is a requirement.

More Is *Caught* Than Taught — Curriculum

In too many instances, however, the existence of a curriculum has little impact on the structure of the program or daily activities. Just as it is challenging to develop a comprehensive business plan for the child care program, it is even more challenging to develop a plan (curriculum) which adequately addresses the needs, conditions, and opportunities of unique groups of children, families and community settings.

Complicating matters even more is the fact that a curriculum is not or should not be a static document, nor a document that is created only for the purpose of documenting its own existence. The curriculum is the product born out of a desire to answer several fundamental questions that should be addressed by those who set out to provide care for the children of others. "What is my/our vision for the care and, by necessity, the development of the children in my/our care?" "What is my/our strategy or plan for caring for the children?" "What is my/our program for growth and development of the children in my/our care?" How will you systematically and consistently offer experiences to children which are appropriate to the age and capacity of each child and which enables each child to achieve her/his fullest potential. These are curriculum questions. As you continually learn more about the care and development of young children, your plan (curriculum) might need to be upgraded. Changes in prevailing attitudes, needs and wishes of parents and community leaders might require changes in your curriculum. Changes in the demographics of the population of children and families served by your program may also demand changes in your curriculum.

If your curriculum is your guide to caring for children and serving their families, it will be an instrumental tool for training staff, orienting volunteers, promoting the business, educating parents and community leaders, and advocating the advancement of the industry. In a business that is characterized by too little time, too little money, and too few resources, the very question of a relevant curriculum document is often overwhelming. Thus, providers often rely on a changing pattern of activities based on whatever experience, knowledge and resources they possess.

The *More Is Caught Than Taught* program sets forth the notion that the care of our children is too important, the potential of children is too precious, the window of greatest impact is too small, and the process of providing appropriate experiences for young children is too complex to be approached without a sound plan – a relevant curriculum built upon a lofty vision, sound philosophy of the development of young children, and age-appropriate approaches and activities.

> The new curriculum would take into account ethnic groups. It would take into account the differences in culture and how children are raised. One of the problems that I found with curriculums is that sometimes they just don't fit our needs. There are going to have to be some changes here, but I think it's good that we are trying to create something that will be a little more geared toward our children.
>
> –Carol Samuel, Teacher, Joyland Child Development Center

A curriculum can be viewed as a wonderful and exceedingly valuable product, and acquiring one can be viewed as an ongoing journey which requires the growth and transformation of all who choose to undertake the journey. We recommend that you view the acquisition or development of your curriculum from both perspectives.

Expected Outcomes

Participants will

- Evaluate a variety of curriculum materials including lesson plans and child assessment programs.

- Through sharing and discussion, participants will identify elements of the materials that support their vision.

- Agree upon specific curriculum materials or approaches that seem right for the program.

- Affirm the existing curriculum, modify the existing curriculum, or chose a new curriculum.

- Chose supporting lesson plans and child assessment instruments.

Preparing

Who will participate?

All members of the site team, staff, parents, and community leaders.

It's crucial that the person who will be the facilitator at this meeting be passionate about the importance and relevance of vision to this program and to the lives of participants and children. The facilitator must have real energy and commitment and must be able to convey these feelings to the other participants. Without the fire of a facilitator who feels and "lives" the session, the participants will come up short.

How long will it take?

All of your work has been leading to this critical point, and it is at this point that you will need to establish the fact that quality is to be desired over quantity. This process will require participants to learn new things, analyze complex options, negotiate sensitive issues, compare and contrast similar and dissimilar things, and, most importantly, explore their deepest held values and examine and share their own early childhood experiences and the belief system that evolved from those experiences.

As you will want discussions to be based on broad and relevant data, it will be necessary for participants to prepare by reading before or during the sessions. This one decision, for example, will have a dramatic impact on the duration of this session. Your approach and supporting activities will determine the overall time of the experience. Again, remember that how you approach the objectives of this module is extremely important. You will want to engage participants in this process. Help them see the challenges of the process and the value of the product. Prepare well for the curriculum work.

Where will it take place?

The "Curriculum" module is not site-specific. It can take place anywhere that is comfortable, convenient for participants, and free of noise and other distractions. A site where chairs can be freely moved about and where newsprint paper can be taped to the walls is an important consideration.

When will it take place?

You will have already set the dates for this and future meetings, but you will want to send out a reminder to program participants including the date, time, and place of the Curriculum, Lesson Planning, and Assessment sessions.

How will you document this module?

It is a good idea to touch base with the person who agreed during the "Getting Started" module to document the meeting so as to make sure s/he has all the necessary materials and equipment for the documentation method that you have chosen (audio taping, video taping, taking photographs and taking good notes are some of the options).

What will you need to bring to the session?

Some suggestions:

   a. Your Vision Statement

   b. Your curriculum, including all lesson plans and assessment tools

   c. Sample curriculums

   d. Early childhood books and articles

   e. Newsprint

> Often people adopt someone else's theory and they say, "This is the way, this is the way," and then they find out after a period of time that it is not the right way for them. What we have done is much better: take as much as you can from as much as you can and throw away the things that you don't like and the things that don't work for you. And be open to the approaches others have used.
>
> –Jude Peterson, Community Leader, Joyland Child Development Center

f. Markers

g. Loose paper

h. Pencils or pens

i. Masking tape

j. Documentation materials and equipment

k. Attendance sheet

l. Agendas

m. Handouts

n. Evaluation forms

o. Food and drinks for meal or snack

What else?

Is there anything else you need to do to prepare for the Curriculum, Lesson Planning, and Assessment module?

Challenges of this Module

Perhaps the greatest challenge is to get participants to prepare for this module. This module will require participants to discuss specific philosophies, approaches, and strategies for teaching, training, nurturing and guiding the growth and development of children. It is necessary that participants become informed activists rather than passive witnesses in the process of curriculum building. Another challenge is acquiring and surveying the mountains of very good material available that will be essential to your building a curriculum that fits your vision. Although it is a lot of work to translate your vision for children into an appropriate curriculum, this work may be the most exciting and rewarding of the *MCTT* process.

Putting this Module into Action

"Curriculum" Meeting # 1

The facilitator will lead the session by introducing exercises, establishing times for each exercise, and, most importantly, creating a fun, energetic, and connected environment for the session.

Basic approach:

1. **Introduce the "Curriculum, Lesson Planning, and Assessment" module by connecting it to the rest of the *MCTT* program and your work with children.**

More Is *Caught* Than Taught
Curriculum   Page 177

- Define the objectives for the session clearly. Invite participants to discuss the objectives of the session until all are unified in their understanding of the objectives.
    - Objective: To enable each participant to gain a clear understanding of the objectives, expected outcomes and the activities of the "Curriculum" module.
    - Objective: To help each participant prepare for the process of identifying materials that support the vision statement of the program.
    - Objective: To help each individual develop a plan with timelines for guiding their exploration of materials and approaches for inclusion in the curriculum.

2. **Introduce and discuss the following:**
    - What are the purpose, value and our expectations of a curriculum?
    - How will the curriculum help to achieve the goals of the program?
    - What will it look like physically (how large, degree of detail, etc.)?
    - Will it have components (assessment, evaluation, lesson plans, etc.) and, if so, what might be the major ones?
    - Will we look at the development of the curriculum as a process as well as at the development of a product?

3. **Introduce and discuss the existing curriculum or guiding principles of the program.**

4. **Discuss the basic strategy (below) for developing the curriculum.**
   - Basic plan to achieve the objectives of the "Curriculum" module
     - study other curriculum <u>documents</u> as well as study curriculums in action
     - evaluate your existing curriculum
     - select models or prototypes that will bring focus to what the document will look like and what it will include

     Other considerations:
     - parent friendliness
     - publishing and communicating
     - complexity
     - how the curriculum will be used with teachers and parents
     - how the work (writing) will get done
     - who will advise/assist/support the writer/developer

5. **Explore the options for individuals (and groups) to prepare for the next session.**
   - reading books, articles and studying existing curricula
   - interviewing teachers and directors from other programs (curriculums in action)
   - interviewing educators and agency professionals
   - attending training seminars with fellow child care providers
   - meeting with other participants in small groups to process and consolidate what they are learning
   - inviting early childhood scholars and practitioners to speak to the group

6. **Introduce and discuss the questions that can frame and guide preparation activities of participants. (Page 193)**

7. **Invite participants to develop individual plans to prepare themselves to work on the curriculum at the next session.**

   Their plans might include:

   - A list of special areas of interest, i.e., role of teachers, culture, discipline, child directed learning, small and large motor development, teaching values
   - individuals targeted for interviews
   - books, articles, and videos to evaluate
   - child care settings to observe
   - timeline for activities

8. **Next steps.**

   - Review the basic plan (4 above) and insure that each person understands what will happen at the next session. Help them envision how the room will be laid out and the activities that will take place.
   - Invite each person to bring all materials that they discover in their exploration. Care must be taken to tag or mark each item so that it can be returned.
   - Plan well for the next session. You will need ample time, space, and freedom from distractions. A full day is the very minimum.
   - Evaluate the session using evaluation forms.

"Curriculum" Meeting # 2

The facilitator will lead the session by introducing exercises, establishing times for each exercise, and, most importantly, creating a fun, energetic, and connected environment for the session.

Basic approach:

1. **Review the "Curriculum, Lesson Planning, and Assessment" module by connecting it to the rest of the *MCTT* program and your work with children.**

   - Define the objectives for the session clearly. Invite participants to discuss the objectives and plan for the session.
     - Objective: Identify materials that support the vision statement of the program and that will be used to select, create, or modify, a curriculum.

> If they keep hearing the same things over and over again but in different ways and on different levels, then I think by the time they get up to the five-year-old class they might think, "Well, Ms. Davis said this is supposed to be done this way," or "This is right, and this is wrong."
>
> –Coronda Davis, Teacher, Miller's Toulminville Day Care Center

- Objective: Develop a plan for writing and polishing the final document.

2. **Review preparation activities.**

3. **Introduce the curriculum materials.**

4. **Assessment and selection of materials:**
   - You will want every person to get deeply involved in reading and discussing the curriculum materials. Although it is a good idea to bring in educators and other resource persons to aid and enrich discussion and evaluation, all participants should be encouraged to act with the knowledge, skills and inspiration that prior sessions have developed.
   - To cover as much as possible, the group should spend most of their time in small group settings selecting materials and exchanging ideas.
   - This session can be very exciting as small groups discover exciting ideas and approaches in the materials. From time to time, bring the small groups back to the large group setting for processing their findings and sharing sources.
     - Some questions for processing are: What have you found that you like? Why do you like it? How does it fit our vision?

5. **Evaluating and summarizing:**
   - From the large group, ask participants to categorize and summarize their findings. The following can be used as categories for comments, references and selections.
     - Program philosophy
     - Program vision
     - Program theory
     - Program values
     - Program goals
     - Program objectives
     - Teacher roles and strategies
     - Program structure or components
     - Order of program components

- Program approaches
- Program activities
- Child development monitoring and assessment
- Program evaluation
- Program administration

• Post a sheet of chart paper for each of the categories, and ask participants to call out the things that they like which they found in the materials. Challenge the whole group to help place the items in the most appropriate category. Encourage participants to share why they liked the item. Remember that much of this discussion has taken place in the small groups, and many of the offerings have some consensus. Do not allow the group to get hung up splitting hairs concerning the "right" category. It is much more important to get at what is liked and disliked by participants and record their positions.

• When this process is done you will know if your task is to: a) affirm your existing curriculum, b) modify your existing curriculum, c) modify an existing curriculum, or d) create a new curriculum. To support this work, you will have a working outline for doing any of the above.

6. **Next steps.**

It is not likely that the group will be able to make their final selection of a curriculum or to build a new curriculum. Therefore, it will be necessary to identify persons who will assemble the work from this session and organize it for presentation to the site team for discussion and approval.

> I just try to do the best I can do and try to learn all I can learn, if it's going to help me with my boys. I just sit down and kinda sort it out. It's like religion. If you go into a bunch of different churches, you hear all kind of different beliefs about God and who He is and what He did. You know, you just kind of have to listen and decide on your own, "Well, what should I do, what should I believe? Let me pick up a Bible and read and try to interpret from my understanding."
>
> –Aurelia Martin, Parent, Miller's Toulminville Day Care Center

- If necessary, spend the next session on lesson planning, child assessment, and other intricate components of the curriculum.

- Discuss the following three points and agree upon what will be done and by whom.

  o Write up all the lists generated during the meeting, send copies to all *MCTT* participants and bring copies to the next session.

  o Develop and send to participants either: a) an affirmation statement of your existing curriculum with supporting rationale, b) a modified version of your existing curriculum, c) a modified version of an existing curriculum, or d) a well developed draft of a new curriculum.

  o Invite participants to study the document in light of the Vision Statement and categorized statements from the last session.

7. **Evaluate the session using evaluation forms.**

"Curriculum" Meeting # 3

The facilitator will lead the session by introducing exercises, establishing times for each exercise, and, most importantly, creating a fun, energetic, and connected environment for the session.

Basic approach:

1. **Review the "Curriculum, Lesson Planning, and Assessment" module by connecting it to the rest of the *MCTT* program and your work with children.**

   - Define the objectives for the session clearly.

     o Objective: To refine and develop consensus and to affirm the curriculum.

2. **Present an overview of the curriculum document.**

3. **Begin a discussion by inviting participants to ask questions about the document. Resolve as many questions as possible.**

4. **List on chart paper the questions and issues that the group cannot easily find consensus on. These may reflect conflicting ideas, values, philosophy, approach, etc.**

5. **Divide these questions and issues among small groups, and challenge them to come up with compromises and resolutions.**

   Next steps.

   - As you prepare for "Work Planning," the final *MCTT* module, the evaluations of each session as well as notes made, will prove their value. Invite participants to review their notes and evaluations of past sessions. Encourage them to carefully review the "Work Planning" module.

Resources

Books and Magazines:

Administrator's Guide to an Individualized Performance Results Curriculum, William E. Stradley

Ages and Stages, Karen Miller

Alike and Different: Exploring Our Humanity with Young Children, Bonnie Neugebauer

The Anti-Bias Curriculum: Tools for Empowering Young Children, Louise Derman-Sparks

Approaches to Preschool Curriculum, Michael C. Anziano, *et al.*

Black Children: Their Roots, Culture & Learning Styles, Janice E. Hale-Benson. Chapter 7: "Toward a Curriculum Relevant to African-Americans"

Caring for Infants and Toddlers: A Supervised Self-Instructional Training Program, Diane Trister Dodge

Children and Books I: African American Story Books and Activities for All Children, Patricia Buerke Moll

Creative Resources for the Early Childhood Classroom, Judy Herr, Yvonne Libby

Developmentally Appropriate Practices in Early Childhood Programs: Serving Children from Birth through Age 8, Sue Bredekamp

Diversity in the Classroom: A Multi-Cultural Approach to the Education of Young Children, Frances E. Kendall

Empowering African-American Males to Succeed: A Ten-Step Approach for Parents and Teachers, Mychal Wynn

The Giant Encyclopedia of Theme Activities for Children 2 to 5, Kathy Charnek

Growing Pains: Helping Children Deal with Everyday Problems through Reading, Maureen Caddigan, Mary Beth Hanson

Infants and Toddlers: Curriculum and Teaching, LaVisa Wilson

Learning Environments for Children, Henry Sanoff, Joan Sanoff

A Multicultural Guide to Thematic Units for Young Children, Dr. Jeri A. Carroll, Dr. Dennis J. Kear

Observing Development of the Young Child, Janice J. Beaty

The Outside Play and Learning Book, Karen Miller

Places and Spaces for Preschool and Primary (Outdoors), Jeanne Vergeront

Planning Activities for Child Care: A Curriculum Guide for Early Childhood Education, Caroline Spang Rosser

The Portfolio and Its Use: Developmentally Appropriate Assessment of Young Children, Cathy Grace and Elizabeth Shores

Practical Solutions to Practically Every Problem: The Early Childhood Teacher's Manual, Steffen Saifer

Principles of Parenting, H. Wallace Goddard

Resources for Creative Teaching in Early Childhood Education, Darlene Softley Hamilton, Bonnie Mack Fleming

Roots and Wings: Affirming Culture in Early Childhood Programs, Stacey York

Stories in the Classroom: Storytelling, Reading Aloud, and Role-playing with Children, Bob Barton and David Booth

A Survival Guide for the Preschool Teacher, Jean R. Feldman

Teaching About Native Americans, Karen D. Harvey, Lisa D. Harjo, Jane K. Jackson

Training Teachers: A Harvest of Theory and Practice, Margie Carter and Deb Curtis

Understanding Assessment and Evaluation in Early Childhood Education, Dominic F. Gullo

Valuing Diversity: The Primary Years, Janet Brown McCracken

The Whole Child, Joanne Hendrick

Catalogues/Bibliographies:

Resources for Early Childhood Training: An Annotated Bibliography (Council for Early Childhood Professional Recognition)

Venture into Cultures: A Resource Book of Multicultural Materials and Programs, Carla D. Hayden

Support Materials

- Agendas for all MCTT participants.

- Expanded agendas for members of the MCTT Site Team. These expanded agendas will provide you with helpful information as you go through the meetings.

- Documents resulting from the Curriculum meeting with Joyland, Kiddy Land, and Miller's centers. These are included to give you a sense of what to expect. It's a good idea to share these with the facilitator and the Site Team but not with the whole group, because they might influence their own work.

Agenda

More Is Caught Than Taught Program

Curriculum, Lesson Planning, and Assessment

Meeting #1

1. Welcome
2. Introductions
3. **Explanation of the meeting agenda**

    Purpose of the meeting
    - To enable each participant to gain a clear understanding of the objectives, expected outcomes, and the activities of the "Curriculum" module
    - To help each participant prepare for the process of identifying materials that support the vision statement of the program
    - To help each individual develop a plan with timelines for guiding their exploration of materials and approaches for inclusion in the curriculum

4. **Next Steps**
5. **Closing**

Expanded Agenda

More Is Caught Than Taught Program
Curriculum, Lesson Planning, and Assessment

Meeting #1

1. **Welcome**

2. **Introductions**

3. **Explanation of the meeting agenda**

   Purpose of the meeting

   - This session is about preparing. Emphasize that when participants leave the meeting they are expected to have a very clear understanding of the process that will be used to develop the curriculum and a very clear idea as to how each one of them will participate in the process. Inform the participants that they will be expected to write down for themselves a simple plan of action for their exploration of materials for the curriculum. Note the fact that your Vision Statement is central to this process.

   - You will want to have a good discussion on 5 topics:

     1. What curriculum is, what one typically looks like, and how it can/will be used by the program

     2. Questions central to early childhood development (Use the sheet on page 193)

     3. Your present curriculum or guiding principles (If you are not proud of what you have or don't have as a curriculum, do not mislead the group. Simply put this fact out as your starting point.)

     4. Basic plan to achieve the objectives of the "Curriculum" module

        a. study other curriculum <u>documents</u> as well as study curriculums in action

        b. evaluate your existing curriculum

        c. select models or prototypes that will bring focus to what the document will look like and what it will include

     Other considerations:

     a. parent friendliness

b. publishing and communicating
   c. complexity
   d. how the curriculum will be used with teachers and parents
   e. how the work (writing) will get done
   f. who will advise/assist/support the writer/developer
   5. Individuals' plans for the exploration of the curricular issues

4. **Next Steps**

   - Encourage participants to bring ALL curriculum materials that they find to the next session. They might have to photocopy, borrow, or purchase the material. They should know that simply "bringing back the idea" will not be adequate in most cases. Advise participants to work together where ever possible in their exploration efforts.

5. **Closing**

   - Fill out evaluation forms.
   - Review the date and time for the next meeting.
   - Express appreciation for and affirmation of the meeting and the meeting participants.

Agenda

More Is Caught Than Taught Program

Curriculum, Lesson Planning, and Assessment

Meeting # 2

1. Welcome

2. Introductions

3. Explanation of the meeting agenda

    Purpose of the meeting

    - To identify materials that support the Vision Statement, of the program and that will be used to select, create, or modify a curriculum and to develop a plan for writing and polishing the final document.

4. Next Steps

5. Closing

Expanded Agenda

More Is Caught Than Taught Program
Curriculum, Lesson Planning, and Assessment

Meeting # 2

1. **Welcome**

2. **Introductions**

3. **Explanation of the meeting agenda**

   Purpose of the meeting

   - To identify materials that support the Vision Statement of the program and that will be used to select, create, or modify, a curriculum, and to develop a plan for writing and polishing the final document.
     - Prepare the room well. Arrange seating so that people can work in clusters of 3 to 5 individuals. Provide plenty of table space for laying out all of the curriculum materials as well as room for working. Set out refreshments so that people can work, munch, and share. As participants will be doing a lot of reading, lighting is very important.
     - Organize the work. Hang the chart paper with the categories, organize the materials into groups such as curriculums, support materials, misalliance articles, books, and "must read" resources.
     - Use about half of your time for discovery and sharing. Divide the remaining time between organizing those things that participants like or recommend. Use the chart papers with your categories. With the time that is left, address the tasks of refining the work, assigning tasks, and planning the next session.

4. **Next Steps**

5. **Closing**
   - Fill out evaluation forms.
   - Review the date and time for the next meeting.
   - Express appreciation and affirmation of the meeting and meeting participants.

Agenda

More Is Caught Than Taught Program

Curriculum, Lesson Planning, and Assessment

Meeting # 3

1. **Welcome**
2. **Introductions**
3. **Explanation of the meeting agenda**

   Purpose of the meeting
   - Objective: To develop consensus and then refine and affirm the curriculum.
4. **Next Steps**
5. **Closing**

Expanded Agenda

More Is Caught Than Taught Program
Curriculum, Lesson Planning, and Assessment

Meeting # 3

1. **Welcome**

2. **Introductions**

3. **Explanation of the meeting agenda**

   Purpose of the meeting
   - To develop consensus and then refine and affirm the curriculum.
     - The purpose of this session is to bring the work to a "final draft" stage. At this point, all participants should be very familiar with the curriculum document and have relatively clear ideas for final changes.
     - From the large group, ask the participants to identify the areas in the document where they wish to see changes. Again, the chart paper with categories is a good tool to keep people talking about the same kinds of changes. Negotiate the differences.

4. **Next Steps**
   - Review the approach of the "Work Planning" module and help participants prepare for the final session(s).

5. **Closing**
   - Fill out evaluation forms.
   - Review the date and time for the next meeting.
   - Express appreciation for and affirmation of the meeting and the meeting participants.

Curriculum Questions

1. Is there a need for curriculum? If so, why? If not, why not?

2. What is age appropriateness? Is this concept important to our program? Why? Why not?

3. Will our curriculum be born out of the specific needs of our children or children in general? Does it make a difference? Why? Why not?

4. Is it useful to make connections between curriculum and teacher selection and training? Why? Why not?

5. If you had to favor one of the following positions, which would you chose as an emphasis for the program: **content** (facts, skills and ideas, attitudes, knowledge) or **process** (ways of being or ways of doing - thinking, expressing, probing, coping behavior)?

6. What value do you place on children choosing and directing their own learning? Why?

7. Which direction would you prefer for the program: spending resources to help teachers and parents alter the way they think and feel about caring for children or spending resources to help teachers and parents follow a well-defined program of care for children? Why?

8. Is it necessary that a caregiver be able to articulate or clearly describe her/his program for children? Why? Why not?

9. Is it possible to have an individual program of development for every child in a program? Is it necessary?

10. Should efforts be made to deal with the culture of the child and family through the curriculum? Why? Why not?

11. Is play something that just happens with children that needs no special attention, or is play something to spend money and energy learning about? Why?

12. Would you rather have a teacher with children who relies on experience and knowledge to perform her/his duties or a teacher who relies on a curriculum? Why?

13. Cognitive development, physical development, social development, and emotional development are ways of categorizing and looking at the way that children grow and develop. Should the curriculum address these areas? Why? Why not? If so, how?

14. To what level of detail should the curriculum address such things as choice of classroom materials, arrangement of indoor and outdoor areas, color of paint on the walls, etc.?

15. If the program keeps an up-to-date list of activities for the children each day, would this be a satisfactory curriculum? Why? Why not?

16. Is there a particular value in the sequencing and combining of activities and experiences for children (for example, to make sure certain activities and experiences precede some activities and follow other experience)? Why? Why not? Is this an item for the curriculum?

17. What are things you favor regarding the concept of "molding behavior" and the concept of modeling?

FOCAL
Celebrating Twenty-four Years
Of Service To Children

WORK PLANNING MODULE

"If there is no struggle, there is no progress."

Frederick Douglass

What Is this Module?

The "Work Planning" module is where it all comes together. As you implemented the previous seven modules, you discovered problem areas that needed fixing and opportunities to improve the program. You did not stop the *MCTT* process to "fix" things; instead, you made notes in your Planner In this module, you will use your Planner to develop a comprehensive improvement plan for the program. In order for your program to match your vision your and your supporters may spend considerable time and energy. Thus, your plan may require several years to implement. Don't be discouraged. A sound plan, mobilization of all available resources, and imaginative utilization of resources will give birth to the program of your vision. It will only be a matter of time.

Expected Outcomes

Participants will develop a comprehensive plan for the improvement of the program that includes these outcomes:

- Enriched relationships between and among parents, teachers, children, administrators, community leaders.
- Enriched program for children.
- Improved facilities.
- Identification and utilization of all available resources that are needed to implement the plan.
- A timeline for activities, with assignments of responsibilities to individuals.
- Naming of and description of barriers to achieving this plan.
- A system for monitoring the progress of the plan.
- A financial budget. This is necessary to overcome the barriers and produce leaders in tomorrow's world.

Preparing

Who will participate?

All members of the site team, staff, parents, and community leaders.

The planning process can be a difficult and exasperating experience. If you do not have experience leading a planning process,

> We also have to give thought to what they give us from the state office, that's been "the Bible" for us to use. For us to make a change, I guess we'd have to have a dialogue. Even the assessment forms, it's not something that we decide–they have given us these forms to make it easier for them to come and monitor the assessments. When we make changes here, we're going to have to do some negotiating.
>
> –Clara Card, Director, Joyland Child Development Center

you might want to call upon an experienced facilitator. When a facilitator is used, all of the energy and attention of the group members can be directed towards the content of the planning rather than the process – for example, being sure that all persons are contributing, processing hurt feelings, confusion, and the like. It must be remembered, if a facilitator is used, that the role of the facilitator is to <u>help</u> the group plan, not to <u>do</u> the planning. It is you and the members of your site team who have walked through the *MCTT* process, it is you who have the vision, and it is you who will shoulder the opportunity and responsibility for change. Do not give up this responsibility simply because others might have facilitation or process skills. Hold on to the fact that you have vision and knowledge.

How long will it take?

The planning process can be very involved. Many important things will happen. Therefore, this work should be viewed as "developmental," like the work of the other modules. As you plan, your vision will likely become more refined and stronger. The nature of problems and the connections between these problems and administrative procedures are likely to become clearer. For example, staff development training may be connected to hiring strategies, which might be connected to financial resources, which might be connected to relationships with leaders in the community and their support of the program. Therefore, a realistic plan to improve the quality of classroom activity may begin with a financial campaign to upgrade salaries. A successful campaign might have its roots in the site team and the community leaders who have worked with you throughout the *MCTT* process.

You should choose quality time and ample hours for the planning process. Two or three Saturdays or one or two weekends would not be out of the ordinary.

Where will it take place?

The "Work Planning" module can take place anywhere you will feel comfortable, that is convenient for participants, and that will be free of noise and other distractions. A site where chairs can be freely moved about and where newsprint can be taped to the walls is an important consideration.

When will it take place?

You will want the full site team present for development of the work plan. Therefore, the availability of your team members will dictate the time for the "Work Planning" module.

How will you document this module?

Your plan will be the product of this module and will, in some way, document this module. On the other hand, you will be learning from the process of developing the plan and therefore you might consider documenting this module as you did the others. A final consideration that could be the most important is that a lot of good ideas are developed in the planning process. Sometimes in the speed and heat of generating plans, these ideas are lost or key elements come up missing. If you arrange to record your sessions, valuable ideas and precious time can be preserved.

What will you need to bring to these meetings?

- All of the Planner notes, miscellaneous notes, and newsprint from previous modules.
- Newsprint. This works very well in this session; creating a banner-sized Vision Statement with the articulated vision of participants written large for all to see really gives strength to the process and makes the Vision Statement a powerful common property.
- Markers
- Loose paper
- Pencils or pens
- Masking tape
- Documentation materials and equipment
- Attendance sheet
- Agendas
- Food and drinks for meal or snack

Other possible materials include:

- Photographs of participants' children or children close to them.
- Photographs of women and men of vision

What else?

Is there anything else you need to think about or map out in your mind before going ahead?

Challenges of this Module

Staying with the planning process until it is completely finished is the greatest challenge of this module. The temptation will be to lay out broad goals and objectives in detail and to give less attention to timelines, identification of tasks and activities that support goals and objectives, and the assignment of individual responsibilities. Another challenge is to put the plan on paper. Often the act of thinking through a set of activities lulls one into believing that these activities and the ideas that support them have been memorized or internalized. No matter how "good" the planning session might be, no matter how clear everyone was and no matter how much agreement and unity was developed, some of the planning will be forgotten and lost if it is not written down. After spending time with the previous modules, some team members will feel like it is all over. The planning process will feel redundant. They must come to the realization that the planning process is the greatest insurance that all of their work and sacrifice will come to fruition.

Putting this Module into Action

The "Work Planning" Session

The facilitator will lead the session by reviewing the *MCTT* process, the materials covered, and the resources that are available for the planning process. An agenda to guide the planning process will be offered, evaluated, modified if necessary, and accepted. The agenda should include a projected time frame.

Basic approach:

1. See that everyone is introduced. Start a fun activity to get people comfortable with each other.

2. Evaluate the agenda and identify outcomes expected from the planning process.

- Discuss the Comprehensive Planning Diagram. In the process, invite participants to affirm their commitment to finish the final module and the *MCTT* program.

3. Reach agreement as to how closely the group will follow the Comprehensive Planning Diagram.

4. Invite participants to complete Step One of the "Comprehensive Planning Diagram." Address the remaining three steps in subsequent sessions.

5. Discuss the next steps.

Setting the time and place of the next meeting is the main objective of this discussion.

The agenda and expanded agenda (page 200-202) can be used a model for remaining sessions that address developing goals and objectives, setting the goals, objectives, activities and tasks on a time-line, and developing the evaluation plan.

6. Evaluate the session using prepared forms.

Follow-up

Compile the notes from the meeting (newsprint and personal notes) and organize them for the next meeting. Check with individuals who have agreed to carry out tasks for the next meeting.

Resources

Books:

- *The Fifth Discipline Fieldbook: Strategies and Tools for Building a Learning Organization,* Peter M. Senge, Art Kleiner, Charkotte Roberts, Richard B. Ross, Bryan J. Smith
- *Change Management: Creating the Dynamic Organization Through Whole System Architecture,* Lawrence M. Miller and Helene F. Uhlfelder, Ph.D.

Support Materials

- Agenda for all MCTT participants at the "Work Planning" session(s).
- Expanded Agenda for members of the MCTT Site Team. This expanded version will provide you with helpful information as you go through the module.
- The Comprehensive Planning Guide.
- Goals, Objectives, Activities, and Tasks Forms.

Agenda

More Is Caught Than Taught **Program**
"Work Planning" Meeting

1. **Welcome**

2. **Introductions**

3. **Explanation of the meeting agenda**

4. **Purpose of the meeting**
   - To review as a group our understanding of the planning process
   - To confirm our commitment to the planning process
   - To define/affirm the approaches to planning that will be taken
   - To establish a schedule for the next 3 to 5 meetings of the planning process
   - To begin development of the plan

5. **Starting the planning process**

6. **Setting a schedule for upcoming meetings**

7. **Next steps**

8. **Closing**

Expanded Agenda

More Is Caught Than Taught Program
"Work Planning" Meeting

1. **Welcome**

2. **Introductions**

3. **Explanation of the meeting agenda**

4. **Purpose of the meeting**

   - To review as a group our understanding of the planning process
     - This review can be facilitated by discussing the Comprehensive Planning Diagram. This tool is not the same as the Planner, although there are some similarities. The Comprehensive Planning Diagram is used to guide the planning process for this module. The Planner was used to capture the ideas, learning, concerns, etc., as the group worked through the previous seven modules.

   - To confirm our commitment to the planning process
     - This is at once a new, different and final phase of the *MCTT* program. It is necessary for participants to recommit themselves for the final push. Discussions and comment can be drawn directly from the vision of the group and the commitment to make a significant contribution to children, families and the community. The objective is to raise the planning process to a level of principle.

   - To define/affirm the approaches to planning that will be taken
     - The discussions that have taken place to this point will provide options for outlining the way that the group will proceed in the planning. The idea is for the group to create for itself an approach to planning that works for the group.

   - To establish a schedule for the next 3 to 4 meetings of the planning process

   - To begin development of the plan

5. **Starting the planning process**

   - Use the Comprehensive Planning Diagram or the customized version that you may have created to begin the planning process. It is important to set time limits for this first phase of planning and to set limited and achievable objectives so that success is likely for this first session.

6. Setting a schedule for upcoming meetings

7. Next steps

8. Closing

Comprehensive Planning Diagram

Planning is often made easier if the components of the process are identified and separated. To be sure, these components, or steps, cannot be completely separated, and it is not desirable to spend a lot of energy struggling to keep all components "pure." Seeking a balance, this diagram will identify major components and assist in keeping them separated. The benefits of this approach will likely become apparent as you continue through the planning process.

Step One - Developing a Mission Statement, a Universe of Needs Statement, and a Bank of Resources Statement

The outcome of this session will be: a) a Mission statement, b) a Universe of Needs statement, and c) Bank of Resources statement.

A good beginning for this step is to review the Vision Statement and the environment necessary to grow the children of your vision. From this foundation, spend some time (no more than 30 minutes) developing a mission statement for the program. This task is difficult for a group. It is like a committee trying to write a letter. Individual writing styles and word usage gets in the way. A better approach is to use the group to make broad statements and assign one or two individuals to develop a statement to which the group can respond. It is not important that the statement be developed at this session. Writing the mission statement can be carried over in several sessions.

Developing the Universe of Needs statement is essentially a brainstorming session except that you already have a wealth of ideas and needs that reside in your Planners. You might begin by posting on the walls 10 sheets of newsprint with the following headings to categorize the needs:

- Relationship Between Parents and Providers
- In the Classroom Activities
- In the Home Activities
- Relationships with the Community
- The Child Care Center/the Home of the Care Giver
- The Home of the Child
- The Curriculum/Assessment Tools/Lesson Plans
- Administration
- Staff Development
- Parent Education

The purpose of this exercise is to develop a comprehensive list of needs. This process is not simply taking the needs for the Planners and putting them on the walls, but a process that will generate new ideas, synthesize existing ideas and create energy in the group.

During this process, an effort should be made to capture all ideas rather that categorize ideas or reject poor ideas. Ideas or needs that are not well conceived will not make it through the planning process unless personalities or position unduly influence consultations. The needs list should be left open for additions as the process goes along.

With additional sheets of newsprint, list all available resources. This includes resources than are immediately at hand and resources that need reasonable development. The list might be categorized as Resources Available Now and Resources Available With Reasonable Work. As with the needs list, energy should be placed on identifying resources and possible resources rather than struggling to categorize and reject items.

Step Two - Developing Goals and Objectives

The outcome of this session will be the development of well-defined goals and objectives. Setting goals is a "dance" that requires mixing and blending the resource list with the needs list and creating a sense of possibility. You cannot allow available resources to dictate what you can and will do, for sometimes victory lies beyond what is "at hand." Conversely, realism requires careful assessment of available resources. Thus, we have the "dance." Sometimes doing what is necessary for children requires the "impossible." Sometimes doing what is necessary for children requires being very pragmatic. In the planning process, you want the advantages of both of these strategies.

In this Planning Diagram you will be encouraged to develop **goals**, supporting **objectives**, supporting **activities,** and supporting **tasks.** Although this process is time and energy consuming, breaking down the work of improving the program to this level greatly facilitates assigning responsibilities, monitoring progress, and allocating financial resources.

Goals are rather broad statements of things to do. Objectives are less broad, more focused, and more precisely measurable. Activities are even more focused and specific. Tasks are very narrowly defined pieces of work, specific and limited.

Return to the list of needs and prioritize the items. Efforts should be made to keep participants from lumping items together, except for needs that are very close in their meaning or intent. Therefore this might be the first step. In each category the question could be: "If only one thing from this category can be done, what should it be?" This need will be labeled "1." The question is asked again with this modification: "If only one additional need could be addressed, what should it be?" Continue down the category and proceed to the next category.

After the needs in each category are prioritized, the categories themselves (Relationship Between Parents and Providers, In the Classroom Activities, In the Home Activities, Relationships with the Community, The Child Care Center/the Home of the Care-giver, The Home of the Child, The Curriculum/Assessment Tools/Lesson Plans, Administration, Staff Development, Parent Education) can be broken down.

When the needs are prioritized, the plan begins to take shape. You know what is most important to you and supporters of the program. And you know something of the relationships between needs.

Setting goals begins with addressing the greatest or most pressing needs. Your goal statements should be measurable. For example: "To increase the participation of parents in program activities by 15% within the next program year." This statement is measurable as it tells us by how much and when. Other goals statements might look like the following: a) To raise the budget by $14,000.00 b) to provide training in classroom management for 4 staff persons within the next 6 months, c) to gain the support and involvement, this program year, of 5 new community leaders who will raise funds for the program.

Setting goals is sometimes easier if you separate goals into two or three categories. You might consider "Long Range Goals" and "Short Range Goals." Or long, medium and short range as categories. Short might be 12 to 18 months. Medium might be 18 months to 3 years. Long might be 3 to 5 years. If two categories are used, short might be 1 to 2 or 3 years and long might be 2 or 3 to 5 years.

Your objective is to build a series of pyramids, each with one goal statement on top supported by several objectives, which are in turn supported by activities with tasks as the foundation for each set of activities. This is the objective in a "perfect" planning process. In the real world we seldom reach perfection and we often compromise. You must make the decision as to whether all activities must be supported with tasks, or whether a goal is really an objective, etc. If you must err, lean towards more specificity rather than less.

As with developing the mission statement, you might wish to get close to writing your statement of goals and objectives and then assign a small team to work out the kinks in the statement and present it to the group at the next session for final touches. Remember, all elements of the plan can be modified at a later date.

Step Three - Setting the Goals, Objectives, Activities, and Tasks on a Timeline and Assigning Responsibilities

The outcome of this session is to have a set of documents which, when combined, will essentially be your comprehensive plan. It will lack only your monitoring and evaluation activities. (Refer to the sample planning documents that follow.)

This is a crucial step in the planning process. The tendency here might be to assign too many responsibilities to too few persons with too short a time span for completion of the work. By now the needs are staring you right in the face. You can see what is possible. You might be feeling a little anxious or even a little guilty for not having addressed the needs sooner or better. In any case, the sure formula for failure is to not assign responsibilities based on past experiences and the demonstrated ability of persons to perform similar tasks. Do make room in your plan for the unexpected.

At this point you are deep into the planning process and it is easy to go astray. You can get lost in objectives, tasks, activities and so on. As a way of keeping on course, you should take one or two goals completely through the process of stating the (measurable) goal, supporting the goal with objectives, the objectives with activities, and the activities with tasks. Complete the process by assigning responsibility and setting start and completion dates. Spend time getting these goals to the point where you are pleased with them and your ability to accomplish this task. This will be your model and compass. Keep them before the group for instruction and inspiration.

Do not be surprised if at this point you begin to lose people. Some personality types are simply better suited for this work that others. Stay with the planning process, however, and give your best to finishing the plan with all goals addressed and assigned. Remember, an individual or a small committee might be used to work on details while the large group provides direction and affirms the work of the committee.

Step Four - Developing the Evaluation Plan

The outcome of this session is to develop a monitoring and evaluation program which will complete your comprehensive plan.

The essential questions to be answered in the evaluation program are these:

- What outcomes will we measure?
- Who will look for or who will evaluate the outcomes?
- At what point or when will the evaluation take place?
- What happens if outcomes fall short of plans?
- What happens if outcomes exceed plans?

The following are some considerations for each question.

What outcomes will you measure?

If your goals and objectives are measurable and set on a time line, the outcomes that are to be evaluated become apparent. If the goal is to start recruiting 5 community leaders to support the fundraising campaign in March and to have them on board in June, at any point after March we might ask the question, "How many new community leaders have we recruited?" Well-defined goals and objectives set on a time line with assignments to individuals pay for the time and energy spent in their development when it comes time to monitor and evaluate program progress.

Evaluation activities are also defined and assigned to individuals and are integrated into the comprehensive plan along with other goals, objectives, activities, and tasks.

Who will look for or who will evaluate the outcomes?

Surely, persons from the site team should be used as evaluators. No one knows the program better or has a clearer vision than these individuals. In addition, persons from "outside" the program can bring objectivity and perspective to the evaluation process. Ideally, a balance of parents, staff and community leaders would cover all bases. These individuals could be drawn from within and from outside of the program.

At what point or when will evaluation take place?

Program evaluation might take place at two levels. One is the staff level and the other is the "advisory board" level. The staff might come together and check progress each month or more often. This activity can be integrated into ongoing work of the staff with minimum difficulty. On the other hand, getting advisory level evaluators may not be reasonable more than two to four times a year.

What happens if outcomes fall short of plans?

One objective of evaluation is to catch activities that are falling behind schedule. When this is done, some action should be automatic or preplanned. For example, persons who put the plan together, in this case your site team, might be called together to offer revisions to the plan by extending the time for completing objectives, revising or scrapping objectives, or reassigning activities and tasks. In any case, you will want to be following a plan that is achievable and up-to-date.

What happens if outcomes exceed plans?

In this case, you will want to revise your plan. Only this time be sure to include a little celebration as you move expectations outward towards the edge of the ability of people to achieve success. For many, the stretch to achieve difficult goals develops capacity and adds challenge and excitement to the work.

Congratulations on a difficult job well done!

It is now time for a real celebration, since you have reached a very significant milestone. Your plan, if attended to, will take you step by step to your vision for the children in your care. If by chance you are not entirely pleased with your plan, take heart. Such things happen. Set it aside, reflect on the barriers that you experienced, and come back to your plan later. Set aside quality time, which may be short periods, to polish the plan. If you get stuck, consider getting help with the planning process. Resource persons can be found in educational institutions, businesses and human service agencies who will help you evaluate the methods that you are using and barriers that are getting in the way. If you are more or less on tract to this point and you have all of the raw material that you need, you may find that only a little technical assistance can push you over the top. However you get there, a comprehensive plan to address program needs and problems is an exceedingly valuable tool and a medal of honor as you strive to build a program that honors your vision and the potential of children in your care.

Work Planner

Program Name: _____ Date: _____ Page Number: ___

Mission Statement:

Program Goal	Start	Finish
	:	

Assignments	Program Objective	Start	Finish

Assignments	Program Activities	Start	Finish

Assignments	Program Tasks	Start	Finish

Facilitator's Guide

A. Jack Guillebeaux

What is Group Facilitation?

Individuals who come together to work on common social problems and issues will find that differences in perceptions, felt needs, preferred strategies, and other considerations will present barriers to identifying and reaching agreed-on goals and objectives. Differences in class, gender, race, age and religion usually broaden the diversity of perceptions and felt needs, as well as the preferred actions and expected outcomes. As diversity increases, so does the likelihood of misunderstandings, confusion and conflict.

On the beneficial side, diversity contributes richness and strength to the process of collective action. Problems and issues important enough to draw individuals across cultural lines generally are both highly valued and difficult to resolve. All available community resources are often needed to resolve such situations. However, diversity can also clarify vision, refine the definition of problems and issues, expand and reinforce the principles by which actions are guided, and encourage people to commit more human energy to tasks defined for collective action.

Unity and its corollary, strength, do not come without a cost. As individuals come together to work as groups, it is often necessary, especially if the group is culturally diverse, for a person or persons to assume the role of *facilitator*. The definition of "facilitate" is basic: "to make easier." Thus, in the case of a diverse group attempting to work in unity and harmony, the role of the *facilitator* is to "make" any communicating, sharing, hearing, listening, taking in and working together "easier."

Group facilitation can also be thought of as an art, given that we think of an art as a "a system of principles and methods employed in the performance of a set of activities." This handbook is prepared as a tool to identify and examine principles, methods and activities necessary to facilitating the process of diverse groups working together in unity and harmony.

The Role of Group Facilitator

To better understand the role of group *facilitator*, one might ask "What are the tasks before the *facilitator*?" The individual tasks that a *facilitator* might perform are numerous. The expectations of individuals involved, the objectives of the group, the level of experienced individuals, and the physical setting are only a few of the many elements that dictate the tasks of the *facilitator*. This discussion will cover only the basic tasks of the *facilitator*. Careful thinking about the basics offered here and further experimentation with these ideas will expose the secrets of the art of group facilitation.

It should be noted that facilitating the progressive movement of a group from one point to another is often a spontaneous act performed in whole or in part by random members of the group. Indeed, in some cases the goals or objectives of the group are not clearly defined. However, our objective here is to focus on facilitating a group that comes together to work on explicit and defined objectives, thus limiting the scope of this discussion.

Primary Tasks Of Group Facilitators

Developing a clear understanding of the stated goals and objectives of the group is normally an essential task of the *facilitator*. Given that the fundamental work of the *facilitator* is to cause the group to work smoothly, effectively and productively and that the work of the group is to achieve the stated goals, the *facilitator* becomes, in varying degrees, the rudder that guides the craft on a true course. Following this ship analogy, the group becomes the "captain" who sets the goals and the rudder an instrument that turns the vessel. This distinction of roles is very important, and *facilitators* should carefully consider whether or not they agree with the purpose and projected outcome of the group's work before agreeing to assume the responsibility to facilitate.

It is not ethical to agree to facilitate with the hidden purpose of changing the stated course of the group. If one wants to direct the group in this manner, it is better that the individual join the group and become a member or leader. Another option is for the individual to assume the explicit role of teacher or mentor for the group. From these roles, directing the course of a group is expected.

One might draw from this statement the impression that a *facilitator* is not expected to register any impact on the group. This is not so. The *facilitator* will bring vision, a set of values and expectations. These offerings cannot and should not be left behind by the *facilitator*. These things will have a substantial effect on the group process. The point is that another task of the *facilitator* is to be aware of the "stuff" that s/he brings to the process and to manage her/his own desires in such a way that her/his "stuff" adds to their ability to steer the ship, not direct the course of the group.

As the *facilitator* will focus on the *process* and not the *product,* another task of the *facilitator* is to listen to the outer and inner meaning of communications and help the group "hear" each member. Given that some individuals are naturally more talkative or less talkative than others, it is necessary for the *facilitator* to assist the group in regulating its conversation so that all members can be heard.

One constant enemy of collective action is time. As a rule, group members do not have enough time to attend meetings and serve at a level that is needed for the group to achieve its objectives. The *facilitator* will monitor the passing of time and help the group utilize it wisely.

Often, the *facilitator* will be given the responsibility of setting the tone for the work of a group. The *facilitator* can do much to establish the climate, and there are many options. The *facilitator* can achieve a tone that communicates: a) an easygoing, laid-back atmosphere; b) a business-like "let's get to work" attitude; c) an anxious "this is something to be feared" concern; d) or an unrealistic "pie-in-the-sky" or "let's pretend" approach. As one might imagine, there are many, many variations on these options, and there are also countless other possibilities. A task of the *facilitator*, then, is to identify a climate that is appropriate to the situation and to work to create such a climate. The identification of the appropriate climate is done in collaboration with the "captain" as goals and expected outcomes are defined.

In summary, the task of the *facilitator* is to be sensitive to and **manage the process** of the group, moving from one step to the next in such a fashion that the group can concentrate more on achieving the goals and objectives that have been designated by the group.

In this discussion of roles, it is important that an explicit understanding of the role of the *facilitator* be shared by the group or its leaders. Put another way, a CONTRACT, formal or informal, should exist between the *facilitator* and the leadership/organizers of the group.

Principles

The question of right and wrong principles, or –put another way– greater and lesser principles, is inevitably subjective. Having no way, then, to identify and talk about the ultimately correct principles or hierarchy of principles, what we offer here are the admittedly subjective views of this writer.

Certain principles govern the process of effectively enabling a group to work through differences more effectively. The first and most important principle is honesty. Honesty is the foundation of all other principles necessary to guide the work of group facilitation. In addition to the conscious agreement involved in accepting the facilitating role in the first place, we add a few more elements. One is not to lie or misrepresent the truth about the motivations, skills, objectives and planned strategy of the *facilitator* of the group.

Another principle necessary for the facilitator to embody is genuine love and respect for the "humanness" of each of the group's members. Sometimes it is very difficult to love and respect all persons in a group. However, it is absolutely necessary that the negative personal feelings of the *facilitator* towards individual members of the group be set aside. To help make this possible, the *facilitator* might focus on the higher truths and realities of individuals of the group. Some of these include the following: a) the person was motivated to come to the group; b) the person's thoughts and ideas are a part of a system of belief and are not "the person"; c) one should not be quick to judge a person in whose shoes one has not walked; d) only with enough information does all behavior make sense; and e) within all human beings is the image of God.

The *facilitator* must strive not to allow her/his prejudices of class, race, gender, etc., to support the false notion of inherent superiority and inherent inferiority of individuals and groups. To whatever degree possible, the principle of the equality of all peoples must be observed. Offering one's behavior as a model of how to interact is better than inviting the group to "do as you say." For example, showing love and respect, listening attentively, being flexible, and being agreeable and patient are behaviors that the *facilitator* should *practice*, not *preach*. One need not be a perfect model, but the standard is not to allow one's words to exceed one's deeds.

The success of group facilitation is greatly enhanced if the *facilitator* loves and values the group process and the role of *facilitator*s. Facilitating the progress of a group or helping a group to achieve lofty goals is worthy of praise. This work can and should be a source of pride.

Also, "humor is the spice of life"; use it generously when appropriate.

Responsibilities

One of the prime responsibilities of the *facilitator* is to provide protection for individual group members. This function is an important one to explore during the development of the contract between the *facilitator* and the group's leaders and as an element of the norm or rules of the group. In addition to negative impact on the human spirit, personal attacks on individuals get in the way of the group's progress. Thus, the *facilitator* must work to insure that focus remains on the work of the group and not on the personalities of individuals. A clash of ideas is necessary, expected, and healthy, but the clash of personalities is dysfunctional and undesirable.

When the group veers away from a course that leads towards its goals, the *facilitator* must assume leadership and offer observations and suggestions for getting back on course. The "captain" of the group can change the course or set new goals and objectives. This is her/his right. However, the *facilitator* will want these changes to be explicit and will assume the responsibility of making them explicit.

In keeping with the "contract" of the *facilitator* and the objectives of the group, the *facilitator* should assume responsibility for creating a climate or environment which supports the principles stated above and which is in harmony with the work of the group. One very useful way of doing this is by "contracting" with the group concerning norms, rules, expectations, parameters and expected outcomes.

A final responsibility is that of being emotionally and intellectually present. As the "vessel" is struggling to make headway, it is important that individuals feel that the "rudder" is there doing its job: listening, thinking, feeling, planning, observing, evaluating, and caring about the *way* things are going. When the *facilitator* is no longer willing or able to do this job, for a short period of time or not at all, it is essential that the *facilitator* inform the group and allow for other(s) to carry on the functions of the *facilitator*.

Vision

Vision is one of the most necessary and powerful tools that the *facilitator* brings to the task of facilitating. Vision is also one of the most necessary and powerful tools that the group has at its disposal. Having vision and developing a shared vision as a tool to focus the energy and power of the group falls within the role of the *facilitator*.

Looking at vision from a different perspective, it should be observed that the *facilitator* will enter the group with a vision of expected outcomes, and that each participant will also bring a vision. It is important that the *facilitator* make her/his vision conscious and examine it so that "unconscious" feelings and wishes will not sabotage the "conscious" expectations of the *facilitator* and sabotage the agreement of the *facilitator* with the group or its organizers. Again, here is the place to assess whether or not the facilitation of the work of the particular group is desirable, whether the expectations of the group are realistic, and whether the principles and values of the group and those of the *facilitator* are harmonious.

Assumptions

Closely following the concept of vision is that of assumptions. The *facilitator* and each group member come with certain assumptions about all manner of things. More importantly, they arrive with assumptions about the behavior, attitudes, skills, knowledge, motivation, vision, etc., of other group members or of the group as a whole. Again, diversity makes these assumptions more varied and often more erroneous. The *facilitator* should examine his/her assumptions and be willing to adjust them in the face of new or contradictory information. A good set of assumptions (like principles, they are subjective) that the *facilitator* might bring to the group include the following:

That all individuals can speak.

That all expressions and offerings are valid.

That good ideas and solutions can from come anyone at any time.

That all people (participants) are equally needed and valuable.

That all have thoughts and that all wish to be heard.

That there is enough of everything (time, energy, attention, etc.) if members share, cooperate and establish priorities and standards.

Expectations

Operating from a foundation of positive expectations is a valuable and necessary tool for the *facilitator*. A few basic expectations should be considered: a) that people will cooperate and support the group's rules; b) that the group will finish all reasonable (though difficult) tasks; and c) that the group will find within itself the resources to achieve its goals.

Barriers

Many barriers can impede the progress of a group, most of which we have all experienced. Some of the more pronounced ones have do with prejudices towards groups such as the poor, blacks, whites, men, women, the rich, the educated and so on. A feeling of scarcity of time and attention is a very prevalent barrier to collective action. The belief that "my position and thinking really are best" plays havoc with the group process. Protecting or rescuing other members of the group gets in the way of open communications. Feelings of anger or suspicion held by members toward one another make the job tough.

Though these attitudes and related behaviors are dysfunctional, they are givens. People must and will bring their dysfunctional behavior to the work of the group. The work of the *facilitator* is to help the group manage these givens by expressly offering options and negotiating for behavioral norms that aid the progress of the group.

Dos

By simply comparing the space in this handbook allotted to "how to be and think" as opposed to "what and how to **do**," it should become obvious that the writer believes that the motivation behind what the *facilitator* does is more important than the acts the *facilitator* performs. This is true in the main. However, some activities and techniques do enrich the process. There is no way to come up with a definitive set of Dos that fit all groups and situations, so a set of considerations will be offered with a "soft" priority represented by the order of the set. The following is given in the context of the roles, principles, responsibilities, and barriers discussed above.

- At the beginning of the session, the *facilitator* should help the group agree on goals and expectations and the role of the *facilitator*.

- The *facilitator* should make clarifying remarks that anchor discussion.

- The *facilitator* should "stroke" behavior that supports the rules and norms of the group by pointing it out and thanking participants for their contributions.

- The *facilitator* should be patient.

- The *facilitator* should allow his/her shared honest feelings to be a tool.

- The *facilitator* should make eye contact.

- The *facilitator* should be consistent and trustworthy and treat all persons and situations with equity.

- The *facilitator* should maintain order by inviting the group to observe its stated rules or to change them in some orderly fashion.

- The *facilitator* should move the discussion forward by observing when milestones have been achieved (mini celebrations are in order), when consensus has been reached, or when agreement does not seem likely.

- The *facilitator* should help the group to identify conflicts, problems and options (for example, sharing time, forming in small groups vs. large groups, and pursuing one topic to conclusion vs. addressing a larger number of topics in less depth).

- The *facilitator* should intervene in personality conflicts by stroking the intentions, perspectives, needs, and orientations of both parties and by helping them focus on the issue at hand.

- The *facilitator* should keep a focus on differences of thought, styles, values, expectations, needs, etc., as the valid, valuable and necessary differences that diversity brings.

- The *facilitator* should ask participants to consider using language that affirms the OK-ness of individuals and their groups.

- The *facilitator* should ask participants to consider using language that personalizes their needs and wishes rather than universalizes them.

Examples:	Personal Statements	Universal Statements
	I like . . .	Everybody knows that . . .
	My experience is . . .	Nobody ever . . .
	It seems to me that . . .	The only way for X is to . . .
	I don't understand . . .	We don't understand . . .
	My feelings are . . .	This group is . . .

Intervention and Styles

Methods of intervention are inextricably linked with styles of communicating, comfort levels, levels of awareness, and so on. Each *facilitator* should work to identify and develop her/his own style. Observation and study of the intervention styles of others is advisable. Given these considerations, the offerings that follow are intended to expand the definition or understanding of intervention rather than presenting a pattern to follow. The categories of intervention are 1) giving strokes; 2) getting clarity; and 3) re-establishing norms and expectations. Examples:

- Did you hear that comment?
- Say that again so that we can all hear that.
- Someone make a note of that.
- Your remark was . . .
- If I were to say . . . would this be true for you?
- Would you help us to understand (why, who, when) . . .
- Does that mean that . . .
- Am I right in thinking/feeling that you . . .
- Is another way of saying that . . . ?
- May I ask (someone else) to repeat what you said?
- I think I have a feeling for what you are saying; is . . . what you mean?
- Will you help me see how your behavior supports our "contract"?
- Is this carrying us away from our agreement?
- Do you wish to renegotiate our contract?
- Do you think that others might feel/think . . . ?
- I don't know how to reconcile your position with our contract; will you help me?

Don'ts

- Don't take sides.
- Don't focus on the differences; focus on the issues.
- Don't punish, shame, embarrass, or put down people or ideas.
- Don't discount the thinking and feelings of individuals.

Conclusion

If you are new to the process of facilitating a group's work, please remember that honesty and sensitivity are paramount. All other acts are add-ons. Group facilitation offers one a grand opportunity to develop valuable knowledge of self, people, and people in groups. Set goals for your own growth and development, and work to achieve them as a byproduct of your work as a *facilitator*.

Have the courage not to be understood, not to be heard and not to lead. Have the fortitude to be vulnerable. Rely upon the principles and tools of love, respect, honesty, courage, patience, listening, open-mindedness, questioning, etc. Look for the best in people, and foster this concept in group members. Be generous with praise. Value the essential humanness in all. Ask for help and support when you need it, and, above all, **HAVE FUN!**

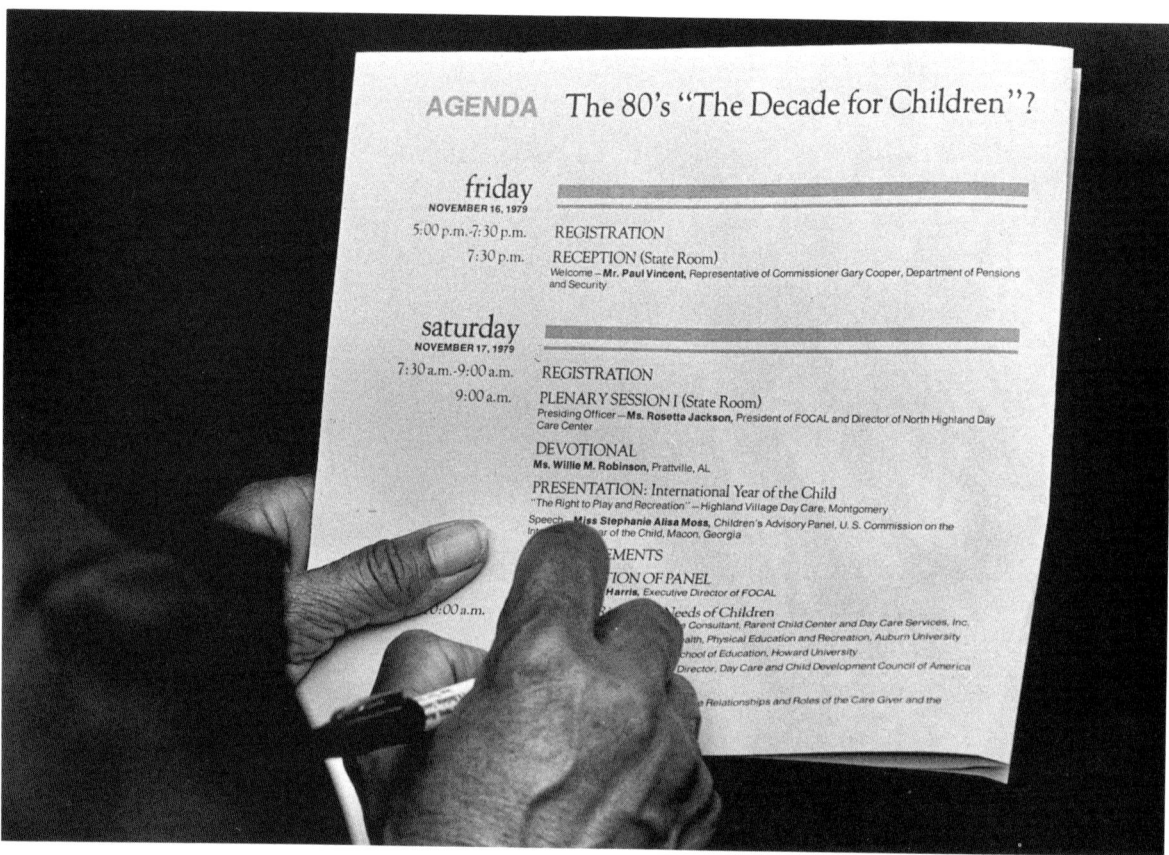

Healing Racism

INTERNALIZED OPPRESSION: What is it?

Institute for the Healing of Racism
Salt Lake City, Utah

Internalized oppression is a phenomenon that happens when people are bombarded with gross misinformation and mistreatment over a period of time. Members of the targeted group internalize the misinformation and the hurtful behavior and turn upon themselves, their family members, and other people of their group.

All people are affected by such internalized oppression: women, people of color, Jews, the physically challenged, the aged, homosexuals, children, men, etc. Because the misinformation is different for each group, the internalized oppression takes a different form in each case. Members within a targeted group internalize the hurtful behavior and misinformation differently, depending on the degree of oppression they have experienced.

Victims of racism can:

- Come to believe the stereotypes and misinformation about their own group

- Accept the standard of beauty and acceptability of the dominant group

- Have difficulty taking pride in their heritage due to a lack of knowledge and appreciation of their group's contributions and heroes

The internalized oppression of racism affects each ethnic group in a distinct way. Some survival behaviors to cope with racism over the years have led to some group patterns of behavior that are also barriers to the full, healthy development of individuals. For example, in the African American community:

- Certain child rearing practices can be traced to slavery and segregation when racism demanded that adults, especially males, were to be submissive. Parents taught their children not to act too proud or powerful and to disguise feelings.

- Certain eating patterns that are a part of culture that stem from racism can be self-destructive; in the early days, slaves ate what was available to them, made it tasty, and learned to like it. But some "soul food," we now know, causes hypertension, high blood pressure, and early death.

- Some people perceive various areas of human activity as "White" because they were once denied to people of African descent, resulting in the limiting of the full range of possibilities for any individual. The fear of being perceived as "acting white" is internalized oppression, as is being criticized for being good at or not good at a particular thing within a narrowly-defined cultural norm.

The internalized oppression can result in:

- Inhibiting the targeted group from taking pride in itself individually and collectively

- Causing members of the targeted group to act out their rage, fear and indignation at each other, resulting in divisiveness and disunity and even the extreme of violence and death

- Causing people to criticize and have unrealistic expectations of other group members who have had the courage to step forward and assume leadership responsibilities

- Causing targeted people to depreciate their children with criticism and fault-finding, thereby destroying confidence and self-esteem

- Creating patterns of powerlessness and hopelessness which give rise to compulsions to escape through unhealthy activities

The healing of internalized oppression demands:

- A recognition that the problem exists

- A commitment to rooting out one's own internalized oppression by learning to identify and recognize patterns of internalized oppression in relationships and interactions with others.

- A supportive process and group to heal the pain and re-evaluate old decisions regarding oneself and one's group

UNCONSCIOUS RACISM: What is it?

Unconscious racism is a form of individualized racism.

In the United States, unconscious racism is:

- Rooted in misinformation about "people of color"

- Internalized in such a way that the "white" person who carries the misinformation is not conscious that the misinformation is even there

- One of the most difficult, insidious forms of racism, simply because it is unconscious and often the intentions of its perpetrators are good

Recognizing Unconscious Racism

Unconscious racism affects all "whites," however good their intentions. Recognizing one's unconscious racism is like living in Los Angeles and not knowing what smog is until you travel somewhere else and breathe clean air. Racism is so much a part of the society in which we live that it is difficult for "whites" to perceive how they have been conditioned to regard "people of color" and not to notice how everything in society is oriented toward "whites" at the expense of others. (See enclosed article on White Privilege.)

Examples of Unconscious Racism

Uncontrollable thoughts and emotions

- The thoughts that pop into our heads about "people of color" which we recognize as inappropriate and thus don't verbalize

- We may often experience these kinds of thoughts when we are under stress and a person of color is in our general vicinity

- Knee-jerk emotional reactions of fear or suspicion when we are in the presence of members of another racial group, especially when we are in the minority

- Feelings of shame when we are in the presence of people of color

- An unconscious sense of superiority (example: when planning a meeting with a person of color, whites will assume that they have more to contribute to the planning and will therefore assume that they should be in charge.) (See excerpt from The Healing of Racism.)

Inappropriate and limiting actions for others or ourselves

- Avoiding contact

- Noticing the behavior of targeted groups that wouldn't be noticed in whites (example: a white male driving a big expensive car versus a black male driving the same car. If it were a white male, we might automatically assume that he must be educated, clever, and worked hard to get what he has. On the other hand, if it were a man of African heritage, many whites would assume that he sold drugs, pimped, or stole the car.)

- Consciously or unconsciously ignoring the vast inequities in our institutions for people of color versus those for whites (example: black people, who are less than 12% of the population of the United States make up 23% of the people in prison, on trial, or on parole.)

- Using the internalized oppression of particular groups to justify one's misinformation and emotional reactions (example: they are always killing each other, aren't they?)

- Limiting our knowledge of history to a Eurocentric perspective (example: the "discovery" of America)

- Being unable to appreciate physical features of different cultural groups if their physical appearance isn't similar to white features

- Not recognizing the validity or wisdom in a suggestion from a person of color (example: During a discussion, a person of African heritage makes a suggestion. The whites listening discount his comment unconsciously. When the same suggestion is given by a white, the validity of the suggestion is praised.)

- Interrupting or "taking over" and other condescending behavior (example: When a person of color is speaking, a white person cuts the speaker off and continues speaking, not even noticing what he/she has just done.)

- Being patronizing (example: over-enthusiastic commenting on "how intelligent" a person of color is or being "sooooo grateful")

- Offering help when not needed or wanted

- Laughing at and passing on racist jokes and stereotypes

- Saying that African Americans (or other groups) are "too sensitive," especially when they complain about racism

Internalized Oppression: How do we free ourselves of it?

Sandra Robertson
Executive Director,
Georgia Citizens Coalition on Hunger

The visible signs of oppression take many forms: hunger, homelessness, racism, sexism and homophobia; you know the long list. We see the effects of oppression every day. When we drive through some neighborhoods and see all of the symptoms signaled by uninhabitable housing and dreary streets, pimps and prostitutes, drug dealers and drug addicts, children without hope packing guns and selling dope, homeless men epoxied to park benches and church doorways, there is no mistaking what's going on. When you enter this gateway, you know where you are and what you are likely to encounter down this rocky road. It is a mean road of hard knocks and few breaks.

Likewise, when we see the portrayal of women as physical sex objects, who are used to advertise cancer-causing cigarettes to our children; or to show off expensive cars to those who are barely able to afford them; or to hustle alcoholic beverages that dull the senses and slow the mind so that someone can reap the profits from the sweeping sales that these oppressive ads generate, we know that something is going on. And when, even today, a major international business, such as AT&T, can portray African people as gorillas, when Texaco executives joke privately about discrimination, and when in 1994 white men are still writing books that attempt to prove that African people are intellectually and culturally inferior to Caucasians and others, we know that racism is alive in America and that it seeks to destroy us.

Understanding these things on an intellectual level is one thing, but grasping the impact that these ills have on us spiritually, emotionally, and psychologically requires greater insight. The spiritual level is the very essence of ourselves, which is connected to our creations and our creator; the emotional level is our conscious mind; and the psychological level is our unconscious mind. Even when we can intellectualize and articulate how oppression works and what causes it, we often fail to ask how can those who have suffered the sting of oppression and those who have become agents of oppressive systems (often unknowingly) can be healed and can recover from the spiritual, emotional, and psychological damage that it causes.

Recently, I heard a powerful woman named Ms. Cotton speak. She was a dynamic organizer during the Civil Rights Movement of the '60s and '70s. She talked about the power of healing in songs. She sang us songs about pain and told the story of the suffering. These songs were used to touch the human spirit and change the minds of the oppressed so that they could change their own circumstances. There is no denying that songs are powerful vehicles for communicating our joys and our sorrows, and perhaps they are even cathartic, not only for those who sing them but also for those who listen to them. But songs are just not enough to wipe away the severe damage caused by the constant bombardment of erroneous facts and false images projected about the poor, about people of color and about women. Songs will not erase the negative images painted daily on television screens, newspapers, and radio shows across this country. Songs alone will not destroy the lopsided views and intentional deceptions created in our history books that are taught to our children and presented as truth and fact in our colleges and universities.

It is easy to create these false images when you have the capacity to influence massive numbers of people at one time on a daily basis. A black face associated with crime, projected on television every night, three and four times each night, across this country, creates a clear message. Even though most criminals are white males, that is not what we are programmed to think when we hear the word "crime."

We are more often shown a black face or a brown face whenever the issues of welfare and poverty are discussed. Yet, statistically we know that 2/3 of the poor are Caucasian people. Furthermore, increasing numbers of white families are falling into the ranks of poverty. This misleading picture of America's poor is a burden for people of color, but it is also a problem for poor whites who know that they are suffering but who, in their attempt to escape, are ridiculed and scorned so that they will remain silent and obscure.

Purveyors of this prejudicial position pollute the airwaves and print media and create a toxic, inhumane environment. This sewage seeps into our psyches and blocks out the realities and truths we should recognize. When welfare cheats, thieves, and murderers are painted with black and brown faces, the opportunity for inclusion becomes hollow words, and hopes of a better future fall on deaf ears.

How can we be healed, restored, and freed from this terrible curse that has been passed down from generation to generation? I believe in a higher power that can save us from our own self-destruction. I believe that power is within us and can empower us to protect ourselves and others. I also believe that we must become "thinkers." We must become people who can "reason" and know how to distinguish the truth from a lie. We must become lovers of the human spirit and see beyond one another's color and cultures, yet respect and embrace each other's color and culture; and we must become receptors for recognizing people's needs, hopes and desires. We must become storytellers. We must tell our stories and truths and be willing to listen to other people's stories. We must also deny the oppressive forces around us - deny them with our every breath. We must deny them the opportunity to separate us from one another. We must deny them the opportunity to dampen our spirit and usurp our energy. We must refuse to be used as instruments of oppressive systems that do their destructive work. Finally, we must reverse the process of internalized oppression. Internalized oppression is the constant flow of negative, self-destructive data into the psyche, which makes that which is false seem true and causes us to act against our own self interests and the interests of the common good. Internalized oppression makes poor white people join the Ku Klux Klan instead of bonding with other poor people to solve their economic and political problems. Internalized oppression makes talented young black "unemployed business men" sell drugs instead of distributing useful products in their own communities, and it makes them kill and be killed trying to make a quick dollar. Internalized oppression makes a young Japanese teenager commit suicide because he made a C+ on a test instead of an A+, and because the pressure to live up to the false image that all Asians are A+ students is too devastating to bear. Internalized oppression afflicts a teenage Chicano girl who could be an A+ student but who seeks acceptance into a gang in which she believes she will be esteemed and protected, and in which getting A's is not the criteria for membership, while getting pregnant is.

Internalized oppression is the "death angel." It takes false information about groups of people, programs people to believe it, and then makes the false information a self-fulfilling prophesy so that over time it becomes our reality. A lie becomes the truth! In order to stop its sting we must first know that it is happening: we must create ways to re-educate ourselves, tell our own stories and truths, listen to others' stories, lean to recognize not only oppression but also those who allow themselves to become agents of oppression, and deny these forces an opportunity to do their destructive work. We must challenge their lies; confront their destructive deeds, destroy their racist, classist, sexist systems; and stand firmly with those who fight oppression. Finally, I believe we must also have faith that a love greater than our own is able to touch the hearts, minds and souls of humankind.

Identification Crisis

Dr. R. Blanchard Stone
Associate Professor of Education
Alabama State University

One of the most conspicuous absences in the life of African-Americans is a reluctance to think analytically about their subjective condition. Such a failure has the same effect as the conscious intent to remain unaffected by events impacting their lives. The lack of rational motivation leads to a lack of purposeful pursuit. A person going nowhere in life needs no special skills or talents to get him there.

There are two reasons why purpose is in such short supply among those who have no sense of destiny. The first reason involves existing without a continuous awareness of people, places, and things. In other words, it involves existing without a functional past. It is from their past that a people conjure their future purpose. A common past binds people together. This past is brought forward, making the present a meaningful and necessary bridge effectively connecting the past with the future. When the bridge is not, there for whatever reason, there can be no synthesis; thereby a people is effectively marooned, stranded in the present. This temporal isolation makes for a unidimensional existence. Without a past, no future is possible except in the simplest sense. For the isolated and the marooned, the future is not what they move into; instead, it is a condition imposed by those who are shaping the future.

It should come as no surprise that those going nowhere in life need no special skills or talents to get them there. From history comes the perpetual bonding of a people, whether such bonding be in the form of family, clan, tribe, nation, or kingdom. The historical basis of this bonding is homogeneity of race and culture. From the union of historical likemindedness comes what is called the manifest destiny (which, for imperial social groups, is the necessity to prevail universally in one or more given areas of skill and technology). Solidified by the social contract (which makes universal respect among members mandatory), mutual trust and social cooperation are then assured. In this environment, trust flourishes, making cooperation the rule rather than the exception.

Color of skin or hair texture alone conveys no proof of social togetherness. One need only look to Europe and Africa, where like-appearing individuals lay total waste to each other every day. When a person lives or dies in the name of advancing a goal for his particular tribe, whether the tribe lives in Europe or Africa pales into insignificance. Thus, we get the concept of a higher purpose. This condition creates the lesser purpose of the individual, who strives to contribute his bit to the greater or higher purpose. In this crucial situation, the unidimensional individual who must wait for the future to be brought to him can have no role at all in shaping the future. His purpose is limited to the frivolous pursuit he carves out in pursuit of his own selfish desires.

When a person has no purpose requiring skill and knowledge, he pursues information in purely mechanical and imitative ways. The use and need of a thing determines how thoroughly a thing is pursued. Do I need a degree (for example) to get a job, or do I require knowledge in order to do a job? The decision will determine the means and the methods of the pursuit. Once I determine that my purpose is the good of my race (those with whom I am bonded), my pursuit of the purpose takes on added significance. Then, and only then, will the acquisition of the skills of critical thinking make sense. Critical thinking is the analytical process of examining an idea, concept, or process thoroughly in an effort to achieve a needed outcome. Critical thinking and applied science are used to reduce the complexity of a problem to its least common denominator by employing logic. Once critical thought is used, a problem should disappear.

Anyone who is not honing his or her analytical skills in an effort to compete in a world of high technology is a person wishing for a miracle, even though the age of miracles has passed. Because a people have been conditioned, even programmed, to fail is no reason to continue to fail. The "Negro" condition is maintained by **internalized oppression**. This acceptance of the notion of inherent inferiority persists beneath the threshold of consciousness and will continue to exist until a purpose for its expulsion is internally discovered. Such a change can result only from a higher sense of awareness of oneself and a greater acceptance of one's past and one's people. Loving oneself cannot alone expel internalized oppression reinforced by selfishness. Only problems that are known can be addressed, and only those which are understood can be solved. To achieve these lofty levels of awareness requires first an awareness of one's philosophical and historical reality. Only then can a person's concrete reality be known and properly attended to.

What has just been outlined is an example of a critical analysis of a psycho-social problem. To identify the problem is only one component of the analytical process. Before a problem is solved, it must be fully understood. For the same reason, a question must be clearly understood before an answer is possible. Until this level of comprehension is reached, all behavior exists in a kind of free-fall situation in which anything goes. In this topsy-turvy, unidimensional world of appearances, "up" appears as "down," "in" appears as "out," and "stop" takes on the illusion of a command of "go." This latter condition is defined as right brain activity rather than analytical left brain activity. Emotion fuels right brain activity, while reason and calculation emanate from the left brain.

Thought and analytical reasoning are as much products of conditioning and internalized programming as emotions are. Reading, for example, involves exposing an individual to a world of ideas. Prohibition of reading creates a darkness in which only fun and games will seem to have merit. Thus we get two kinds of human beings: one conditioned to move forward and the other to go backwards. The furthest an individual can move backward is to the point of forgetting himself. Historical amnesia would be the clinical psychological term to describe the "Negro" condition. While this "Negro" moves farther and farther from himself and thus his reality, travel through time and space remains constant for persons who know themselves. These are persons with a functional past, which makes their present a comprehensive experience that connects the past with the future. This is the psychologically normal tridimensional existence of a people with a past, present, and future. The thoughts of such groups are analytical and their activity is purposeful. These people generally share a common interest and are thereby largely driven by necessity. A purpose fueled by necessity is among the most powerful forces on earth. A purpose fueled by necessity is second only to natural forces as an agent of change. This means analysis, logic, and persistence must consistently be the means for attaining progress.

To go from a unidimensional mind-set to tridimensional mind-set requires a revolution of mind and spirit by those suffering from the "Negro" syndrome. "Up" must once again become up, and "down" must be seen as the degrading and declining position and condition that it is. The African-American primary sufferer of the "Negro" condition must reject almost every view which he and she holds sacred. To suggest that the Negro was not coaxed into his present behavior is being disingenuous. Even though no visible second or third party is present, the Negro is not alone.

To have no self-interest is to have no need of programs to meet those needs. Such apathy forces an individual to relate solely to the interests of others. These interests may be proper for others, but, because of the psycho-social position of African-Americans such interest could be wholly unsuitable, as is the case today with much public school activity.

All persons must have a known center which resolves all contradictions concerning a people's major developmental needs. Knowing what Chinese people need is helpful only if one is Chinese. Objective analysis can only make sense if one has mastered the subjective nature of one's existence. Critical thinking must be an exercise of discovery made on the basis of one's psycho-social reality. It has little benefit otherwise. This is so because critical thought requires a conscious purpose lest it become thought void of analysis.

The above analysis serves to explain the results printed in the recently published book <u>The Bell Curve</u> and replaces the theory of inferiority based on race with an explanation of inferiority based on subjugation of the will of a people and the subsequent internalization of the subjugation. Learning in such a posture is overtly instructionally-dependent, making memory, not analysis, the primary means of achieving academic results. This is a process that only mimics the analytical process. In schools and colleges, logic is offered as a course and not as a practice. This tendency favors those whose existence is based on a practice of inductive and deductive logic and who, as a matter of practice, understand syllogistic reasoning. But what of those who have no functional history, period, to say nothing of a history of logical and analytical thought? What of those who seek the appearance of a thing rather than the thing itself? How does the acquisition of knowledge as a pursuit of excellence replace acquisition of a degree as a purpose of college? The fact is, if a pursuit has no purpose, the pursuit will be poorly pursued. Too often in our schools and colleges, students face few demands to think analytically, and if no purpose for doing so were ever present, it would matter little if they did.

Teachers of uncritical minds depend heavily on obedience to instruction to validate their students' rote response to the poorly understood instruction they earlier received. Such teachers rely on a "do as I say" approach rather than on anything resembling the Socratic method (of inviting the learner to think by introducing questions and problems, hypothetical or otherwise). To deduce from a general premise or to induce from a specific one is the foundation of a scientific mind. Contemporary students, however, are expected to swallow (without digesting) the conclusions of others. They are not asked to examine the nature and contents of the materials ingested. It's "swallow and regurgitate" at test time. This means that no digestion (or learning) takes place. Students briefly memorize details but then forget them. Such line-and-verse recitation is not only anachronistic but will eventually weaken the minds of those allowed to become so thought-dependent.

Thinking is critical only when it is done conceptually. Conceptual learning refers to understanding not only as a function but as a purpose as well. "Freedom," for example, conveys a word to some and a concept to others. A limited definition of the word "freedom" would be a state of not being held. Another could be an ability to come and go; still another meaning would suggest that a person not confined by iron bars and brick walls is free. The concept of freedom, however is much broader. It involves less an ability to come and go than an ability to perform a meaningful task or make a significant contribution as one strives to fulfill one's purpose in life. When we fail to teach and learn conceptually, we fail to learn the basics of the lesson. Today the physical chains that once restrained the Negro have been removed, but sadly the internalized oppression that maintains him in a state of inertia still remains.

Reflection On The "Cooperative Mode"
Dr. Josephine Boynes-Lewis

Introductory Note:

A. Jack Guillebeaux

The Cooperative Mode is a pattern for evolving cooperative relationships and a framework for evaluating relationships. It is built on the assumption of abundance as opposed to scarcity. Only seven items comprise the overarching concept of cooperation, all fitting on a single page. It is very easy to miss the power (or discount the breadth) of the Cooperative Mode. You are encouraged to make a substantial investment in understanding and unlocking the potential of this model for governing the interactions of individuals in groups. We have used the Cooperative Mode at FOCAL for many years and found its principles and approaches essential to creating a workplace that reflects our vision. Implementing the Cooperative Mode requires effort and motivation. Operating our agency in a competitive mode, however, requires even more energy, and the results are less productive and less pleasing.

The Cooperative Mode is an alternative to competitive modes of group interaction. Thus, because the Cooperative Mode *is* cooperative, it can not be successfully imposed on individuals or on a group but must be chosen. Consequently, the Cooperative Mode is best presented as an option, an alternative, or a strategy to improve the quality of one's personal life and the quality of interactions between individuals groups. A very powerful incentive for embracing the Cooperative Mode is its capacity to empower the individual. Your study of the Cooperative Mode will reveal that the individual will benefit from it, even if the group as a whole has not endorsed it.

This paper was prepared from audio tapes made at a workshop given by Dr. Josephine Boynes-Lewis. In our editing of her lengthy and detailed presentation for this very brief overview of the Cooperative Mode, we tried to maintain the spirit of her presentation by keeping her "voice" in the statement. This presentation (again, severely shortened) tries to convey a sense of Dr. Lewis "talking" to friends about the Cooperative Mode. I invite you to "hear" the voice of an exceptionally powerful psychotherapist, trainer, and group facilitator sharing insights and experiences relevant to the Cooperative Mode.

The Cooperative Mode

Dr. Josephine Boynes-Lewis
Center for Cooperative Change
Atlanta Georgia

The basic premise of the Cooperative Mode is that "there is enough." In our society, where commodities are presumed to be scarce, it is no wonder that, even in our relationships, competition is often more prevalent than cooperation. When commodities are assumed to be plentiful, there is no need for competition. The major commodities in relationships are time and energy. Since we all have the same amount of time, the only question is how much we are going to use our time to be with each other in any given relationship and how much energy we are going to give to each other at any given point in our relationship. The other commodity, of course, is strokes (positive affirmation, for being, having, and doing affirmations which can be expressed both verbally and physically). In a competitive relationship, strokes are seen as scarce and are used as a currency for manipulation and exploitation. In a cooperative relationship, strokes become the currency that is freely exchanged, as if they don't run out. Some call strokes the "fuel for life."

The second basic premise of cooperation and cooperative relationships is that the needs of each person are of equal importance. That means you don't have to prioritize your needs, because the assumption is that they <u>can</u> be met. Nor do you have to defer indefinitely to the other person's needs so that one person's needs are important all the time and the other person's needs are not as important all the time. Now, I use the word "needs". Let me stick in " wants," "wishes," "fantasies," and "intuitions" also. One way we try to get around the word "needs" is to say, "That wasn't exactly a need, that was a want." For this discussion of cooperation, wants, wishes, fantasies, and intuitions can be thought of as needs. Even little fleeting thoughts – each person's everything is of equal importance. When these two assumptions are not present (I want to know that my needs are as important as yours, and I want you to know that your needs are as important as mine) either implicitly or explicitly, three results that will occur and promote competition.

1. **Power plays will occur.**
2. **Rescues will occur.**
3. **There will be secrets and lies.**

Power Plays

A power play is an attempt to make another person do something s/he doesn't want to do or they haven't decided they want to do as yet. The rather strict definition of a power play is <u>an attempt to make another person do something s/he doesn't want to do</u>. The reason that I add the part about having not decided yet is that in a relationship where both people are invested (I say "both" because it is easier; any individual's investment could be 5% or 50%), both individuals won't mind doing just about anything if they have the time or realize the benefit to them for doing it. Part of the power play is "Hurry up and do it and act like you want to do it," and that becomes the issue more than whether the person really wants to do it.

So the significant part of the power play sometimes is not so much the attempt to make persons do what they don't want to do as it is the attempt to make them hurry up and do it and to act as if they want to do it before they have had time to come around. On the other hand, sometimes the power play strictly attempts to get people to do things that they do not want to do. Another aspect or characteristic of the power play can involve an attempt to make people give up things they have that they don't want to (or haven't decided to) give up. Such things could be time, strokes, energy, position, or anything else. In any case, they have got it, and it is yours to get. You can use a power play to get it; power plays don't work for very long.

There are two kinds of power plays. There is the "one up" power play which is initiated by the person who is perceived as the most powerful in rank or in an ostensible war at a social level. A power play initiated from a "one up" position has several characteristics. One is a "hurry up" facet, which makes persons in the "one down" position think fast, to justify what they want. People in "one up" positions assume they are right and will use muscle, a loud voice, fancy words, guilt, psychoanalytic language, patronizing attitudes, pseudo-nurturing attitudes, intrusion upon body space, and just plain violations of the other person. Sometimes, for example, they use commodities such as money or space. Whatever tactic they choose, they use it from a "one up" position. Sometimes in terms of commodities it is from a "one up" position. They have the money and they own the space, for example.

A "one down" power play (or one that is initiated from a "one down" position) creates the impression of wasting the time and energy of the person perceived to be "one up"; it elicits guilt and is aimed to be hurtful. We might see power plays from the one down position, for example, when a secretary "dutifully" puts Ms. Knowitall's airline tickets on her desk, but places them in a pile of papers that have not been touched in weeks; or when an aide "forgets" to put gas in the car, causing Mr. Important to have to stop as he streaks for the airport, or when an administrative assistant who "competently" receives calls for Mr. Neverseesmyimportance, and tells his boss that he is away from the office shopping for a birthday gift.

In cooperative relationships, people simply contract against power plays, so that each person asks for 100 percent of what they want 100 percent of the time. And since time doesn't run out, you don't have to ask for something the minute you want it. You can mull it over for a while. Similarly, each person does not always have to accept what s/he doesn't want. Instead, s/he might consider accepting part (or more) of it later. A cooperative relationship is like wearing a sign saying, "I'm available to be asked but I have the right to say 'no.'" I'm glad I said that. The "no" comment is very important. The myth in relationships is that because "no" is forever, it is an unsafe word that seems real scary and frightening. "No," however, <u>can</u> be changed into a "maybe" or into a "yes" – hence the need for negotiating.

A rescue is defined as doing anything you don't want to do or doing it before you know you want to. Rescuing has to do with the business of giving what <u>you want</u> when the other person might not want that. Doing what you want to do before you realize the benefit of doing it or simply doing what you do not want to do are other aspects of rescues. Rescuing means acting as if you are doing something from some kind of compulsion, as opposed to some assessment of the other person's needs. In descriptions and discussions of rescues, you may also hear a statement like "doing more than 50 percent of the 'work.'" That phrase should not be taken literally. There is nothing sacred about 50 percent. If you want to do 100 percent yourself, that isn't a rescue. Instead, it just means that you want to do 100 percent. If you want someone to stay out of the kitchen because you want to do 100 percent of the cooking, then cook. Or if you want the place perfectly clean and you'd rather do it yourself, do it. That's not a rescue. Doing your perception of your share plus the other person's share and being unwilling to negotiate is a rescue.

A more subtle rescue occurs when one person complains and the other person spends an hour trying to make the person complaining feel better and spends two hours justifying his or her own behavior. That, too, is a rescue, because there is no way to speak to what the other person wants if that person hasn't said it. Another subtle way of rescuing is to take a bunch of negative strokes (or positive strokes for that matter) that you don't want to take in order to keep the other person from feeling bad. It is a rescue to accept strokes that you don't want. It can also be a rescue to not ask for what you <u>do</u> want or to say, "I don't want to impose."

Rescues imply that the rescuer is inherently superior to the one being rescued. The message is that "I," the rescuer, "can do this better than you, can finish your sentence better than you, or am better at this than you." The rescuer expects to get positive strokes for the effort but generally will get punished. In other words, people don't like to be told that they just don't cut it, or that they are inferior, and they will find a way to blemish or punish the rescuer, even when they seem to issue an explicit or implicit "invitation" to be rescued. The best options for the rescuer are to ask if help is needed and to negotiate the provision of help.

Secrets and Lies

Let's begin with terms. As to secrets and lies, I'm not really talking about <u>overt</u> lying; instead, I mean pretending that you are happy when you are not or pretending to be angry when you stopped being angry an hour ago but find it's useful to let the impression of anger hang on. Such lying can also involve pretending you don't want something when you do, or pretending you do want something when you don't. That's the kind of lies we are talking about in relationships – the withholding of data. The same is true for secrets. Misrepresenting your feelings and withholding information are among my definitions of secrets. One problem with keeping secrets and telling lies is that doing so discounts the intuitions of the other persons. Another problem is that the energy around those secrets and around those lies is energy that might be used to enhance the relationship. Secrets and lies tie up energy in the process of covering up stuff, thereby preventing one from giving the main currency of a relationship, which is energy and strokes. Trying to cover one's tracks and making sure that certain subjects are not mentioned takes energy. In any kind of relationship, people intuit everything, which means that truth is rarely completely hidden. We may not know exactly what the truth is or we may not know its content, but we do know when another person's energy is withheld and a contact between ourselves and someone else is complicated somehow. The more we depend on lies and secrets, the more we distort our contact with others. The results of secrets and lies include suspicion, confusion, distrust and, often, a resolve not be too close to one who resorts to secrets and lies.

On the other hand, when everything is clear and free, you just know it. You feel it. It's just like the first stage of a marvelous romance, because (among other reasons) you don't even see all the flaws yet. All you see is just straight-on contact, and you haven't had these little arguments and short circuits. You just don't have all that accumulated "stuff." That is the best way I know to explain how to make full contact with another person and just not have any "stuff" in there. It's just clear.

There are ways to be in a cooperative relationship and still maintain your own space (your own privacy of thinking) without distorting the contact at all. One way is to respond to people's intuitions. If they ask, "What's wrong?" instead of replying, "Oh, nothing," it might he useful to take a minute to figure out what it might be. This kind of reaction can be summed up in the word "account." Part of accounting may be to say, "You're right on: I am a little out of sorts and I don't want to talk about it now." And it is usually pretty neat to say, "I will return to the subject at . . ." and give a time when you are willing to come back to the subject. The "I don't want to talk about it" is usually centered around fear of what's going to happen if you do, so the place to start is to ask for protection, so that whatever you fear can be neutralized with protection. Sometimes it takes persons some time to identify and acknowledge their fear. So far, I have not experienced anyone's truth that is more shattering that sensing someone is withholding and not having the data to support or contradict my feelings.

The competition that we see in relationships is simply a manifestation of the internal competition occurring in a person's head between "ego states" or parts of the person's psyche. So people who seem to be fighting with others and competing with others are often fighting just as much internally as you see them fighting externally. Such internal conflicts reflect alienation, isolation, and oppression. There is generally a part of a person that thinks another part of that person is more important than the first part. Let's run that by again: a person who hears an internal message saying "my needs are not important" will operate primarily from a "parent" orientation and will not pay attention to their "child" needs. On those subjects and issues which involve needs that such a person considers unimportant, the person will repress certain thoughts and feelings. Unfortunately, the person's mate or the people who work around the person will sometime play into (or in some way affirm) the "my needs are not important" position.

What I really want you to do is think about how the absence of cooperation in relationships may simply manifest an absence of cooperation between ego states within an individual.

However, since we've been so brainwashed into thinking competitively, displaying and internalizing oppression, discounting our awareness, and discounting our intuition, very often, we need a little help in getting our thoughts together. A particular structure which I call "process time" can help us gather out thoughts. "Process time" is simply time set aside (anybody can call it, or you can set aside a special time) for sharing resentments and checking out paranoid fantasies.

Sharing Resentments

Sharing of resentments is primarily for the benefit of the person doing the sharing. It is secondarily for the benefit of the person who might be willing to listen. One might begin simply by saying "I have a resentment," and then by asking "Are you willing to hear it?" One benefit of prefacing the sharing in this way is that doing so gives the intended receiver of the resentment the option of hearing it at a time when that person can really take it in. Thus, if the person doesn't want to hear it at the moment, s/he might be willing to hear it later. One should negotiate for a time when one's resentment can be heard. If, however, the resentment seems likely to burst out, one can go into a rest-room or the kitchen and share it. One can express the resentment in this way but then come on back and do something else. It is very important to know that sharing a resentment primarily benefits the person who has it. In fact, I would guess that about 95 percent of all resentments reflect not another person's behavior itself but our fantasies about that person's behavior.

Checking out Paranoid Fantasies

Sometime we observe a person's behavior and jump to conclusions that are not even related to that behavior. This kind of false judgment can be prevented if we analyze our fantasies. For an example, I might say "My fantasy is that when you didn't meet me at the door and tell me how nice the flowers were, I concluded that you didn't appreciate them and all you wanted to do was dump problems on me. Is that true?" Keeping with the commitment to tell the truth and not keep our feelings secret, the other person might respond by saying, "Well, yes, it's true that at the time I didn't appreciate the flowers because they just gave me some more work to do. I had to find a vase and put them in water when my computer is down. So, yes, that part of your fantasy is true. I didn't at the time appreciate the flowers. But it is not true that all I want to do is dump problems on you. I do want you to look at my computer now. And, now that you mention it, the flowers <u>are</u> lovely, and I thank you for them."

What I am looking for when I listen to fantasies being shared is <u>both</u> sides. I want as much to hear the part that is true as to hear the part that isn't true. There <u>is</u> always something that's "true" – the basis of the hunch or intuition. Now, you don't have to be digging and searching for the "truth" of another person's intuition about you. You can just say, "No, that invitation is not true, and that response is all I can think of at the moment." I'm really not encouraging pop-psychology navel gazers to "seek the truth." You don't have to dig way down. Instead, just share your present feelings, and maybe later you'll think of the other side of the coin and perceive the "true" basis of the paranoid fantasy of the other person. This tactic is helpful in working with people who are highly suspicious, too, because their intuition is usually really heightened and you can believe that at least part of what they are saying is true. When someone does something that causes us to have a paranoid fantasy, the Cooperative Mode calls for checking the fantasy's possible truth out. We should seek information and gather data about the incident. This information-gathering process produces better results when anger, sadness, and fear are set aside. In other words, we should give the other person the benefit of the doubt. We should not behave out of anger, sadness, or fear because we assume that we "know" what the other person meant, or believed, or intended, or wanted, or whatever (fill in the blank). When we set such feelings aside, the other person is more likely to respond to our questions rather than responding to our feelings. After the facts have been established, there is always time to share our feelings of anger, sadness, and fear.

Strokes

Perhaps the most important part of the Cooperative Mode involves giving strokes. For our discussion, I am defining a "stroke" as a unit of recognition. Any behavior that recognizes another person (a smile, a spoken word, a hug, or even a blow) is an indication that the other person exists and that you recognize the other person. The use of the currency of strokes involves offering strokes and receiving strokes, fully asking for strokes and even self-stroking, or refusing strokes you don't want. In families and at our places of work we create what might be called a "stroke economy." A group in which individuals share a lot of positive strokes, in which there is a sense of abundance of recognition, affirmation, attention, and positive confrontation, might be thought of as having a rich stroke economy. Each of us contributes to the "stroke economy" of the groups in which we are members. Our contribution or pattern of giving and receiving strokes either helps to enrich the stroke economy or helps to impoverish it. We should also remember that human beings need strokes. Receiving positive strokes or strokes that affirm our being and that affirm the good things that we do and have are essential to our well-being. In fact, responses from others are so important that we will even seek and live on negative strokes if we can not get positive affirmations of ourselves.

Strokes can be categorized four ways. I have mentioned positive and negative strokes. These two categories can be divided into two additional categories: conditional and unconditional. Thus, strokes can be positive conditional and positive unconditional, and negative conditional and negative unconditional. Three of these four categories of strokes are kinds of strokes that we should use. Negative unconditional strokes, however, should be avoided, because they are attacks on a person's being. In such cases we are saying something like "I hate you" or "You should not have been born" or "You will never amount to anything." I have not found any justification for these kinds of strokes. On the other hand, conditional positive and negative strokes, strokes for having and for doing, are strokes we should use freely. The stroke economy is richer when we find ways to use more positive conditional than negative conditional strokes, but, even negative conditional strokes can provide others with valuable information and are necessary if we hope to set limits and establish boundaries.

We can deal with strokes in five basic ways. We can give them, receive them, reject them, and ask for them, and we can even-self stroke (that is, give ourselves strokes). Most of us, however, have not been prepared to freely use strokes in all five ways. For example, usually we are told that we should never ask for affirmation or recognition. We are told that we should be suspicious of people who offer strokes because they probably want something. Other messages tell us not to accept strokes because we might get a "big head." Our challenge is to discover or rediscover the truth and power of strokes and learn to use strokes appropriately in all of these ways, both in relation to others and in relation to ourselves. Make no mistake, it is difficult to change the patterns we learned in earliest childhood, but the good news is that we can influence and enrich the stroke economy in all of the groups to which we belong.

Confidentiality

The last element of the Cooperative Mode, confidentiality, is essential to the creation of an environment that invites people to examine their thinking, feelings and behavior honestly and critically and to try out new and different ways of being together in a group. As participants explore the Cooperative Mode and try out its different elements, they probably will expose attitudes, prejudices, and patterns of behavior which can be used by others to disparage, blemish, or otherwise penalize them. In the process of discovery, individuals might tap into thoughts, feelings, and behaviors that arouse anger, sadness, fear, shame, guilt, and confusion. Because <u>changing</u> outdated and dysfunctional thinking and behavior is the objective of the Cooperative Mode, making the environment safe for all persons to express themselves honestly must be the highest priority. In order for everyone to understand fully the contract for confidentiality, offering some examples like the following might be necessary: a) "It is agreed that no one here will take what is shared here and use it negatively in any way"; b) "If anyone wants to respond to something that was offered by someone else, s/he will ask the person who shared for permission to respond and will give that person the freedom to say 'no'"; c) "Even if you are speaking privately with someone away from this setting where the Cooperative Mode is in operation, you should ask permission to bring up things that happened at the session."

The Cooperative Mode is a very powerful instrument for change. Although it is certainly helpful for all members of a group to participate, full participation is not necessary for significant benefits to be realized. The Cooperative Mode is directed towards empowering the individual, recognizing that each individual is 50 percent of all transactions with another person. When the principles of the Cooperative Mode are lived out by one individual, they will have a positive impact on all relationships. Most importantly, however, they will raise the self-esteem, enhance the communication, and generally improve the quality of human interactions of the individual who chooses to learn and apply the tools of the Cooperative Mode.

More Is Caught Than Taught Resource Guide

This resource guide is intended to offer you a variety of materials to choose from as you go through the *MCTT* modules and beyond. There is an enormous amount of resource material available, and this guide is not meant to be comprehensive or limiting. If you have a great resource we haven't included, follow what you know and use it! Better yet, send us a postcard with the title so that we'll know about it, too.

The materials listed here are written from a wide variety of perspectives and represent many different viewpoints. In some cases we have noted in our annotation things which may be of special interest to *MCTT* participants. We have also noted if there is something missing that *MCTT* participants might be seeking. In general, we encourage you to choose those resources which reflect your vision, goals, and program and those which you believe represent the spirit of *MCTT*. We also leave it to you to take what you need and want from these resources – if one chapter speaks to you and the rest do not, keep what's valuable for you and disregard what's not. Resources are meant to help you in putting together your own curriculum and program, and that is the spirit in which we offer you this guide.

This guide is divided into sections for books, catalogues, bibliographies, and videos. For the most part, each selection contains title, author, date, publication information, price, and a brief explanatory text. In cases where the resource is not readily available in bookstores or other stores, we have included information as to where it can be obtained. Finally, each entry contains a reference to the *MCTT* module(s) we believe it fits the best. Often these resources apply to more than one module, and occasionally we identify specific chapters or sections as relevant to specific modules. Again, we hope you will take from this guide what you want and find it useful as you build and supplement your new curriculum.

BOOKS

An Administrator's Guide to an Individualized Performance Results Curriculum,

William E. Stradley

(Curriculum, Lesson Planning, and Assessment)

Affirming Culture in Early Childhood Programs, Stacey York, Toys N' Things Press, 1991. Distributed by Gryphon House. 205 pages. $22.95. (Roots and Wings Book Store)

The belief behind this book is that by endowing children with the courage of their cultural roots you give them the power of wings to soar above prejudice. The book includes over 60 hands-on activities for increasing children's understanding of differences. Topics include a step-by-step plan for implementing multicultural education, how to train a staff to integrate cultural awareness, and ideas for talking with children about culture.

(Curriculum, Lesson Planning, and Assessment)

Ages and Stages, Karen Miller. Telshare Publishing Co., 1985. 153 pages. $12.95.

(Available through Redleaf Press)

A useful guide to the behavior of young children in groups. Short, clear descriptions of the behavior of young children (birth-8) at different stages, and an extensive list of age-appropriate activities.

(Early Childhood Theory; Curriculum, Lesson Planning, and Assessment)

Alike and Different: Exploring Our Humanity with Young Children, Bonnie Neugebauer, ed. NAEYC, 1992. 186 pages. $10.95.

A collection of writings on diversity and cultural awareness in early childhood programs by Louise Derman-Sparks (Anti-Bias Curriculum), Karen Miller (Ages and Stages), Margie Carter (Training Teachers) and others. The book is divided into chapters including "Meeting the Needs of All Children," "Staffing with Diversity," "Learning from Parents; Living in a Changing World," and "Considering Our Resources."

(How to BE Together; Curriculum, Lesson Planning, and Assessment)

The Anti-Bias Curriculum: Tools for Empowering Young Children, Louise Derman-Sparks and the A.B.C. Task Force. NAEYC, 1989. 150 pages. $8.95.

A widely used and well-respected curriculum for integrating anti-bias practices and beliefs into the early childhood classroom or home. The author specifically distinguishes an "anti-bias" from a "multicultural" approach. A focus on multiculturalism, she feels, often results in a "tourist curriculum" in which the food, customs, and holidays of other countries and cultures are celebrated but are distinguished from the main body of the curriculum, which remains centered on White Americans. An anti-bias curriculum integrates diversity and exploration of difference into every activity. The book is clearly written, with helpful stories and a useful chart for selecting children's books that address diversity.

(Early Childhood Theory; Curriculum, Lesson Planning, and Assessment)

Approaches to Preschool Curriculum, Michael C. Anziano, Jane Billman, Marjorie J. Kostelnik and Cathleen S. Soundy. Glencoe/McGraw-Hill, 1995. 448 pages. $22.

This book describes the various leading approaches to preschool curriculum and discusses the focus, goals, structure, and implementation techniques of each approach. The book also illustrates how curriculum goals can be developed by teachers and how different kinds of classroom activities can help meet these goals. Each chapter contains illustrative examples and a helpful review section with a summary, questions, and list of resources for further information.

(Work Planning)

Beginnings: The Social and Affective Development of Black Children, Margaret B. Spencer, Geraldine K. Brookins and Walter R. Allen, eds. Lawrence Erlbaum Associates, 365 Broadway, Hillsdale, NJ, 07642; 1985. 375 pages. $36.

This collection of essays about African-American children's development offers theories, paradigms, empirical studies and commentaries by psychologists, sociologists, historians, and others. The book's aim is to enlarge the reader's understanding by providing fact-based assessments of the environmental conditions, social relationships, and psychological states which influence Black children's growth and development.

(Early Childhood Theory)

Beyond Self-Esteem: Developing a Genuine Sense of Human Value, N.E. Curry, C.N. Johnson. NAEYC, 1990.

(Early Childhood Theory)

Black and White Styles in Conflict, Tom Kochman. University of Chicago Press. $8.95.

(How To BE Together)

Black Children: Their Roots, Culture and Learning Styles, Janice E. Hale-Benson. Johns Hopkins University Press, 1982. Revised edition. 215 pages. $14.95.

In this book, early-childhood professor Hale-Benson argues that American educators have largely failed to recognize the crucial significance of culture in the education of Black children. She draws on the fields on anthropology, sociology, history, and psychology to explore the effects of African-American culture on a child's intellectual development, and she argues that cultural factors produce group differences which must be addressed in the educational process.

(Early Childhood Theory; Internalized Oppression)

Black in Selma, J.L. Chestnut, Jr. and Julia Cass. Farrar, Straus, and Giroux, 1990. 431 pages. $22.95.

In this autobiography, J.L. "Chess" Chestnut talks about his youth in segregated Selma, his experiences as Selma's first Black lawyer, his participation in the Civil Rights movement, and his thoughts on politics and race in Alabama today.

(Vision)

A Black Parent's Handbook To Educating Your Children (Outside of the Classroom), Baruti K. Kafele. Baruti Publishing, P.O. Box 434, Fords, NJ 08863, (201) 433-9484;1991. 76 pages. $5.95.

This book was written to provide Black parents with ideas, suggestions, strategies and techniques for supporting and continuing children's education at home. It includes chapters on parent-teacher-child partnership, peer group influence, studying and test-taking strategies, and goals.

(Vision)

The Bluest Eye, Toni Morrison. NAL/Dutton, 1994. $12.95.

(Internalized Oppression)

Bus Ride To Justice, Fred Gray. Black Belt Press, 1995. $25.

(Vision)

Caring Communities: Supporting Young Children and Families, National Task Force on School Readiness. National Association of State Boards of Education, (703) 684-4000; 1991. $10.

This report highlights the national goals for school readiness and promoting school readiness through caring communities. Among the topics discussed are the need for comprehensive support for young children and families and the development of parent involvement and family-focused policies and services. The booklet illustrates the goals with stories from different schools. This is a good resource for learning about national policy and advocacy for children.

(Work Planning)

Caring for Infants and Toddlers: A Supervised Self-Instructional Training Program, Diane Trister Dodge, Amy Dombro and Derry Gosselin Koralek, volumes 1 and 2. Teaching Strategies. 360 pages. $34.95.

A comprehensive, self-paced set of training materials that covers the 13 functional areas in the Child Development Associate (CDA) Competency Standards.

(Curriculum, Lesson Planning and Assessment; Work Planning)

Child Development: Instructor's Annotated Edition. Glencoe, a division of Macmillan/McGraw-Hill, 1995. $54.75.

This is a valuable book for learning about various early childhood theories regarding children's physical, social, intellectual, and emotional development, as well as the impact of the family and other factors. It is divided into sections on infants, toddlers, preschoolers, and school-age children, with an initial overview section. The work of theorists such as Piaget, Erikson, Skinner, and Freud is well-covered, although Montessori's theory is discussed less fully. Each chapter contains illustrative examples and a helpful review section with a summary, questions, and list of resources for further information. The teacher's annotated edition also has helpful information and discussion questions at the bottom of each page.

(Early Childhood Theory)

Child Health Talk, The National Black Child Development Institute.

(Environment)

Child Observation Record: High Scope Child Observation Record for Ages 2½-6, High/Scope Educational Research Foundation, 1992.

(Curriculum, Lesson Planning, and Assessment)

Childhood and Society (2nd edition), Erik Erikson. Norton Books, 1963. $11.95.

In this book, Erikson lays out his theory of the social and emotional development of human beings, the "eight stages of man." The first stage, "trust versus mistrus;" the second stage, "autonomy versus shame and doubt;" and the third stage, "initiative versus guilt," occur approximately in the child's first six years, according to Erikson.

(Early Childhood Theory)

Children and Books I: African American Story Books and Activities for All Children, Patrcia Buerke Moll. Hampton Mae Institute, 4104 Lynn Avenue, Tampa, FL 33603, 1991. $14.95.

This book contains many stories for and about African-American children, accompanied by suggestions for fun activities including puppet shows, baking, acting out the story, dancing, and visiting a museum.

(Curriculum, Lesson Planning, and Assessment)

The Color Purple, Alice Walker. Pocket Books, 1985. $12.

(Vision)

The Complete Book of Forms for Managing the Early Childhood Program, Kathleen Watkins and Lucius Durant. 1990. $34.95.

(Work Planning)

Creating Newsletters, Brochures, and Pamphlets: A How-To-Do-It Manual, Barbara Radke Blake, Barbara L. Stein. Neal-Schuman Publishers, 100 Varick Street, New York, NY 10013. 1992.

This guide includes information for novices and experienced newsletter editors on planning and budgeting decisions, design, paper, production, writing tips, developing ideas and sources, and equipment.

(Work Planning)

The Creative Curriculum, Diane Trister Dodge. Teaching Strategies, 1988. $29.95.

(Curriculum, Lesson Planning, and Assessment; Work Planning)

Creative Resources for the Early Childhood Classroom, Judy Herr, Yvonne Libby. Delmar Publishers, 1995. 2nd edition. 624 pages. $35.95. (Available through Gryphon House)

With ready-to-use activities organized into 57 themes – including gardens, construction tools, zoo animals, and hats – this resource book provides a child-centered approach to learning. Each weekly section has a ready-to-copy letter for parents suggesting activities they can use at home to extend the week's learning. Every unit includes a flow chart, theme goals, concepts for the children to learn, vocabulary words, how to integrate the themes into learning centers, and resource books.

(Curriculum, Lesson Planning, and Assessment)

Crews: Gang Members Talk to Maria Hinojosa. Harcourt Brace and Company, 1995. 168 pages. $9.

This is a series of interviews with teenage gang members in which they talk about their lives, what their gangs or "crews" mean to them, and what they believe their future holds. It is an excellent tool for learning about the challenges facing our children and our society today and for examining the phenomenon of internalized oppression. Tapes of the original interviews can also be purchased from National Public Radio. This is a valuable resource for teenagers as well as adults.

(Internalized Oppression)

Day Care Do-It-Yourself Staff Growth Program, Polly Greenberg. The Growth Program, 1975.

(Work Planning)

Developing Cross-Cultural Competence: A Guide for Working with Young Children and Their Families, E.W. Lynch and M.J. Hanson. Paul H. Brooks Publishing Co., 1992. 404 pages. $37.25 (Available through Redleaf Press)

This book helps child care providers be aware of their own culture-specific attitudes and practices and the issues that arise when working with diverse cultures. The book introduces eight U.S. groups with different cultural roots by describing each group's history, values, and beliefs. The final section contains suggestions for successfully interacting with people from different cultures.

("How to BE Together")

Developing Individualized Family Support Plans, Tess Bennett, Barbara V. Lingerfelt and Donna E. Nelson. Brookline Books, P. O. Box 1046, Cambridge, MA 02238-1046. $24.95.

A training manual to accompany Enabling and Empowering Families *by Dunst, Trivett, and Deal. Focusing on partnerships between child care providers and families, it provides functional and practical materials to train professionals about implementing family-centered individualized family support plans. Chapters include: Working with Families, Needs and Aspirations; Strengths and Capabilities, Support and Resources, The Effective Help-Giver, Writing Family Support Plans, and Case Studies. Each chapter has trainer's notes, points to look for, and relevant activities. Also included are assessment and IFSP forms, a training checklist, and a list of resources.*

(Work Planning)

Developmental Psychology of the Black Child, Amos N. Wilson. Africana Research Publication, 2580 Adam Clayton Powell, Jr. Blvd, New York, NY 10039; 1978.

This book addresses some of the compelling issues of child development and racial differences from a Black perspective. The author looks at various stages of children's development and at how racism and poverty affect children at each stage. Among other thing he examines the role of Black English in communication, the socialization of Black children, and the "hidden agenda" of IQ and other standardized tests. The book's style and tone are quite academic, but there are many strong, interesting facts and persuasive arguments to interest all readers.

(Internalized Oppression [Chapter 3 especially]; Early Childhood Theory)

Developmentally Appropriate Practice in Early Childhood Programs: Serving Children from Birth through Age 8, Sue Bredekamp, ed. NAEYC, 1987. Expanded edition. 92 pages. $5.50.

(Early Childhood Theory; Curriculum, Lesson Planning, and Assessment; Work Planning)

Dialogue: Racism, the Monster in Our Midst, Rita Starr. Self-evaluation Consultants, P.O. Box 110, Evanston, IL 60204; (708) 492-0123.1993.

This is the first program in a three-part series developed to foster local community leadership to educate communities about the inherent goodness of human beings and how they are conditioned to perpetuate racism, sexism, anti-Semitism, etc. Communities who wish to participate in the 12-week program to educate, heal, and move toward the elimination of racism can purchase a facilitator's manual and a 300-page resource binder. The manual has clear, helpful definitions and exercises.

(Internalized Oppression)

Different and Wonderful: Raising Black Children in a Race-Conscious Society, Dr. Darlene Powell Hopson and Dr. Derek S. Hopson. Fireside, a division of Simon & Schuster, 1990. 242 pages. $10.

This book by two African-American psychologists is full of stories, insightful questions, and personal quizzes to help Black parents prepare their children for the race-consciousness that pervades

American society. The authors make many suggestions for how to promote self-esteem, pride, and positive racial identity throughout the child's youth. There is a helpful, age-appropriate resource guide of books, educational materials, dolls, and games.

(Vision; Environment; Internalized Oppression)

Diversity in the Classroom: A Multicultural Approach to the Education of Young Children, Frances E. Kendall. Teachers College Press, 1983. 111 pages. $14.95.

In this book Frances Kendall focuses on classroom activities and on the attitudes of the adults who interact with the children, addressing both the development of children's racial attitudes and the relationship between an individual teacher's racial attitudes and institutional racism. At the heart of this book is the assumption that these two aspects of multicultural education – teachers' racial attitudes and a multicultural classroom environment – cannot be separated if our goal is positive, growth-producing education for all children.

(Internalized Oppression; Curriculum, Lesson Planning, and Assessment)

Early Violence Prevention: Tools for Teachers of Young Children, Ronald Slaby, Wendy Roedell, Diane Arezzo and Kate Hendrix. NAEYC, 1995. $7.

(Curriculum, Lesson Planning, and Assessment)

Empowering African-American Males to Succeed: A Ten-Step Approach for Parents and Teachers, Mychal Wynn. Rising Sun Publishing. $15.95.

(Vision; Curriculum, Lesson Planning, and Assessment)

Enabling and Empowering Families: Principles and Guidelines for Practice, Carol Dunst, Carol Trivette, and Angela Deal. Brookline Books, 1988. $24.95.

("How to BE Together"; Work Planning)

Essentials For Child Development: Associates Working With Young Children, Carol Brunson-Phillips. Council for Early Childhood Professional Recognition. $30.

(Curriculum, Lesson Planning, and Assessment)

Explorations with Young Children, Anne Mitchell and Judy Davis, eds. 1992.

(Curriculum, Lesson Planning, and Assessment)

Families and Early Childhood Programs, Douglas R. Pell. NAEYC, 1989. $6.

("How to BE Together"; Work Planning)

The Giant Encyclopedia of Theme Activities for Children 2 to 5, Kathy Charnek, ed. Gryphon House, 1993. 512 pages $29.95.

This book contains over 600 "favorite activities" created by teachers for teachers. The result of a nationwide competition, the book covers 48 themes, which have all been tested by teachers and children.

(Curriculum, Lesson Planning, and Assessment)

A Great Place to Work, Paul Jorde Bloom. NAEYC, 1988. $15.

This book helps us define more precisely what our problems may be as a group and points a way toward solutions that staff and supervisory people can work out together. How is your program in terms of collegiality, professional growth, supervisor support, clarity, reward system, decision-making, task orientation, physical setting, and innovativeness? This book touches on all these topics in an easy-to-digest style.

("How to be Together")

Growing Pains: Helping Children Deal with Everyday Problems through Reading, Maureen Caddigan and Mary Beth Hanson. American Library Association. $51.30.

(Early Childhood Theory; Curriculum, Lesson Planning, and Assessment)

A Guide for Supervisors and Trainers on Implementing the Creative Curriculum, Diane Trister Dodge and Laura J. Colker. Teaching Strategies, 1988. $29.95

(Curriculum, Lesson Planning, and Assessment; Work Planning)

Helping Young Children Understand Peace, War, and the Nuclear Threat, Nancy Carlsson-Paige, Diane E. Levin. NAEYC, 1985. $3.

This book offers parents and teachers ways to assist children growing up in the nuclear age. It is divided into four chapters: "Young Children's Thinking" "Children's Thinking about War" "Talking with Children about War and Peace" and "Creating a Classroom to Foster Children's Understanding of War and Peace." It also has an annotated bibliography of resources addressing issues of war and peace.

(Environment)

How to Generate Values in Young Children: Integrity, Honesty, Individuality, Self-Confidence, and Wisdom, Sue Spayth Riley. NAEYC, 1984. $4.50.

(Vision; Environment)

How to Talk So Kids Will Listen and Listen So Kids Will Talk, Adele Faber and Elaine Mazlish. Avon Books, 1980. 242 pages. $7.95.

This book is a superb resource for adults to examine how they interact with children and to develop new means of communicating that will encourage and respect both the children and themselves. It is filled with helpful stories, illustrations, and exercises and is written in an informal, convincing style.

(Environment, "How to BE Together")

I Know Why the Caged Bird Sings, Maya Angelou. Mass Market Paperback, 1971. $5.50.

(Vision; Environment)

Implementing Family-Centered Services in Early Intervention: A Team-Based Model for Change, Donald B. Bailey, Jr., P.J. McWilliam, Pamela J. Winton and Rune J. Simeonsson. Brookline Books, 1992.

This book describes a team-based decision-making workshop for implementing family-centered services in early intervention. The purpose of the workshop is to provide a structure for teams to identify the concrete aspects of a family-centered approach, to assess their current programs in light of this identification, and to implement whatever changes they choose for making their program family-centered. Included in the book are activities and suggestions related to key questions about family-centered services.

(Work Planning)

In a Different Voice: Psychological Theory and Women's Development, Carol Gilligan. Harvard University Press, 1982. $10.95.

In this book, Harvard professor Gilligan asserts that Piaget's concepts of moral development in children are one-sided because they are based primarily on observation of boys. Gilligan believes that boys and girls respond differently to situations requiring moral judgment: boys tend to reason based on logical consistency, while girls reason with a more caring approach, focusing on group needs and consensus.

(Early Childhood Theory)

In My Place, Charlayne Hunter-Gault, Farrar, Straus and Giroux. 1992, 257 pages. $19.

Charlayne Hunter-Gault, now a national correspondent for PBS's MacNeil/Lehrer News Hour, describes in this autobiography her childhood in Georgia and her role as one of two Black students to desegregate the University of Georgia. This is an inspiring, compelling story of a young woman with vision, courage, and the belief that her "place" is wherever she wants it to be.

(Vision)

Infants and Toddlers: Curriculum and Teaching, LaVisa Cam Wilson. Delmar Publishers, 1986. 328 pages. $10.

This book provides information to help caregivers select and use curriculum appropriately individualized for each child in their care. With sections on infant and toddler care, designing infant and toddler curriculum, and matching caregiver strategies to child development, the book focuses on curriculum which provides for the physical, emotional, social, and cognitive development of the child.

(Early Childhood Theory; Curriculum, Lesson Planning, and Assessment)

Learning Centers for Young Children, Georgia Bradley Houle. Consortium Publishing, 1987. Third edition. 90 pages. $21.95. (Available through Redleaf Press)

A practical approach to understanding the role of learning centers in the early childhood classroom. For each of the 17 centers, information is provided: educational values, material to be available in the center, general comments, layouts, and vignettes. The vignettes describe the centers in use by real children and highlight the value of the centers in children's learning. Some of the centers include Staff and Parent Area; Painting and Sculpture, Collage and Construction; Water and Sand; Mathematics; Living Things; Family Life; and Dramatic Play.

(Environment)

Learning Environments for Children, Henry Sanoff and Joan Sanoff. Humanics Learning, 1981. $22.95.

(Environment; Curriculum, Lesson Planning, and Assessment)

Manchild in the Promised Land, Claude Brown. NAL/Dutton, 1976. $6.99.

(Environment)

Maria Montessori: Dr. Montessori's Own Handbook, A Short Guide to Her Ideas and Materials, Maria Montessori. Schocken Books, N.Y., 1965. 190 pages, $8.95.

This is the book that Maria Montessori wrote in response to requests from thousands of American parents and teachers. A short, illustrated guide for the use of Montessori classroom materials, it shows how to set up a "children's house," an environment for learning where children can be their own masters, free to learn at their own pace. It also discusses self-correcting learning tools which stimulate children's powers of observation, recognition, judgment, and classification.

(Early Childhood Theory)

The Measure of Our Success: A Letter to My Children and Yours, Marian Wright Edelman. Beacon Press, 1992. 97 pages. $15.

An inspiring book by the head of the Children's Defense Fund. In this letter to her three sons, Marian Wright Edelman shares her love, moral conviction, and vision of a better world for all of America's children. Her twenty-five lessons for life, which include "There is no free lunch," "Set goals and work quietly and systematically toward them," and "Don't be afraid of taking risks or of being criticized," are lessons for us all.

(Vision)

Multicultural Crafts for Kids. Lakeshore. 1-800-421-5354

(Curriculum, Lesson Planning, and Assessment)

A Multicultural Guide to Thematic Units for Young Children, Dr. Jeri A. Carroll and Dr. Dennis J. Kear. Good Apple, 1204 Buchanan St., Box 299, Carthage, IL 62321-0299; 1993.

This book for teaching young children about different cultures emphasizes how people value many of the same things, although in various ways. Topics included are celebrations, birthdays, food, family, and clothes.

(Curriculum, Lesson Planning, and Assessment)

Nutrition, Health and Safety for Preschool Children, Roberta Duyff, Susan Giarrantano and Mary Zuzich. Glencoe/ McGraw-Hill, 1995. $22.

(Curriculum, Lesson Planning, and Assessment)

Nutrition, Health and Safety for Preschool Children (Study Guide), Roberta Duyff, Susan Giarrantano and Mary Zuzich. Glencoe/McGraw-Hill, 1995.

(Work Planning)

Observing Development of the Young Child, Janice J. Beaty Merrill, 1986. 2nd edition. 386 pages. $21.

This book presents a system for observing and recording the development of young children in an early childhood setting. It focuses on observation of the six major aspects of child development: emotional, social, motor, cognitive, language, and creative. The text includes a child skills checklist with activities for children described after each checklist item.

(Curriculum, Lesson Planning, and Assessment)

Our World: A Planning Guide For the Kindergarten and First Grade Curriculum, Ann Overton and Jeanne James. 1989.

(Curriculum, Lesson Planning, and Assessment)

The Outside Play and Learning Book, Karen Miller. Gryphon House, 1990. 254 pages. $14.95.

This book contains hundreds of age-appropriate and challenging activities and games to engage the toddler or preschooler. Chapters include "Splish and Splash: Things To Do with Water" and "Dig it! Things To Do with Sand and Mud." Each activity includes ways of extending the play and discusses what children learn from the play.

(Curriculum, Lesson Planning, and Assessment)

A Parent's Guide to Early Childhood Education, Diane Trister Dodge and Joanna Phinney. Teaching Strategies, 22 pages. $1.75.

In concise language and clear illustrations, this handbook explains the goals of a developmentally appropriate program, what children learn from activities, the learning environment, daily schedule and conversations. The handbook also explains how parents and teachers can work together to help children acquire the skills, attitudes, and habits to excel in school and throughout life.

(Getting Started)

Parents Unite! The Complete Guide for Shaking Up Your Children's School, Philip and Susan Jones. Wideview, 1976. 263 pages. $4.95.

This is a how-to book for parents who want more say in their children's schools. The attention is on K-12 schools and not child care centers, and the tone of the book is quite confrontational: "How to pit parent power against teacher power" is one example. The book does have some helpful advice for starting and revitalizing parents' groups, raising money, and empowering parents to participate more fully in children's education.

("How to BE Together"; Work Planning)

Perceptual-Motor Development Guide, Melinda Bossenmeyer. Front Row Experience, 1988. $10.

(Curriculum, Lesson Planning, and Assessment)

The Piaget Handbook for Teachers and Parents, Rosemary Peterson and Victoria Felton-Collins. Teachers College Press, 1986. 72 pages. $12.95. (Available through Redleaf Press).

This handbook provides an overview of Piaget's theory in relation to early childhood learning. Activities with everyday materials are suggested which encourage parents and teachers to observe how children think as well as what they learn. A glossary fully explains the terminology of Piaget's work.

(Early Childhood Theory)

Places and Spaces for Preschool and Primary (Outdoors), Jeanne Vergeront. NAEYC, 1988. $3.

(Curriculum, Lesson Planning, and Assessment)

Planning Activities for Child Care: A Curriculum Guide for Early Childhood Education, Caroline Spang Rosser. The Goodheart-Willcox Company, 1993. 504 pages. $31. (Available through Gryphon House)

This is a collection of over 378 activities grouped into six units: community helpers, friends, me, I'm special, nursery rhymes, pets, and transportation. It includes a discussion of how to plan, set up, and implement a play program for 2-, 3-, 4-, and 5-year-old-children. Included are sample daily schedules, themes, sample letters, and bibliographies for each unit, accompanied by lots of graphics and drawings.

(Curriculum, Lesson Planning, and Assessment)

The Portfolio and Its Use: Developmentally Appropriate Assessment of Young Children, Cathy Grace and Elizabeth Shores. Southern Early Childhood Association, 1994. $10.

(Curriculum, Lesson Planning, and Assessment)

Practical Solutions to Practically Every Problem: The Early Childhood Teacher's Manual, Steffen Saifer. Redleaf Press, 1990. 190 pages. $24.95

Hundreds of practical, tested solutions for a wide range of problems in the child care setting. Based on child development theory, these suggestions are arranged into chapters including Daily Dilemmas, Classroom Concerns, Children Who Are Challenging, Working with Parents, Working with Other Staff, Your Own Needs, and Promoting Yourself as a Professional.

(Curriculum, Lesson Planning, and Assessment; Work Planning)

Principles of Parenting, H. Wallace Goddard. Alabama Cooperative Extension Service, Auburn University, AL 36849-5612.

This is a series of circulars for parents with direct, useful strategies and advice for helping children develop, enjoying each child as an individual, building family strengths, dealing with the challenges of parenting, and more. Each circular has personal examples, fun drawings, and a list of resources for more information.

(Environment, Early Childhood Theory; Curriculum, Lesson Planning, and Assessment)

The Promised Land: The Great Black Migration and How It Changed America, Nicholas Lemann. Vintage Books, 1991. 408 pages. $14.

This book documents the great migration of African-Americans from the South to the North between 1940 and 1970. It tells the stories of men and women who left the poverty and oppression of the South for a piece of the American dream in the North, only to find that this region, too, held many false promises for Black Americans. It conveys their dreams, their disappointments, and the way this migration changed and continues to change American society.

(Vision)

Race Matters, Cornel West. Beacon Press, 1993. $15.

(Vision)

Raising Black Children, James Comer and Alvin Poussaint. NAL/Dutton, 1992. $13.95.

More Is *Caught* Than Taught — Appendix D — Page 249

(Early Childhood Theory)

Reaching Potentials: Appropriate Curriculum and Asssessment for Young Children Vol 1., Sue Bredekamp and Teresa Rosegrant. NAEYC, 1992. $7.

(Curriculum, Lesson Planning, and Assessment)

Reconceptualizing the Early Childhood Curriculum, Shirely A. Kessler and Beth Blue Swaener, eds. Teachers College Press, Columbia University, N.Y., 1992. $22.95.

This is a collection of essays, mostly academic in tone, that draw on alternative modes of thinking, such as critical and feminist theory, to re-examine early childhood education. In chapters that discuss, among other things, Afrocentric curricula, the politics of bilingual education, and the implementation of an anti-bias curriculum, the book pays special attention to issues of gender, race, and ethnicity.

(Early Childhood Theory)

Resources for Creative Teaching in Early Childhood Education, Darlene Softley Hamilton, Bonnie Mack Fleming. 1990. $67.25.

(Curriculum, Lesson Planning, and Assessment)

Stories in the Classroom: Storytelling, Reading Aloud, and Roleplaying with Children, Bob Barton and David Booth. Heinemann Educational Books, 70 Court Street, Portsmouth, NH 03801, 1990. $15.

This book talks about the power of stories and storytelling and also suggests how to find, choose, and use specific stories. It discusses the various types of stories – folk tales, picture books, story poems, novels, and more – and includes a "story response repertoire" which has follow-up activities from story talk to retellings, reading of similar stories, dramatizing, and thematic art projects.

(Environment; Curriculum, Lesson Planning, and Assessment)

The Safe, Self-Confident Child, Signal Hills Publications. New Readers Press, 1994. $8.95.

(Curriculum, Lesson Planning, and Assessment)

Social Foundations of Thought and Action: A Social Cognitive Theory, Albert Bandura. Prentice Hall, 1986. $80.

(Early Childhood Theory)

Stand and Deliver, Jaime Escalante.

(Vision)

A Survival Guide for the Preschool Teacher, Jean R. Feldman. The Center for Applied Research in Education, 1991. $27.95.

This book for beginning teachers has advice for establishing learning centers and finding or developing appropriate materials.

(Curriculum, Lesson Planning, and Assessment)

Teacher-Parent Relationships, Jeannette Galambos Stone. NAEYC, 1987.

Stone, a preschool teacher, child care consultant, and parent, presents in this booklet various ways that parents and teachers have found helpful when coping with differing views, needs, and life experiences. She stresses that parents and teachers educate each other when there is true two-way communication; she looks at some problems that get in the way of that communication; and she includes ideas for how to share information openly and how to examine others' points of view without compromising one's own convictions.

(Getting Started; "How to BE Together")

Teaching About Native Americans, Karen D. Harvey and Lisa D. Harjo, Jane K. Jackson. National Council for the Social Studies, Bulletin No. 84, 1990. National Council for the Social Studies, 3501 Newark Street N.W., Washington, D.C. 20016. $12.95.

This is a helpful and necessary book for teaching about Native American people as they really were and really are. It challenges teachers to examine the attitudes about Native Americans that are embedded in how social studies and other subjects are taught and to replace negative and harmful stereotypes with information and communication. The book contains chapters to inform teachers about Native American history, culture, and issues of current interest. Each chapter contains lesson plans that incorporate the information. There is also a chapter on resources for teachers and students and suggestions for evaluating materials about racism and sexism.

(Curriculum, Lesson Planning, and Assessment)

Testing African American Students, Asa G. Hilliard, III, ed. Southern Education Foundation, 135 Auburn Avenue, Atlanta, GA 30303, 1991. $12.95.

This collection of essays addresses the power of standardized tests in American schools, colleges, and life. It also examines how these tests' assumptions, biases, and omissions have an impact on how African-Americans score on them. The essays are scientific and academic in nature but filled with interesting, clear examples.

(Internalized Oppression)

Toys for Early Childhood Development, Berenda W. Abrams and Nancy Allen Kauffman. Center For Applied Research in Education, 1990. $27.95.

(Curriculum, Lesson Planning, and Assessment)

Training Teachers: A Harvest of Theory and Practice, Margie Carter and Deb Curtis. Redleaf Press, 1994. 288 pages. $32.95.

This book is a valuable resource for child care providers and teachers. It provides helpful teaching tools and training strategies in areas ranging from child-centered curriculum practices to cultural sensitivity and anti-bias practices. The authors' goal is to "teach teachers in ways consistent with how we want them to teach the children in their care." It has sections containing forms and charts for observation, training, and evaluation.

(Early Childhood Theory; Curriculum, Lesson Planning, and Assessment; Work Planning)

Understanding Assessment and Evaluation in Early Childhood Education, Dominic F. Gullo. Teachers College Press, Columbia University, NY, 1994. 143 pages.

(Curriculum, Lesson Planning, and Assessment)

Valuing Diversity: The Primary Years, Janet Brown McCracken. NAEYC, 1993. $5.

This book provides helpful tools for exploring how and what children are learning in classrooms and for integrating diversity into the classroom. In chapters entitled "Liberating the Human Spirit," "Preparing a Diverse Environment," and "Teaching Strategies," the author explores internalized oppression, how children learn, how to foster pride in each child's heritage, and how to respect, value, and find strength in diversity.

(Internalized Oppression; "How To BE Together"; Curriculum, Lesson Planning, and Assessment)

The Virtues Guide: A Handbook for Parents Teaching Virtues, Linda Kavelin, Dan Popov, and John Havelin. Personal Power Press International.

(Curriculum, Lesson Planning, and Assessment)

Who Am I in the Lives of Children?, S. Feeney, D. Christenson, and E. Moravick. MacMillan Publishing Co., 1991. $62.

(Getting Started; Vision)

The Whole Child: Developmental Education in the Early Years, Joanne Hendrick. Prentice Hall, 1995. $52.

(Getting Started; Curriculum, Lesson Planning, and Assessment)

Working and Caring, T.B. Brazelton. Addison-Wesley Publishing Co., 1992. $13.

(Getting Started; Vision)

Your Home is a Learning Place, Pamela Weinberg. Signal Hill Publishers, 1993. $6.95.

(Curriculum, Lesson Planning, and Assessment)

Your Preschooler (Ages 3&4), Richard Rubin and John Fisher III. 1982.

(Curriculum, Lesson Planning, and Assessment)

CATALOGUES/BIBLIOGRAPHIES

Beyond the Stereotypes: A Guide to Resources for Black Girls and Young Women.

In Her Own Image: Films and Videos Empowering Women for the Future. Media Network, 39 West 14th Street, Suite 403, New York, NY 10011; (212) 929-2663. $11.50.

This helpful guide lists 82 films and videos under eight categories: Food, Clothing, and Shelter; All Work and No Pay; The Body Politic; War and Peace; Confronting Violence; Transitions; Changing Roles; and Educate, Agitate, Organize! The films and videos present the experiences, perspectives, and activism of women all around the world. The listing for each selection includes a review and information regarding price, length, and distributor. It also has helpful indexes for subject (Access to Resources, The Family, Race, Rape, Sexuality, etc.) and for audience (Activists, Adolescents, etc.)

(Vision, Environment, Internalized Oppression)

A Reality Check on the American Dream: The Guide to Anti-Poverty Film and Video. Media Network, 39 W14th Street, Suite 403, New York, NY 10011; (212) 929-2663. $11.50.

This guide is divided into eight sections: neglected communities; housing and homelessness; health care access; labor struggles; education in crisis; women among the poor; growing up poor; anti-poverty strategies. It lists 75 films, each with a brief review and information regarding price, length, and distributor. It also has helpful indexes for subjects (African-American Studies, Building Self-Worth, Child and Adolescent Welfare, etc.) and for audiences (Activists, Children, Educators, etc.)

(Vision, Environment, Internalized Oppression)

Resources for Early Childhood Training: An Annotated Bibliography. Council for Early Childhood Professional Recognition, (202) 265-9090, 1993. Revised Edition. 162 pages. $5.

This annotated bibliography is designed around the Child Development Associate (CDA) Program. The extensive index of resources is organized into the 13 CDA functional areas and into various child care settings. The guide contains information about written materials and about video and audio tapes. This is a valuable guide for choosing resources appropriate for your program and needs. It also contains appendices explaining the CDA Program and describing demonstration projects at various sites.

(Curriculum, Lesson Planning and Assessment; Work Planning)

Venture into Cultures: A Resource Book of Multicultural Materials and Programs, Carla D. Hayden, ed. American Library Association, (800) 545-2433, 1992. $25.

This book is divided into sections on African American, Arabic, Asian, Hispanic, Jewish, Native American, and Persian cultures. Each section contains a bibliography of works and program references.

(Curriculum, Lesson Planning, and Assessment)

The Video Project: Films and Videos for a Safe and Sustainable World. The Video Project, 5332 College Avenue, Suite 101, Oakland, CA 94618; (800) 4-PLANET.

This catalogue is split into three sections: The Environment, Nuclear Issues, and Global Concerns. Within these sections are smaller categories such as "Kids and the Planet," "Sustainable Development," "Ethics and Values," "Human Rights," and "Youth Concerns." The catalog has clear descriptions of each video, accompanied by information regarding length and price. The prices are, in general, very reasonable.

(Environment)

Women Make Movies. Women Make Movies, 462 Broadway, Suite 500 C, New York, NY 10013; (212) 925-0606.

Women Make Movies is an organization dedicated to changing the representation of women in the media by promoting a diversity of styles, subjects, and perspectives in women's media. This catalogue contains listings for over a hundred films by and about women which are separated into the following categories: Sex Equity, Health, Gender, Global Perspectives and Cultural Identity, and

Arts. Videos of interest include: *Visionary Voices: Women on Power, Trade Secrets: Blue Collar Women Speak Out,* and *A Place of Rage (a celebration of African American women and their achievements),* among many others. Both fiction and documentary films are included in the catalog.

(Vision, Environment, Internalized Oppression)

VIDEOS

A Class Divided, Documentary Consortium of Public Television Stations. Distributed by PBS Video. 1984-93. 57 minutes.

This remarkable video traces an Idaho teacher's two-day lesson in discrimination for her all-White, all-Christian third-graders. By dividing her students into "blue eyes" and "brown eyes" and discriminating against each group on successive days, this teacher did much more than talk about the harmful effects of discrimination–she allowed her students to experience them for themselves. Originally filmed in 1970, this version includes a reunion in 1985 in which the students come back and talk about the positive impact this lesson has had on their lives. This video is an invaluable tool for any discussion of prejudice and its effects on children.

(Internalized Oppression)

Color Adjustment, 1991, California Newsreel. #149 9th Street/420, San Francisco, CA 94103; (415) 621-6196. 87 minutes. $59.95.

This video explores prejudice in the United States by examining images of Black Americans during the television age – from Amos and Andy *to* The Cosby Show. *Revisiting such popular favorites as* Beulah, The Nat King Cole Show, Julia, I Spy, Good Times, *and* Roots, *viewers see how bitter racial conflict was absorbed into the non-controversial formats of the prime-time series. Throughout the video, we see how television images of African Americans have much more to do with society's perceptions than with the reality and diversity of African Americans' experience.*

(Internalized Oppression)

The Color of Fear, Lee Mun Wah. 1994, Stir Fry Productions, 1904 Virginia Street, Berkeley, CA 94709; (510) 548-9695. 90 minutes.

This video is an incredibly powerful look at men's attitudes about race in the United States. It captures a weekend retreat by a group of men – African American, Asian, Latino, and White – who discuss and grapple with racism between Whites and people of color and among people of color themselves. As these men discuss their fear, rage, confusion, and hopes, they learn a lot about themselves and each other. We highly recommend this video.

(Internalized Oppression)

Ethnic Notions: Black People in White Minds. 1987, California Newsreel, 149 9th Street/420, San Francisco, CA 94103; (415) 621-6196. 57 minutes. $49.95.

This powerful, extremely moving video traces the evolution of the deeply rooted stereotypes which have fueled anti-Black prejudice in the United States. Through cartoons, advertisements, children's rhymes, feature films, and household artifacts, the video shows how the dehumanizing caricatures of loyal Toms, carefree Sambos, faithful Mammies and others were developed and perpetuated from the 1820s to the Civil Rights era.. Narration by Ester Rolle and commentary by respected scholars shed light on the origins and devastating consequences of this 150-year-long parade of bigotry.

(Internalized Oppression)

Eyes On the Prize. PBS, Item number: EYPZ103. $49.95

In 1960, large numbers of college students and young people began to get involved in the black freedom struggle. The focus of black protest changed from legal battles to personal and group challenges against racial inequities. This program focuses on four related stories: the lunch counter sit-ins of 1960; the formation of the Student Nonviolent Coordinating Committee (SNCC); the impact of the movement on the 1960 presidential campaign; and the freedom rides of 1961. Produced by Blackside, Inc., 1986.

(Vision)

The Killing Culture. 1992, Kurtis Productions, Ltd. and Arts & Entertainment Network. Available through New Video Group, 419 Park Avenue South, New York, NY 10016; (212) 532-3392. 50 minutes.

This documentary offers an introspective look into what has made the U.S. murder rate so high, and it explores the relationship between guns and homicide.

(Environment)

One Woman, One Vote (Produced by Ruth Pollak). 1995, Educational Film Center. Distributed by PBS Video. 106 minutes.

This film documents the struggle by American women to achieve the right to vote. From Elizabeth Cady Stanton's call for women's rights in 1948 to the passage of the Nineteenth Amendment to the Constitution in 1920, the film depicts the heroines of the woman's suffrage movement, their various strategies, their setbacks, and their victories. It is a powerful piece about American women's fight for democracy and equality. One drawback: the role played by African-American women in this movement is given too little attention, in our view.

(Vision)

The Promised Land. 1995, British Broadcasting Corporation. Available through the Discovery Enterprises Group, Bethesda, MD 20814. Three 90-minute videos.

This video series documents the great migration of African Americans from the South to the North between 1940 and 1970. It tells the stories of men and women who left the poverty and oppression of the South for a piece of the American dream in the North, only to find that even this Promised Land held many false promises for Black Americans. Narrated by Morgan Freeman and containing many interviews with people who made the journey, this video conveys their dreams, their disappointments, and the way this migration changed and continues to change American society.

(Vision)

ANNOTATED BIBLIOGRAPHY OF SUGGESTED BOOKS FOR CHILDREN

The following is a partial list from a bibliography compiled and annotated by Ellen Wolpert. This list of recommended books is a "work in progress" and by no means all-inclusive. Books designated with an asterisk (*) appear in The Slide Show: Anti-bias Curriculum at The Washington-Beech Community Preschool.

*Aladdin, The Magic Carpet Ride. Walt Disney Company. This book can be used to illustrate stereotypes: The color black and Semitic features are used in negative ways, while the color white and European features appear in positive ways.

Alef Is One: A Hebrew Alphabet Counting Book, by Katherine Janus Kahn; Kar-Ben Copies, Rockville, Md. Hebrew letters introduce the concept of counting from one lion to 400 parrots.

All The Colors We Are/Todos Los Colores De Nuestra Piel: The Story Of How We Get Our Skin Color/La Historia De Por Que Tenemos Diferentes Colores De Piel, Katie Kissinger; Redleaf Press. Containing beautiful photographs and a simple text, this book carefully and clearly explains how we get our skin color. Several relevant activities are suggested to go with the book.

*Amazing Grace, by Mary Hoffman. Dial Books for Young Readers, USA. About a young African American girl who wants to be Peter Pan in the school play. A classmate tells her she can't play that role because Peter Pan isn't Black. Grace's family provide the support she needs to be what she wants to be.

Amelia's Road, by Linda Jacobs Altman, Enrique O. Sanchez. Lee & Low Books. About a young girl in a migrant farmworker family. Tired of moving around so much, Amelia dreams of a stable home.

*Angel Child, Dragon Child, by Michele Maria Surat. Scholastic. A young girl experiences discrimination because of her Vietnamese clothing and accent. A young boy confronts and changes his prejudice towards his classmate and in the end helps her with a problem. There is a problem that needs discussion: At one point in the story, Raymond the teaser tells Ut, "Hoa!" He shouted. "You said my name. You didn't use funny words." 'I say English,' I answered proudly..." I think this leaves the message that languages other than English sound "funny" rather than simply different and that pride comes with learning English and not from both learning English and maintaining one's first language. (In slide show.)

*Asha's Mums, by Rosamund Elwin & Michele Paulse. Women's Press. The teacher tells Asha, "You can't have two mums." The story includes a wonderful class discussion and debate about whether or not, and why and why not, you can or cannot have two same-gender parents.

Ashraf Of Africa, by Ingrid Mennen, Songolo Books, South Africa. Challenging stereotypes about Africa, the story is about Ashraf, who lives in an African city and has only seen "wild and untamed animals in a book borrowed from the city library."

Atariba & Niguayona, Children's Book Press, Bilingual (English & Spanish) folk tale from Puerto Rico.

Babushka Baba Yaga, by Patricia Polacco. Philomel Books. About stereotyping. The villagers are afraid of her, so the legendary Baba Yaga disguises herself as an old woman in order to know the joys of being a grandmother. Fear of discovery forces her back into the forest. A child loses a grandmother, and the village babushkas lose a friend. In the end they discover how wonderful the Baba Yaga, is and she is welcomed back to the village.

Be Good To Eddie Lee, by Virginia Flemming. Philomel Books. About friendship and diverse physical abilities.

Being With You This Way, by W. Nikola-Lisa. Lee & Low Books. On a beautiful day, a little girl visits the park and rounds up a group of her friends. As they play they celebrate their diversity (straight hair, curly hair; light skin, dark skin) with wonderful rhyming verse.

Belinda's Bouquet, by Leslea Newman. Alyson Wonderland. A child, teased about being fat, is aided by a friend who has two moms.

Best Friends, by Miriam Cohen; Aladdin Books, Macmillan Publishing Co., N.Y. Young friends fight and make up.

Black Like Kyra, White Like Me, by Judith Vigna. Albert Whitman & Co., Illinois. A Black family moves into an all-White neighborhood. Christy, who is White, faces peer pressure to reject her friend. Both she and her family confront the prejudice and maintain their friendship with Kyra's family, even though they are rejected by White friends. This book is one of the few available stories dealing directly with racism. The book needs editing in the beginning. According to the story, Kyra's family wants to move because of the crime in their present neighborhood. There are many reasons why a Black family would want to move - the need for a larger home, for example. The inclusion of these negative references to a "bad neighborhood" perpetuates a stereotype of high crime in Black neighborhoods.

Boundless Grace, by Mary Hoffman and Caroline Binch. Dial Books for Young Readers. Grace has negative feelings about the composition of her family, especially since her mother and father are separated. Grace goes to visit her father in Africa and deals with feelings of jealousy. This is a sequel to Amazing Grace.

The Bracelet, by Yoshiko Uchida; Philomel Books. Emi and her family were being sent to a prison camp because they were Japanese-Americans. The U.S. was at war with Japan. The family hadn't done anything wrong, but they were being treated like the enemy just because they looked like the enemy. Emi's best friend comes to say goodbye and brings her a bracelet so she will remember their friendship.

Bread, Bread, Bread, by Ann Morris. Photos by Ken Heyman. Lothrop, Lee & Shepard Books, New York. Excellent photographs illustrate a cross-cultural theme.

Building An Igloo, by Ulli Steltzer. A Meadow Mouse Paperback, Groundwood/Douglas & McIntyre, Toronto/Vancouver. Tookillkee Kiguktak does not live in an igloo; like most Inuit of today, he lives in a house of wood. But when Tookillkee was a little child he lived in an igloo, and when he was a boy he learned how to build one. If he goes hunting far away for a musk ox or a polar bear, he builds an igloo for shelter.

The Carousel, by Liz Rosenberg and Jim LaMarche. Harcourt Brace & Company. Two sisters find that the horses of a broken carousel have come alive in the rain. The story is a fantasy of courage and adventure that weaves in the sisters' memories of their mother, who "had been someone who could fix anything, from leaky faucets to broken porch lights and banisters, washing machines, and more." The sisters have acquired their mother's skills, and they use what she has taught them to fix the broken carousel.

Chicken Sunday, by Patricia Polacco. Philomel Books. The story of a White child's close relationship with a Black family. There is an elderly Jewish man who has a hat store. The children want to get a special Easter hat for grandmother, but the store owner, who is oftened teased by neighborhood children, thinks that they are the culprits.

Children Don't Divorce, by Rosemary Stone. Dinosaur, UK. This book is about families and divorce.

Children Just Like Me, by Barnabus and Anabel Kindersley in association with UNICEF. Dorling Kindersley. Wonderful photographs and family stories of children from all over the globe. Most of the children are dressed in typical daily wear as they talk about daily activities. I recommend buying more than one copy and using one for making games and then keeping the other copy of the book to look at and talk about.

Children's Home, by Hoonie Feltham and Margaret Robson. A & C Black, London. About a child living in institutional care.

The Children We Remember by Children from the Holocaust.

Colors Around Me, by Vivian Church. Afro-Am Publishing Company. About the diversity of color of Black people. Children of different tones of brown, black, and beige are compared to positive, pleasing things in their environment.

Come Sit by Me, by Margaret Merrifield. Women's Press. About friendship and AIDS.

Cornrows, by Camille Yarbrough. Illustrated by Carole Byard. About African American hair styling.

A Country Far Away, by Nigel Gray & Philippe Dupasquier. Magi Publications. Two children in very different places tell similar stories about their day. Bilingual (Hindi and English).

Daddy and Me, by Jeanne Moutoussamy-Ashe. A photographic story of the relationship between Arthur Ashe and his daughter, Camera, that thrived even in the face of AIDS.

Daddy's Roommate, by Michael Willhoite. Alyson Wonderland. About a boy who lives with his two fathers.

The Day Of Ahmed's Secret, by Florence Parry Heide & Judith Heide Gilliland. Lothrop, Lee & Shepard Books, New York.. This beautifully illustrated book shows daily life in an Arab city as Ahmed waits to tell his family his secret: He has learned to write his name.

Dulcie Dando, Soccer Star, by Sue Stops. Henry Holt and Company. Dulcie is a wonderful soccer player, but the boys don't want her on the team. In the end, the team needs Dulcie, who scores the winning goal.

Eating Fractions, by Bruce McMillan. Two close friends (one White, one Black) are pictured throughout the illustrations of food and fractions.

*Family Portraits In Changing Times, by Helen Nestor. New Sage Press, Oregon. This book has a fabulous collection of photographs of a wide variety of families. I recommend buying more than one copy and using one for making games and then keeping a copy of the other book to look at and talk about.

*Fat Fat Rose Marie, by Lisa Passen. Henry Holt & Company, NY. Rose Marie is teased because of her size. Her friend, Claire, is coaxed away to join the teasers. Claire eventually stands up for her friend, risking the disapproval of the teasers. The story illustrates the difficulties children encounter in situations like these but shows that they can still take positive action.

Finding the Green Stone, by Alice Walker; Harcourt Brace Jovanovich.

Finger Foods, by Chris Despande, photographs by Prodeepta Das. A & C Black, London. A school class has a cross-cultural picnic of foods they can eat with their fingers.

Fly Away Home, by Eve Bunting. Clarion Books. A homeless boy, Andrew, lives in an airport with his father, moving from terminal to terminal, and trying not to be noticed. Andrew's father works as a janitor on weekends. He is searching for an apartment but has been unable to find one he can afford.

Follow The Drinking Gourd, by Jeanette Winter. Alfred A. Knopf. By following the directions in a song, "The Drinking Gourd," runaway slaves journey north along the Underground Railroad to freedom in Canada.

Food For Sharing, by Ruth Fahlman, Jocelyn Graeme, and May Henderdson. Addison-Wesley.

A Forever Family, by Roslyn Banish with Jennifer Jordan-Wong. Harper Collins Publishers. About adoption.

Friends From The Other Side/Amigos Del Otro Lado, by Gloria Anzaldua. Children's Book Press. About Joaquin, who has crossed the Rio Grande River into Texas with his mother in search of a better life. It is about Joaquin's friendship with Prietita, a brave Mexican-American girl, who defends Joaquin from the neighborhood kids when they taunt him with shouts of "mojado" or "wetback" and who finds a way to protect Joaquin and his mother from the Border Patrol.

Friday Night Is Papa Night, by Ruth Sonneborn. Puffin Books, Viking Penguin. A father who works a distance from home comes home every Friday night.

* Generations: A Universal Family Album, edited by Anna R. Cohn and Lucinda A. Leach. Pantheon Books, Smithsonian Institution, Washington D.C. Generations contains lots of wonderful photographs. It can be used as is, or the pictures can be mounted on sturdy cardboard for playing games.

Gita Will Be A Dancer, by Barbara & Eberhard Fischer. UNICEF. Bilingual (English & Hindi). A story about a young girl and a classical Indian dance.

Going Fishing, by Rachel Warner. A&C Black, London. About the daily activities of a family in Bangladesh.

Good Morning Franny, Good Night Franny, by Emily Hearn. The Women's Press. Franny is an active young girl in a wheelchair who forms a friendship with Ting. The illustrations of Ting and her mother are disappointing. Their eyes are portrayed as slits rather than full eyes.

Haitian Days: Ti Djo Remembers, by Marcus Plaisimond. Sundance Publishers. This book is trilingual (in English, French, and Kreyol). Ti Djo remembers the things he used to do in Haiti. The illustrations are beautiful paintings by various Haitian artists.

Halmoni and the Picnic, by Sook Nyul Choi. Houghton Mifflin Company. Yunmi's grandmother has just moved to New York City from Korea, and she's finding it difficult to feel comfortable. The customs are very different, and she is too shy to speak English. When her grandmother is invited to join her third grade class picnic, Yunmi worries that her classmates will make fun of her grandmother's traditional dress and Korean food. Instead, the picnic is a wonderful experience, and Yunmi's grandmother feels much more comfortable after the event.

Harriet Tubman: They Called Me Moses, by Linda D. Meyer.

The Hating Book, by Charlotte Zolotow. Harper Trophy of Harper Collins. About conflict. Two girl friends have a misunderstanding. "When I moved over in the school bus, she sat somewhere else. 'Ask her,' my mother said, 'ask your friend why.'" She finally takes her mother's advice and asks her friend why. The females in the story play in traditional gender roles.

Hats Hats Hats, by Ann Morris. Lothrop, Lee & Shepard Books, N.Y. Beautiful photographs with simple text illustrate a cross-cultural theme.

Hats Off To Hair!, by Virginia Kroll. Charlesbridge. This book discusses different ways we wear our hair - long, short, curly, knotted, twisted, braided, beaded, etc.

Here Comes Kate!, by Judy Carlson. Steck-Vaughn Company. Kate just loves to go fast in her wheelchair but often goes too fast and causes a variety of difficulties for others. She becomes interested in wheelchair races that she sees on TV.

Hiroshima No Pika, by Toshi Maruki. Lothrop, Lee & Shepard Books, N.Y. About devastation of the atomic bomb on Hiroshima. Gives a sense of what war really is in a sensitive way for children.

Houses And Homes, by Ann Morris, photos by Ken Heyman. Lothrop, Lee & Shepard Books. Cross-cultural collection. Different kinds of houses and what makes them homes.

I'm Not Frightened of Ghosts, by Juliet & Charles Snape. Prentice Hall Books for Young Readers. A young girl, unafraid, enters alone a big old house with ghosts.

I'm The Big Sister Now, by Michelle Emmert. Albert Whitman & Company, Illinois. Michelle's older sister was born with cerebral palsy. Michelle tells her sister's story.

*Indian Two Feet And His Horse, by Margaret Friskey. Grolier International, Connecticut. I recommend this book only for doing exercises in recognizing stereotypes about Native Americans.

It Takes A Village, by Jane Cowen-Fletcher. Scholastic. New York mother goes to market with two children, knowing that other people will help look out for them.

Jambo Means Hello: Swahili Alphabet Book by Muriel Feelings. Dial Press. From A to Z, Swahili words re-create the traditions of East African village life. It is important to balance this book's depiction of African life with urban images of Africa as well.

Jennifer Has Two Daddies, by Priscilla Galloway. The Womens' Press. Jennifer's parents are divorced. One week she lives with Mummy and Michael, and the next week with the man who was her daddy when she was born.

Jeremy's Dreidel, by Ellie Gellman. Kar-Ben Copies. About celebrations, diverse physical abilities, and blindness.

Leila, by Sue Alexander & George Lemoine. Hamish Hamilton, London. Leila's brother dies and her father forbids anyone to say his name again. Leila convinces her father that it helps to remember. A familiar theme experienced by a family in another country.

Less Than Half, More Than Whole, by Kathleen and Michael Lacapa. Northland Publishing Co. About Native American identity.

Lights On The River, by Jane Resh Thomas. Hyperion Books for Children. A story of migrant farmworkers from Mexico working on U.S. farms. The story illustrates the power of family as well as the difficult life and mistreatment that farmworkers face. A story for young children of farmworkers organizing against some of the mistreatment would be a helpful companion.

The Little Weaver Of Thai-Yen Village, by Tran-Khanh-Tuyet. Children's Book Press. The story is about a young Vietnamese girl. She lives in a village that helps another that has been bombed. Then her village gets bombed, too. The young girl's parents are killed. She is wounded and taken to the U.S. and continues to help Vietnam by weaving and sending blankets.

Living In Two Worlds, by Maxine B. Rosenberg. Lothrop, Lee & Shepard Books, N.Y. About biracial families, race and racism

The Lorax, by Dr. Suess. Random House. This is a good book for reconsidering cooperative strategies. Discussion with children could have them examine alternative ways the Lorax could have fought the pollution caused by the Once-ler as he manufactures Thneeds. The Lorax tries to stop the pollution. He speaks for the trees, and he's in charge of the Bar-ba-loots and the Swomee-Swans and the Humming-Fish, all of whom he has to send away because of the pollution which he is unsuccessful in stopping before it's too late. Perhaps, instead of sending them away, he could have helped bring them all together to organize against the pollution.

Louise Builds A House, by Louise Pfanner. Orchard Books, New York. Fanciful girl does interesting things. She builds a house, gives it to her sister, and goes on to build a boat.

Marshmallows, Monsters And Mice, by Wendy Hartma. Songololo Books, South Africa. About nightmares and a young girl taking control.

Matthew And Tilly, by Rebecca C. Jones. Dutton's Children's Books, N.Y. Close friends have a disagreement and resolve their conflict.

Max, by Rachel Isadora. Collier Books, Macmillan Publishing Company, N.Y. About a boy who gets into ballet dancing.

Mrs. Katz And Tush, by Patricia Polacco. A Bantam Little Rooster Book, Bantam Doubleday Dell. Young African American boy's friendship with an elderly Jewish woman.

My Dad Takes Care Of Me, by Patricia Quinlan. Annick Press, Toronto. Luke's father is unemployed. Luke tells everyone he's a pilot. The story shows some of the changes the family has had to make because of unemployment.

My Grandma Has Black Hair, by Mary Hoffman & Joanna Burroughs. Beaver Books, UK. This book contrasts "my grandma" with all of the typical stereotypes.

My Grandson Lew, by Charlotte Zolotow. Harper & Row. Lewis remembers lots of wonderful things about his grandfather who has died.

Moja Means One: Swahili Counting Book, by Muriel Feelings. Dial Press. Beautiful counting book in Swahili picturing East African village life. Needs to be balanced with urban images of Africa as well.

My Mom Can't Read, by Muriel Staner. Albert Whitman & Company. A young girl learning to read at school discovers that her mom can't read. A teacher responds with sensitivity and helps her mom get into reading classes at the community center.

My Mother The Mail Carrier/Mi Mama La Cartera, by Inez Maury. The Feminist Press. A five-year-old describes the loving and close relationship she has with her mother, a mail carrier, and also relates some aspects of her mother's job.

My Sister Is Different, by About Retardation.

Mum Can Fix It, by Non-traditional Gender Roles.

The National Civil Rights Museum Celebrates Everyday People, by Alice Faye Duncan. BrideWater Books.

New Friends, by Ron Harper. Hodja's Australian Stories for Kids. Reunion of a Vietnamese family.

*The Nose Book, by Al Perkins. Pantheon Books, NY. This book illustrates stereotypes, particularly a picture that includes all animal noses and one stereotypical Native American nose.

The Nutmeg Princess, by Richardo Keens-Douglas. Annick Press. A fantasy story set in Grenada about two children who manage to see the Nutmeg Princess (unseen by others except Petite Mama) because of their unselfishness and friendship.

Oliver Button Is A Sissy, by Tomie dePaola. Harcourt Brace Jovanovich. Oliver is teased for doing ballet, but the taunts don't stop him from doing what he likes best. In the end, the teasers decide he's a star.

On The Go, by Ann Morris, photographs by Ken Heyman. Lothrop, Lee & Shepard Books. Cross-cultural collection of wonderful photographs of the many ways we transport people and things.

Our Teacher's in a Wheelchair, by Mary Ellen Powerd. Albert Whitman & Company. Brian Hanson teaches in a day-care center. The book shows what he can do with his wheelchair. It also talks about childrens' fears of "catching it." Like other teachers, Brian helps children learn, play, and do their best, although sometimes he feels sad he will never run again.

The Owl And The Woodpecker, by Brian Goldsmith. Oxford University Press. About conflict resolution. The woodpecker pecks and disturbs the owl, who sleeps during the day. The other animals get involved in their dispute.

The Paper Bag Princess, by Robert N. Munsch. Elizabeth, a young princess, is about to marry Prince Ronald. Unfortunately, a dragon burned all her clothes and carried off Prince Ronald. Dressed only in a paper bag, Elizabeth follows and outsmarts the dragon and releases the prince. Elizabeth then rejects the ungrateful prince, who was more concerned with the fact that she smells like ashes and is dressed in a dirty paper bag than with her bravery or his own freedom.

Papou And The Magician, by Ron Harpe. Hodja Educational Resources Cooperative Limited, 135 Church St. Richmond 3121, Australia. About an extended family.

Paul And Sebastian, by Rene Escudie & Ulises Wensell. Kane/Miller Book Publishers. Paul, who lives in a trailer, and Sebastian, who lives in an apartment, are discouraged from playing with each other by their mothers, who each feel disdainful of the other's living situation. They discover that even though their homes are different, they can be friends.

Pearl Moscowitz's Last Stand, by Arthur A. Levine. Tambourine Books. Pearl Moscowitz, an elderly Jewish woman living in a diverse urban neighborhood, takes a stand, supported by her neighbors, when the city government tries to chop down the last gingko tree on the street. She chains herself to the tree and refuses to move.

*People, by Peter Spier. Doubleday & Company, N.Y. This book, while clearly an attempt to present diversity, actually perpetuates stereotypes. It is useful for doing exercises in recognizing stereotypes. People of color are generally represented as exotic, not from the United States, and existing primarily in non-urban settings. One page illustrating the wonderful diversity of language features a picture of one person next to each language example, whereas no one person can represent the diversity of people who speak most languages.

The People Who Hugged The Trees, adapted by Deborah Lee Rose. Roberts Rinehart. A young girl leads her community to stand up against the soldiers of the Maharajah to prevent their cutting down the trees that protect the village from sand storms.

Pueblo Story Teller, by Diane Hoyt-Goldsmith. Holiday House, New York. The book illustrates present day pottery-making, bread baking; story-telling, drum-making, and learning the Buffalo Dance.

Purnima's Parrot, by Feroza Mathieson. Magi Publications, London. Purnima wishes her parrot could talk instead of just saying things like "Craark." She discovers it can talk but in a language she can't understand.

The Puzzle Place: Go Team, by Michi Fujimoto. Price Stern Sloan. Why is it that the boys keep losing to the girls at tug-of-war? Isn't it a "manly" rope game, and not like the silly jumping rope games that girls play? The boys learn that the girls' valuable secret of working together is the best strategy of all and that rope-jumping is for both boys and girls.

The Puzzle Place: I Can't Sleep! by Michi Fujimoto. Price Stern Sloan. During a slumber party, the kids find that they can't get to sleep without their regular bedtime routines. Each child has different habits. With a little ingenuity and a lot of cooperation, they manage to do what each of them needs to fall asleep.

The Puzzle Place: Kyle Can, Can You? by Michi Fujimoto. Price Stern Sloan. Skye's best friend, Kyle, loves to dance and play sports. The kids are surprised to find that Kyle uses a wheelchair. The children learn that there are many different ways people live and that we often do the same things in different ways.

Race You, Franny, by Emily Hern. Women's Educational Press, Canada. Franny, an active young girl, is confined to (but not by) a wheelchair.

Ragsale, by Artie Ann Bates. Houghton Mifflin Company. Jessann and her family spend Saturday going to the rag sales of their Appalachian town.

The Rainbow Fish, by Marcus Pfister. North-South Books, N.Y. The most beautiful fish in the ocean discovers that the value of sharing and friendship is far greater than being the most beautiful but without friends.

Rainbow Fish To The Rescue, by Marcus Pfister. North-South Books. A striped fish wants to join a group of fish but is left out. Rainbow fish feels bad about excluding this fish, because he remembers what it was like when he was left out. A shark enters the reef and all the fish make it to safety except for the striped one. Rainbow fish organizes the other fish to help the striped fish.

The Rajah's Rice: A Mathematical Folktale From India, adapted by David Barry. W. H. Freeman & Co. On rent collection day in a village in India, the villagers must turn over to the Rajah most of the rice they have grown. Many of the villagers will go hungry. When the Rajah's elephants get sick, Chandra, the official bather of the Rajah's elephants, is the only one who can make them well. To cure them, she demands in exchange what appears to be a very simple mathematical formula of rice for the village. The Rajah agrees, only to discover that the formula multiplies into so much rice that he is unable to pay it. In the end he must agree to give the people of the village the land that they farm and to take only as much rice as he really needs for himself.

The Red Comb, by Fernando Pico. BridgeWater Books. In this story, set in 19th-century Puerto Rico, two women, one old and one young, plot to save a runaway slave.

*The River That Gave Gifts, by Margo Humphrey. Children's Book Press, San Francisco, California. This African-American story concerns three sisters who create beautiful presents for their grandmother before she loses her eyesight. It shows that the best presents are often made with love, not bought with money.

Sachiko Means Happiness, by Kimiko Sakai. Children's Book Press. The story is about a young Japanese girl and her relationship with her grandmother, who has Alzheimer's disease. It's a wonderful story but must be balanced with many other stories that show elderly people leading active lives.

Sam Johnson and The Blue Ribbon Quilt, by Lisa Campbell Ernst. Mulberry Books, N.Y. While mending an awning, Sam discovers that he enjoys sewing the various patches together but meets with ridicule when he asks his wife if he can join her quilting club. Sam forms a men's quilting group. In the end, both groups have to cooperate together to make a quilt.

Sami and The Time of The Troubles, by Florence Parry Heide & Judith Heide Gilliland. Clarion Books. A ten-year-old Lebanese boy goes to school, helps his mother with chores, plays with his friends, and lives with his family in a basement shelter when bombings occur and fighting begins on his street. Giving a positive demonstration of something that can be done in a deplorable situation, the children participate in a protest against war. The illustrations by Ted Lewin are fabulous.

Seeing In Special Ways, by Thomas Bergman. Gareth Stevens. Children's Books. About children and blindness. Interviews with children.

Sitti's Secrets, by Naomi Shibab Nye. Four Winds Press. A young girl describes a visit to see her grandmother in a Palestinian village on the West Bank.

The Sneetches, by Dr. Seuss. Random House. About prejudice based on physical characteristics: "the Star-Belly Sneetches had bellies with stars. The Plain-Belly Sneetches had none. The Star-Belly Sneetches would brag, "We're the best kind of Sneetch on the beaches...We'll have nothing to do with the Plain-Belly sort!"

Stellaluna, by Janell Cannon. Harcourt Brace & Company. A bat (Stellaluna) separated from her mother joins a family of birds. According to the birds, the bat hangs upside down, etc. Stellaluna asks, "How can we be so different and feel so much alike?"

*The Streets Are Free, by Kurusa. Annick Press, New York, Ontario, Canada. About children who organize to get a playground.

Swimmy, by Leo Lionni. Dragonfly Books. Alfred A. Knopf, NY. All the little fish get together to protect themselves from the big fish.

T Is For Terrific/T Es Por Terrifico, by Mahji Hall. Bilingual alphabet book in English and Spanish.

Talk To Me, by Sue Brearley. A & C Black, London. Not everyone starts to speak at the same age or in the same way. Some children have problems speaking clearly. Some can't speak at all and must find a different way of talking. About deafness, sign language, physical differences that inhibit speech, speech therapists, using symbol language; learning slowly, hard work learning to speak. getting frustrated and mixing up words, the need for others to pay attention and to listen, lip-reading, sign language, symbols, and patience.

Tap-Tap, by Karen Lynn Williams. Clarion Books. This is a story of market day in a village in Haiti. Tap-taps are privately owned colorful buses that serve as transportation through much of Haiti.

Teammates, by Peter Golenbock. Harcourt Brace Jovanovich. This story describes the racial prejudice experienced by Jackie Robinson when he joined the Brooklyn Dodgers and became the first Black player in major league baseball. It also depicts the acceptance he received from his White teammate Pee Wee Reese, who challenged some of the racism.

Through My Window, by Tony Bradman and Eileen Browne. Little Mammoth, U.K. Jo is ill. She must stay indoors while Dad looks after her and mum goes to work. Jo's mother is Black and her father is White. The street scenes that Jo can see from her window are racially and culturally diverse and other roles are non-traditional.

True Or False?, by Patricia Ruben, J.B. Lippincott Company/Philadelphia & New York. Photographs with true or false questions.

I Use A Wheelchair, by Althea. Dinosaur Publications, UK.

Up The Tree, by Eileen Browne. About a girl who climbs a tree.

Vietnam, Australia, & Me, by William Kelly. Hodja Educational Resources Cooperative Limited, 135 Church St. Richmond 3121, Australia. Adoption by Australian family of Vietnamese child. The child is teased for being Vietnamese.

Wait And See, by Tony Bradman and Eileen Browne. Oxford University Press. Jo's dad is White and her mom is Black. Jo and her mom go out shopping. Jo's dad stays home and prepares lunch. As they do their errands, they talk to neighbors and shopkeepers who are from diverse races, cultures, and ages.

We Can Do It!, by Laura Dwight. Checkerboard Press. Photo essay about several children with a range of physical challenges.

Welcoming Babies, by Margy Burns Knight. Tilbury House. This book celebrates the diversity of ways babies are welcomed.

What Is Beautiful?, by MaryJean Watson Avery and David M. Avery. Tricycle Press. This book encourages children to recognize different forms of beauty in various individuals and to see what is beautiful about themselves.

Who's In A Family?, by Robert Skutch, Tricycle Press. Illustrates the fact that families can be made up in many different ways. Includes male and female gay and lesbian families.

Willie's Not The Hugging Kind, by Joyce Durham Barett. Harper Trophy Alternative. Discusses gender roles.

Who Belongs Here? An American Story, by Margy Burns Knight. Tilbury House Publishers, Maine. Nary is a young boy who fled with his grandmother from the brutality of Pol Pot and the Khmer Rouge in Cambodia. In the United States, Nary is teased by his classmates. He tells the teacher of his difficulties, and together they plan a lesson that will help other children to understand Nary better. There are parallel anecdotes relating the experiences of other refugees. The format of the book is a little complicated, but it can be adapted. It is also an excellent book to use with staff as a catalyst for discussion about refugees to the United States and related issues.

*William's Doll, by Charlotte Zolowtow. Harper Collins, N.Y. This is about a young boy who loves model trains and basketball but still wants a doll to play with. The book also portrays his grandmother in a positive, non-stereotypical way as the person most sensitive to William's desire for a doll.

The Wonderful Way Home; An Adventure in Haiti, by Stephen Dunn. Published by Stephen and Marbeth Dunn, Printed in Haiti by Le Natal. The book may be obtained from the author by sending $5. to Stephen Dunn, P.O. Box 371275, Miami, FL, 33137-1275. In the Haitian village of Limbe, a brother and sister go to the river, to do the wash. Their laundry accidentally gets pushed into the river and they must chase after it. They end up in a city far from Limbe and are helped in small ways by several different people.

Working Cotton, by Sherley Anne Williams. Harcourt Brace Jovanovich Publishers. A young Black girl relates the daily events of her family's migrant life in the cotton fields of central California.

You Be You I'll Be Me, by Pili Mandelbaum. A Cranky Nell Book, Kane/Miller Book Publishers. An interracial child says, "But daddy, I don't like the color of my face, or of my hands...I want to be like you." "How silly...I would do anything not to have this pale face of mine..." The discussion continues and they talk about mixing paints and then coffee and milk to match their skin tones. Eventually brown-skinned daughter and white-skinned father experiment to see what it would be like to have the other's skin color and hair styles.

Zeynep, by Zeynep Hasbudak and Brian Simons. All London Teachers Against Racism and Facism (ALTARF), available from ALTARF, Panther House, Room 216, 38 Mount Pleasant, London WC1XOAP. There is also a video - details from ALTARF. About a school in London that organized to stop the deportation of two of its students to Turkey.